Inside Intranets and Extranets

Also by James Callaghan

THE MANAGEMENT OF TELECOMMUNICATIONS NETWORKS,
R. Smith, E.H. Mamdani and J. Callaghan (eds), Ellis Horwood Ltd,
Chichester, 1992.

Inside Intranets and Extranets

Knowledge Management and the Struggle for Power

James Callaghan

palgrave

First published 2002 by
PALGRAVE
Houndmills, Basingstoke, Hampshire RG21 6XS and
175 Fifth Avenue, New York, N. Y. 10010
Companies and representatives throughout the world

PALGRAVE is the new global academic imprint of
St. Martin's Press LLC Scholarly and Reference Division and
Palgrave Publishers Ltd (formerly Macmillan Press Ltd).

ISBN 0–333–98743–8

This book is printed on paper suitable for recycling and made from fully managed and sustained forest sources.

A catalogue record for this book is available from the British Library.

Library of Congress Cataloging-in-Publication Data

Callaghan, James, 1964–
    Inside intranets and extranets—knowledge management and the struggle
    for power / James Callaghan.
        p.   cm.
    Based on the author's Ph.D. thesis, University of Cambridge.
    ISBN 0–333–98743–8
    1. Intranets (Computer networks)   2. Extranets (Computer networks)
    3. Knowledge management.   I. Title: Knowledge management and the
    struggle for power.   II. Title.

HD30.385 .C347 2002
658'.05467—dc21

2002019594

10   9   8   7   6   5   4   3   2   1
11   10   09   08   07   06   05   04   03   02

Printed and bound in Great Britain by
Antony Rowe Limited
Chippenham, Wiltshire

Contents

Prologue

A conversation overheard on an early morning train from Ipswich to London, early 1999. John and Carol, middle/senior managers, both aged late 40s to early 50s, discussing the strategy of their company, move on to discuss the use of e-mail, the Internet and how to disseminate information in their organisation ...

Carol: 'Just get Kate to put it on a web page'

John: 'Oh, yes, I never thought of that. Will she be able to do it?'

Carol: 'Oh yes. She's getting quite good at it now. She's even done a page for that estate agent. It's getting hundreds of hits a week from all over the world. They even had an e-mail from Guatemala asking about property in Suffolk'

John: 'Oh really? Yes, but those web pages are only read by the scruffy types. You know those ...'

Carol: 'You mean anoraks?'

John: 'Well, yes. You know the type that collect pictures of trains and things. I don't want any scruffy types reading my web pages ...'

Carol: 'It's not really like that. It's not only anoraks, anyone can read web pages and send e-mail'

John: 'Oh yes, I've got one of those'

Carol: 'One of what?'

John: 'One of those e-mail things. What are they called addresses?'

Carol: 'Yes, addresses'

John: 'Look there it is (shows his business card). It's been on my card for over a year now. 'Course I've never used it. Don't have the time'

Carol: 'Oh you should use it, it's really easy'

John: 'Is it?'

Carol: 'Oh yes. If I'm saying it's easy to use, it must be really easy. Listen, when I get in, I'll send you an e-mail and you'll see how easy it is to use'

John: 'So you'll send me an e-mail? Gosh that's awfully kind...'

Acknowledgements

Grateful acknowledgement is made to the following for permission to reprint copyright material:

The Institution of British Telecommunications Engineers, UK: Figure 1.1 in Chapter 1 from Callaghan, J.G. and Flavin, P.G., 'Intranets – Corporate Nirvana: The End of the Traditional Organisation?' *Journal of the Institution of British Telecommunications Engineers*, 15(3): 224–9, October 1996. Reprinted by permission.

Management Information Systems Research Center (MISRC) of the University of Minnesota and the Society for Information Management (SIM): Figure 2.1 in Chapter 2 from J. Yannis Bakos, and Michael E. Treacy, 'Information Technology and Corporate Strategy: A Research Perspective', *MIS Quarterly*, 10(2): 107–19, June 1986. Copyright © 1986 by the Management Information Systems Research Center (MISRC) of the University of Minnesota and the Society for Information Management (SIM). Reprinted by permission.

There are many others whose assistance with this book, both directly and indirectly, I would like to acknowledge.

Firstly, I would like to express my sincere gratitude to Professor Nick Oliver from the Judge Institute of Management Studies, University of Cambridge. He was my primary supervisor for my Ph.D. research upon which this book is based. I wish to thank him for his valuable advice, support and guidance from the inception of the research through to the successful completion of this book. In addition, I would like to thank Professor Geoff Walsham and Dr Matthew Jones also of the University of Cambridge, for their advice and complementary interpretation of my work. I would also like to acknowledge the counsel and guidance given to me some years ago by William T. Grimson of the Dublin Institute of Technology (Kevin Street Campus) in Ireland.

I am indebted to all those people who participated in the research and in particular to Steve Sim, Dr Steve Jones and Debbie Stone, who acted as facilitators for the case studies presented in this book.

Thanks are also due to Mike Matthews and Dr David McCartney who gave me valuable support and afforded me the opportunity to complete the research. For the facilitation of BT sponsorship throughout the duration of my Ph.D. studies, I would like to acknowledge, with sincerest gratitude, the assistance of Professor Peter Cochrane. The research presented in this book was fully sponsored by BT.

Others who I would like to thank for various reasons are my brother Keith, Peter and Pat Easter, Bob and Pauline Emmett and Brian Tester – you know who you are and how you have helped me – many thanks.

Without doubt, the biggest thanks are due to my wife Gillian and my sons James and Peter for their patience and understanding while I conducted the research and completed this book. The ultimate acknowledgement is to my mother Eileen and to the memory of my father Jimmy who sadly did not live to see the completion of this work.

1
Introduction

In November 1995, the Wall St Journal coined the term 'intranet' to describe the use of Internet technologies by managers in organisations to reform their information technology (IT) strategy. Many commentators, for example Pincince *et al.* (1996), Tomasula (1996) claim that the development of corporate intranet solutions has fuelled the most significant change in corporate infrastructure since the development of the PC in the early 1980s.

Considering that intranets have only been around since 1995, the growth in the level of interest and the degree to which they have been implemented is quite remarkable. Looking back a few years, Forrester Research (1996) reported that 64 per cent of the 50 'Fortune 1000' companies they surveyed already had an intranet and that a further 32 per cent were building one. Haapaniemi (1996b) reported that about two-thirds of the companies in a survey claimed that the Internet is a key part of their IT strategy, and of particular interest were intranets. Basker (1998) pointed out that the interest in intranets is not just confined to the United States. Later figures from KPMG (1998a) indicated that in a survey among 101 major UK companies, 48 per cent of respondents said their organisation currently had an intranet and that a further 37 per cent were planning to install an intranet in the next three years. Similar figures were predicted by Zona Research (1997) for other European countries within the near future.

By the end of the 1990s, the interest in and the publicity surrounding the use of intranets was to a large extent subsumed by the mega-hype generated by the so-called 'dot.coms' and how they would reputedly change the face and future of the way business is conducted. With the subsequent, well-documented, demise of the 'build a website and make a fortune' philosophy and the rapid twist of fate and literal

1

transmogrification of the 'dot.coms' into 'dot.bombs', publicity surrounding the deployment of intranets was hidden under a bushel. In the meantime, intranets have been engaged in a quiet revolution. The functionality offered has grown just as rapidly as the cost of implementation has fallen and the rate of take-up by organisations has grown markedly.

The primary reasons cited for installing an intranet include speedier internal communications (KPMG 1998a), reduced costs of printing and distributing information (Parker and Attwood 1997), support for new ways of working such as virtual teams, and the sharing of corporate knowledge (Coleman 1997a; Scott 1998). The flexibility, ease of use and the low cost of intranets have proved to be very appealing to many companies (Technology Strategies 1996). Another attraction of intranets is the return on investment that is often quoted. A study conducted by IDC (International Data Corporation 1997) among a number of Fortune 1000 companies claimed that business investment in intranet solutions has shown returns on investment (ROI) of over 1000 per cent on average, with pay-back periods in the range of 6–12 weeks. Also, British telecommunications (BT) have reported that their intranet has given actual audited savings in the range of £745–850 million (Network News 1997), these savings being achieved in less than three years.

While such large ROI figures make one sit up and take notice, another point worth highlighting is the remarkably short period of time over which these benefits have reportedly been realised. As intranets use the same technology as the Internet, the rapid development of the Internet has been mirrored by intranets. Indeed, so much has happened in such a short space of time that the notion of an 'Internet timescale' is often used as a way of illustrating how rapid the development has been in comparison to other technologies. Vadapalli and Ramamurthy (1998: 88) in an exploratory study of business use of the Internet provide a nice example of this when they point out that:

> the first round of IT respondents perceived intranet technology to be ... dynamic and cost effective ... a web year is three or four weeks.

In terms of understanding how organisations are actually making use of intranet technology, there has been an avalanche of journalistic articles in the past few years, but little theoretical research. Scott (1998) points out that evidence of the business value of the intranet has been convincing but largely anecdotal.

As the importance and ubiquity of intranets has grown, the time is now appropriate to move beyond the anecdotal and 'death by statistics'

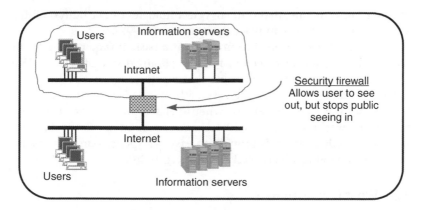

Figure 1.1   Illustration of a simple intranet (from Callaghan and Flavin 1996) .

approach and to present in-depth research on what has actually happened in organisations that have implemented intranets and to attempt an understanding of intranets within cultural and contextual situations. This is the purpose of this book.

However, before presenting an overview of the book, it is useful at this early stage to clarify what an intranet actually is.

1.1   What is an intranet?

An intranet is a closed area of the Internet with added security and guaranteed quality of service. It enables low cost access to information in a wide variety of forms without unnecessary restrictions upon location. The dependency on paper-based information storage can be minimised. In essence, an intranet is an Internet deployed within the confines of an organisation. The intranet differs from the Internet in that it is based on private company-controlled servers and is shielded from the public Internet by a security firewall as shown in Figure 1.1.

Intranets are typically based on standard Internet technology, which is built using open standards and multiple hardware (e.g. PC, Mac, Unix) and software platforms (e.g. Windows 9x, Windows NT, Solaris). Having a standard technology platform has a number of benefits. It is both cheaper and easier to implement than some of the existing technologies used for information publishing and distribution within organisations. For example, if an organisation has a local area network (LAN) running the internet protocol (IP) (which most do) then that can serve as a basic intranet infrastructure, that is the new technologies can be built on infrastructure that is already in place (Bayyigit *et al.* 1997).

Also, the software needed to implement a basic intranet, such as the server software and browser can now be obtained free of charge. This last point is significant as it means that intranets are not restricted to large firms as tended to be the case with other IT innovations – even Groupware was quite expensive when it first came on the scene and thus its use was restricted initially to large organisations. Particularly for small companies, intranets provide an easy, inexpensive means of electronically 'enabling' an enterprise (Taninecz 1996).

1.2   What is an extranet?

As illustrated in Figure 1.1, a 'firewall' is used to allow intranet users to access the public Internet but to prevent unauthorised access to information on the intranet. A firewall is server or router software that filters packets of information coming into the intranet to stop potential malicious or intrusive software and protect information on the intranet. However, a firewall can also be configured to allow authorised access (to some or all of the information on the intranet) by people outside the organisation, for example customers and/or suppliers. In such cases, the term 'extranet' (*ex*tended in*tranet*) is often used (Riggins and Rhee 1998). In essence, there is little difference between an intranet and extranet apart from who has access to the information.

1.3   Intranets/extranets and knowledge management

There is a lot of interest in the use of knowledge in organisations and how 'organisations' can best manage their knowledge (Amidon 1998; Skyrme 1997a, Davenport *et al.* 1996). As Davenport *et al.* (1998: 43) report: 'organisations everywhere are paying attention to knowledge – exploring what it is and how to create, transfer, and use it more effectively. Knowledge management in particular, has recently blossomed'. The current 'knowledge boom' is due to the convergence of multiple factors (Davenport and Prusak 1998; Skyrme and Amidon 1997). In addition to new global competition and economic and social structural changes, many authors such as Davenport and Prusak (1998), Cropley (1998), Ruggles (1998) cite the widespread interest in and the availability of Internet technologies as being instrumental in catalysing the knowledge management movement. Cole (1998) and Leonard (1998) report that these technologies have facilitated dramatic reductions in the costs associated with the transmission of much information and some kinds of knowledge.

This 'joint' interest in knowledge management and the use of intranets/extranets was also evident in the preliminary research conducted for this book, and indeed, as the research progressed, the knowledge management theme became stronger. Thus, one of the perspectives presented both in the literature review and the discussion of the results is knowledge management.

1.4   Overview of the book

As mentioned above, the relatively recent ascent into prominence of intranets means that there is very little in-depth literature addressing the use of intranets/extranets. Thus, the approach taken in this book is to view intranets/extranets as the latest in a (long) line of IT systems and to make use of the existing literature both as a guide to the research and to inform the subsequent discussion of the results. Chapter 2 thus presents a review of the 'traditional' IT literature. However, in order to understand better the issues surrounding the use of intranets and their potential role in knowledge management, Chapter 3 presents a review of the literature relating to various aspects of knowledge management.

Chapter 4 details the research methodology employed and also contains an overview of the three case studies conducted, the data from the case studies being presented in Chapters 5, 6, and 7. The case studies are presented as 'stand-alone' chapters so that the reader can develop his/her own understanding of the issues before the discussion and analysis of the case studies is presented in Chapter 8. Finally, in concluding the main body of the book, Chapter 9 presents a review of the appropriateness of the research methodology employed, together with a discussion of the significance and relevance of the work presented in this book.

In summary, this book presents an in-depth analysis of the use of intranets and extranets in three organisations, identifying and expanding on the key issues that arise. As such, it represents one of the first books to examine this subject through the use of in-depth case studies. It is hoped that the reader will benefit by relating the issues identified with similar issues in his/her own organisation and thus will increase their understanding of how best to exploit the many advantages offered by the use of this rapidly proliferating technology.

2
The Role of IT

In terms of engaging with the literature both as a guide to the research and in order to inform the discussion of the results, the relative infancy of intranets/extranets presents initially some difficulty in that there is a dearth of material specifically addressing intranets/extranets. What literature there is available is either anecdotal or is 'sponsored' by consultants or firms involved heavily in providing 'intranet and extranet solutions' for organisations.

Thus, the approach taken here is to treat intranets/extranets as the latest in a line of IT systems and investigate to what extent their roles and effects in organisations differ from those of other IT systems that have been reported in the literature. Therefore, in guiding the research a fairly 'typical' strand through the literature was taken, covering issues such as integration of IT into corporate strategy, planning and implementing IT, and the evaluation of IT. However, in reviewing the literature it was evident that intranets/extranets could also be viewed as a 'form' of Groupware, and thus it is also useful to review what has been reported in the literature with reference to Groupware.

Furthermore, as extranets facilitate electronic links between organisations, it is also useful to review the literature on interorganisational information systems (IOS). Finally, in an attempt to understand better the organisational changes that may accompany the implementation and use of an intranet/extranet, the information systems (IS) literature on the relationship between IT and organisational issues is also reviewed.

2.1 Issues from the IT literature

As mentioned above, the approach taken in this research is to view intranets/extranets as the latest in a line of IT systems, and in reviewing the literature the following key issues were identified:

- integration of IT into corporate strategy
- the contribution of IT to competitive advantage
- planning and implementing IT/IS
- evaluation of IT/IS
- assessing when benefits accrue.

Each of these areas of the literature is addressed in Sections 2.1.1–2.1.5.

2.1.1 Integration of IT into corporate strategy

Many commentators claim that the use of IT in organisations has evolved from being a simple tool used to automate some manual processes and tasks, to being a strategic resource without which many of today's businesses could simply not function effectively (Venkatraman 1991; Martin and Powell 1992; Mackiewicz and Daniels 1994).

Venkatraman (1991) discusses the emergence of a strategic role for IT in terms of the convergence of two concurrent forces, referred to as technology push and competitive pull. He notes that with respect to technology push, of particular interest are the significant improvements in the cost-performance ratio and the increased connectivity capabilities. The costs of developing and deploying IT-based applications are only a fraction of what prevailed just a few years ago. Also the costs of deploying PCs (both desktop and portable) to individual employees have plummeted in the past few years. These factors, in conjunction with the development of enhanced forms of connectivity such as Groupware, Internet technologies and 'dial-in' capabilities of mobile or remote workers, have contributed to the strength of the force of technology push. Venkatraman (1991) also notes that as markets continue to become more highly competitive, the 'traditional' sources of competitive advantage are diminishing, and managers are increasingly looking for new and innovative mechanisms to obtain differential advantages for their organisations. Information technology perhaps offers the best potential to provide new and powerful sources of gaining such differentials.

Information technology now permeates all functional activities in organisations (Cash *et al.* 1994) and its effects can be felt not only at the level of the individual employee and the organisation (Davenport and Short 1990; Benjamin and Scott-Morton 1988), but right up to the level of the industry (Porter and Millar 1985; Venkatraman 1994).

In recent years, with increasing interest in business process reengineering (BPR) (Johansson *et al.* 1993), IT has been seen as a key enabler of organisational change strategies (Taylor 1994) as it makes radical process redesign possible (Davenport and Short 1990). Furthermore, in a detailed examination of how companies use IT, Dreifus and Daniels (1993: 1) conclude that

> IT is becoming an integral part of corporate strategy. It is helping reduce staff, connecting subsidiaries in different regions, and facilitating new organization structures.

At a fundamental level, this means that the business objectives and the IT objectives must be integrated and the content of IT and business plans must be 'internally consistent and externally valid' (Reich and Benbasat 1996: 55). This integration of IT into the strategy process is also addressed by Rockart *et al.* (1996: 44), who posit that changes in the global competitive environment have:

> led to...major changes in how organizations operate and are managed. All involve major process change. All heavily involve IT. And all are necessary to compete in the new environment.

There is certainly widespread support in the IT management literature for the notion that IT can significantly enable the strategic response (Porter and Miller 1985; MacDonald 1991; Chatfield and Bjørn-Andersen 1997) and as the field of strategic management has expanded, researchers and practitioners have shown a growing interest in the role of IT in strategy formulation and implementation (Sabherwal and King 1991; Holland *et al.* 1992; Henderson and Venkatraman 1993). Perhaps the high level of interest in intranets and their widespread implementation is a sign that they have begun to appear on the strategic horizon of managers in organisations. This issue will be discussed in Chapter 8 in the context of the findings from the case studies.

2.1.2   Contribution of IT/IS to competitive advantage

Before discussing how the use of IT and information systems in general can give a company a competitive advantage, it is useful to recap on what is actually meant by the term competitive advantage. Bakos and Treacy (1986) argue that competitive advantage stems fundamentally from two factors:

1. Comparative efficiency, which allows an organisation to produce its goods or services more cheaply than its competitors; and
2. Bargaining power, which allows a firm to resolve bargaining situations with its customers and suppliers to its own advantage.

As illustrated in Figure 2.1, the comparative efficiency 'component' comprises two elements, internal efficiency and interorganisational efficiency. Internal efficiency relates to the development of efficient and effective organisational structures. In the context of the use of IT it thus refers to the use of, for example, business planning systems, office automation systems, and management information systems.

Interorganisational efficiency refers to the development of efficient and effective mechanisms for working with other organisations, typically customers and suppliers. In the context of the use of IT, this would refer to, for example, the use of electronic data interchange (EDI), or perhaps more proprietary interorganisational information systems (IOS). It could also refer to the use of extranets.

The bargaining power 'component' comprises three elements; search-related costs, unique product features, and switching costs. Bakos and Treacy (1986) note that these factors have implications for an organisation's relationship with its customers and its suppliers. For example, a firm can increase its 'power' by increasing its customer's relative cost of searching for alternative suppliers, by incorporating unique features into its products, and by increasing its customer's costs of switching to alternative suppliers. In the context of the use of IT, this has often been translated into the development of proprietary IOS where customers (and suppliers) are 'locked' into maintaining the existing relationships because of the costs associated with developing a new IOS with alternative suppliers. However, the use of extranets may begin to undermine the capability of managers in firms to use proprietary IOS as a way of sustaining the bargaining power over customers and suppliers.

The goal then for IT is to show how it can influence one or more of these components to such an extent that the net result is an increased competitive advantage (King *et al.* 1989; McKenney *et al.* 1995). However, it is not sufficient that the net result is simply an increased or improved competitive advantage, as Gogan and Cash (1992: 257) point out:

> the ability to use IT as a competitive weapon may be replicated or surpassed. Successful organizations harness IT for sustainable advantage, continuously modifying strategic information systems to maintain their lead in the marketplace.

The challenge for IT thus becomes one of creating a sustainable competitive advantage (Clemons 1986; Ciborra 1994).

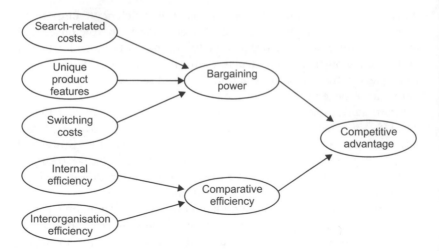

Figure 2.1   A causal model of competitive advantage (Bakos and Treacy 1986).

Interorganisational systems

Some firms, however, look beyond their own boundaries when trying to achieve a competitive advantage. For example, Haapaniemi (1996a: 22) reports that:

> an increasing number of companies are trying to achieve a competitive advantage by using information technology to establish links among their employees, across functions, with their customers, and between data and decision makers.

This point is echoed by Johnston and Vitale (1988) who argue that IOS can bring significant competitive advantages and that it is possible for individual firms to achieve sustainable competitive advantage from the innovative use of IOS. An IOS can be used for relatively simple tasks such as sharing customer data (Konsynski and McFarlan 1990), or for more strategic reasons (Scott-Morton 1991; Bakos 1991b; Short and Venkatraman 1992). In fact, the use of IOS is enabling an increase in the strategic options available to many companies (Holland and Lockett 1994).

The use of IOS in particular is becoming more widespread. This is due to a number of reasons. Firstly, companies are becoming more aware of the potential of these systems and IT in general and since an IOS can be shared by two or more companies (Cash and Konsynski 1985), the potential is there not only for the competitive advantage to be shared amongst the members of the IOS but also for the IOS to have a significant impact on the industry level (Bakos 1991b). Secondly, recent changes in technology as well as increased competition in most industries are leading to growth in the number, variety and scope of IOS (Johnson and Vitale 1988).

However, coverage of the role (and potential) of IT in enabling and supporting interorganisational relationships and networks tends to take a rather narrow focus. For example, Malone *et al.* (1987), Johnston and Vitale (1988), Bakos (1991a), Clemons and Row (1992) all look at IOS from a purely transactions cost perspective and explore how IT reduces coordination costs. However, Clemons and Row (1992: 26) do recognise the potential of IT in enabling 'new cooperative structures' and they point out that 'interactions between firms in the same or related industries that previously were not achievable, due to high coordination costs or high transaction risk, may now be possible'. This point is also echoed by Clark and Stoddard (1996: 350) who add that 'declining connectivity costs have enabled networked-organisation structures to become a viable design for many complex environments', and by Konsynski (1993a: 111) who points out that 'emerging information technologies change the limits of what is possible in the leverage of strategic control through transformation of boundaries, relations, and markets'.

With the rise in interest in emerging technologies such as extranets, their potential for enabling IOS and business networks in ways that were previously infeasible, and the desire of many managers to implement such systems, there is clearly a need for research in this area.

2.1.3 Planning and implementing IT/IS

Strategic information systems planning has been and remains to be one of the key IS management issues (Brancheau and Wetherbe 1987; Galliers 1994; Galliers 1995; Lederer and Salmela 1996). The continued advances in IT, the strategic nature of the impact of IT (Scott-Morton 1991), and the increased competitive pressures that companies are now facing, are putting the strategic IS planning process under greater pressure. Furthermore, as Gogan and Cash (1992: 257) contend:

> formal, top-down planning processes alone do not adequately serve the accelerating requirements of organizations coping with competitive and technological turbulence . . . Although formal planning processes are thorough and systematic, these benefits come at the expense of considerable time.

Unfortunately, for many managers, due to the heightened complexity and uncertainty characteristic of today's business environment, time in which to perform thorough and formal planning is a luxury that they possess in limited quantities.

With the advent of, and ease of implementation of new technologies such as intranets and the Internet in general (Poon and Swatman 1996), there is a need for new approaches to strategic IS planning that will provide companies with the ability to take advantage of the benefits of new technology in shorter timescales. However, in practice many forms of new IT have come in without systematic strategy formation and evaluation. Faxes, mobile phones, applications like Lotus Notes, concepts like BPR have all mushroomed in a short space of time with little formal planning but with major organisational effects.

Facilitators and inhibitors

Despite the importance of strategic IS planning to organisations, some plans never actually get implemented (Lederer and Salmela 1996; Lederer and Sethi 1988). There are many reasons (inhibitors) for this, ranging from lack of necessary resources and organisational resistance (Earl 1993) through to difficulty of recruiting (Galliers 1994). There is clearly a need for research into the implementation of strategic IS plans (Gottschalk 1997). Information systems implementation research can be categorised into three major research streams known as the factor stream, social change activity stream, and the political research stream (Kwon and Zmud 1987). Of the three streams, most studies fall into the factor stream, which tries to identify those factors that inhibit and facilitate IS implementation (King and Grover 1991).

For example, King and Thompson (1996) found that the most important facilitators were innovative needs, competitive position, environment, economies of scale, and top management guidance. Similarly they found that 'the lack of IT drivers, the lack of economies of scale, and the lack of innovative needs are the most important inhibitors' (King and Thomson 1996: 35).

Ginzberg (1981) also attempts to identify some generic facilitators, and concludes that there is consistent evidence of the importance of only two generic issues for success in management information systems (MIS) implementation. These are management support and user involvement. This view is supported by Ives and Olson (1984) who point out that these have been the prominent variables studied. However, with the continued rapid advances in IT, and the increased competitiveness in many industries, it would be useful to re-examine the relevance and subsequent degree of importance of these two variables.

2.1.4 Evaluation of IT/IS

Despite the importance of strategic IS to managers and the interest shown by researchers in the subject, the issue of evaluating and assessing the success of strategic IS and IT in general is still an area that requires further research (Lucas 1981; Jurison 1996). There is little consensus about the nature of IT's business value – or whether IT is capable of creating value (Mooney *et al.* 1995). Furthermore, there is little consensus among IS researchers on the conceptualisation and operationalisation of IS effectiveness (Thong *et al.* 1996). Furthermore, Dreifus and Daniels (1993: 3) report that 'companies are still struggling to develop adequate performance measures for IT investment'. Also Jurison (1996) points out that many senior managers are dissatisfied with their capabilities for evaluating IS impact on organisational performance. Lack of suitable approaches for evaluating the success of IT can often prevent companies from embracing new technologies (Hollis 1996).

Given that levels of IT expenditure in organisations now represent a substantial amount of capital expenditure, and that the pressures on organisations to make better use of IT continue to increase (Pumo 1996), evaluation of IT systems is more important than ever before.

However, evaluating IT success or the effectiveness of an IS is not an easy task (Hamilton and Chervany 1981; Ross *et al.* 1996), and consequently the literature in this area contains a number of different approaches (Srinivasan 1985; Goodhue 1992; Sutherland *et al.* 1995; Lines and Finlay 1995; Thong *et al.* 1996). For example, Raymond (1990: 5) points out that 'research suggests that organisational factors can be as important as individual factors for the success of information systems'. He then goes on to propose a contingency approach relating selected organisational factors (organisational size, maturity, resources, time frame, and IS sophistication) to user satisfaction and system usage. His results indicate that 'while organisational time frame and IS sophistication have a direct effect upon satisfaction and usage, the effect of size, maturity, and resources is mediated by IS sophistication'.

Other authors also put forward their suggestions for factors that influence the success (or otherwise) of IS projects. For example, Ginzberg (1981) found that top management commitment to IS projects and to organisational change can differentiate between successful and unsuccessful IS implementation. Also, Thong *et al.* (1996: 264) in examining the implementation of IS in small businesses conclude that 'while top management support is important for IS implementation, external IS expertise may be even more important in the small business context'.

However, Walsham (1993) points out that the factor approach is inadequate in that it does not account for the dynamics of the process of organisational implementation. Furthermore, Nandhakumar (1996) in discussing executive information systems (EIS) reports that a frequent assumption in the literature is that each factor is assumed to be an independent variable. This assumption thus overlooks the interaction between the factors and 'the interaction with other elements in the social and organisational context' (Nandhakumar 1996: 62).

Actually measuring IT investment payoff is difficult. This is because most IT benefits are qualitative, indirect, and diffuse (Wen *et al.* 1998). However, given that some early adopters of intranet technology reported very large ROI within relatively short periods of time, it will be interesting to see if the characteristics of the benefits delivered by intranets differ from those of more traditional IT systems as discussed in the literature.

2.1.5 Assessing when benefits accrue

Jurison (1996) discusses the dynamic nature of IT benefits and reports on findings of a three-year evaluation of user productivity and organisational effectiveness following the installation of an integrated office information system. He points out that:

> there is a pattern of organisational learning in applying new technology, and that organisations go through several distinct stages before they can really exploit new technology (Jurison, 1996: 76)

Furthermore, he adds that the impact of IT on the individual precedes that on the organisation. He concludes that the role of time has received limited attention and that 'despite (many) recommendations, examples of longitudinal studies are rare' (Jurison, 1996: 76). This is indeed the case, for evidence in the literature that supports the use of time as a variable is conspicuous by its absence. The main reason for this is perhaps the fact that it may take years before the impact of an IT system is felt at the organisational level (Jurison 1996) and longitudinal studies of such duration can be extremely expensive. Time lags between the implementation of IT and the delivery of benefits also make it very difficult to assess the success or effectiveness of the IT system (Brynjolfsson 1993). With some companies who have implemented intranets reporting benefits at the organisational level within periods as short as a few months, time as a variable may begin to appear on many people's research agenda.

Having looked at the general IT literature, the following section now focuses on Groupware as this is an area that is very relevant to a study of intranets/extranets.

2.2   Groupware

The term Groupware was originally coined in 1978 (Johnson-Lentz and Johnson-Lentz 1982) and now describes a large number of computer-based systems that support the work efforts of groups engaged in achieving common tasks or goals (Raisinghani *et al.* 1997).

The term Groupware covers a wide range of technologies (Johansen 1988). Groupware is essentially a software system that enables users to share information (Bock and Marca 1995; Glyn-Jones 1995). It has also been defined by Cameron *et al.* (1995) as technology that communicates and organises unpredictable information, allowing dynamic groups to interact across time and space. It is the support of the group activities that is significant, and thus it should be noted that Groupware is not just an extension of traditional office automation systems (St John Bate and Travell 1994).

According to Cameron *et al.* (1995: 4) there are three types or 'flavours' of Groupware. These are as follows:

1. Transmit – this 'model' includes e-mail. It adds little other than information movement from one person to others.
2. Access – shared e-mail folders, like Microsoft Exchange or Web pages built with Netscape, allow people to pull the information they want. Multiple users can thus share a single piece of information.
3. Discuss – conversations among multiple users are neither push nor pull – conversations actively involve people in an information exchange. These exchanges take place either over time or in real-time.

Groupware is not actually a new idea. Most of the technologies that Groupware comprises have been around for a number of years (Skyrme 1995). However, Groupware never really took off in the 1980s because of a lack of network infrastructure and the relatively high cost. However, the infrastructure is now in place (Opper and Fersko-Weiss 1992) and businesses are becoming aware of the potential of Groupware (Pancucci 1995). Also, the cost of Groupware technology has dropped dramatically or as Schrage (1996: 4) puts it 'the economics of Groupware have turned inside out'. Whereas common practice has been to heavily customise a Groupware product to achieve optimal performance, more affordable shrinked-wrapped Groupware solutions are becoming available (Hook and Baker 1997).

Given that Groupware is not just an extension of traditional office automation systems there are a number of authors who recognise the strategic significance of the use of Groupware (Bock and Marca 1995; King 1996; Williams 1996; Ciborra 1996). However, when viewed in a strategic context, the problem of using Groupware in an organisation becomes much more important (Hildebrand 1996).

The technology element is just one of the factors that impact on the success in using Groupware. The difficulty most organisations encounter with Groupware is not with the technology, but with the relationship between technology and the people in the organisation who have to use Groupware. It is not the technology that is the important factor, but rather how it is used (St John Bate and Travell 1994; Vandenbosch and Ginzberg 1997) and how organisational barriers to its use are overcome (Schrage 1996). This point is echoed by Klinte and Gardiner (1997) who argue that the variables of enough training and technical support while in the initial stages of learning to use the systems were by far the most important in the adoption process of Groupware in an organisation. In a similar vein, Orlikowski (1996) highlights the difficulties of integrating the technology into work practices and points out that this raises issues such as inadequate training, inappropriate expectations, and structural and cultural problems. The integration and use of Groupware into work practices is often referred to as appropriation. This is discussed in more detail below.

2.2.1   Appropriation

In an attempt to describe better how the technology is actually used in organisations, Ciborra (1996: 11) uses the notion of appropriation. 'If actually utilised, a Groupware application can be described as being appropriated by the end users, harnessed to support the requirements of the business and the task.' He describes appropriation as a form of taking 'care' of the innovation in its context of use. He distinguishes three different forms of care:

1. *Perception* – a way of taking care that deals scientifically with natural and human artefacts ... 'perception deals with sanitised, unworlded entities, that have not passed the test of being "fully immersed" in the world and getting "wet" with the everyday practicalities of

organisations'. Users either lack the resources (time, training, expertise) or specific economic incentives to engage in 'perception'. A consequence of deficient perception seems to be the slowness or the lack of exploitation of the Groupware system's potential.

2. *Circumspection* – 'this is the domain where care consists in practical problem solving and incremental learning. It is the realm of use and implementation in situ ... We learn how the organisation reacts and evolves ... The neat world of the scientific models is not at the centre of attention anymore, rather it is the match to be achieved *in vivo* (by getting our hands dirty) between the new system and the local organisational context'. Circumspection is associated with an evolving and richer use of the technology.

3. *Understanding* – 'this is the domain where "things" are granted sense, until new events arise at the horizon. It is the realm of "worlded" things, of systems and practices that effortlessly mingle with the "world" '. Understanding a system means becoming so intimately familiar with the innovation, that the system itself becomes taken for granted or self-evident (fully appropriated) since 'it gets encapsulated into the routines of our daily absorbed coping'.

Ciborra (1996) adds that full appropriation is the outcome of intimate understanding but unfortunately few and fragile instances of this process have been found.

2.2.2 Drifting

Also it is clear from the literature that as organisations experiment with and learn from their use of Groupware, the role of the technology will also evolve. This is referred to as drifting. As Ciborra (1996: 8) points out 'Groupware presents itself as a technology that tends to drift when put to use' but drifting should not be considered as a negative phenomenon as it can occur for both successful and 'failing' applications. He adds that:

drifting can be looked at as the outcome of two intertwined processes. One is given by the openness of the technology, its plasticity in response to the re-inventions carried out by users and specialists, who gradually learn to discover and exploit features and potentialities of Groupware. On the other hand, there is the sheer unfolding of the actors' 'being-in-the-workflow' and the continuous stream of interventions, bricolage and improvisations that 'colour' the entire system life cycle.

Orlikowski (1996) suggests that drifting and the process of allowing organisations to experiment and continue to evolve organisational adaptations around a new technology may be a particularly appropriate process of implementing organisational change around Groupware. She distinguishes between three different types of change that occur around Groupware (Orlikowski 1996: 56):

1. Anticipated changes – changes that are planned ahead of time and occur as intended.
2. Emergent changes – changes that arise spontaneously out of local innovation which are not originally anticipated or intended.
3. Opportunistic changes – changes that are not anticipated ahead of time but are introduced purposely and intentionally during the change process in response to an unexpected opportunity, event, or outcome.

She adds that both anticipated and opportunistic changes involve deliberate action, in contrast to emergent changes which usually arise tacitly out of people's practices with the technology over time. She posits that the effectiveness of this change process suggests that the strategy an organisation should adopt when implementing Groupware is to focus first on initial planned organisational changes, and then to build on these to enact emergent changes in response to the opportunities and conditions occasioned by the planned changes (Orlikowski 1996). However, as will be discussed later, the interplay between the technical and social elements of introducing technology into an organisation does not necessarily mean that the planned changes will actually occur.

There are many discussions and case studies of Groupware implementation and use in the literature, for example Ciborra (1996), Kiely (1993), Orlikowski (1996), Monteiro and Hepsø (1999). One message that comes from these studies is that although Groupware can facilitate collaboration in organisations, its implementation will not guarantee collaboration. As Vandenbosch and Ginzberg (1997: 77) point out:

> it will not mysteriously transform organisations from collections of highly competitive loners to well-integrated, cooperative groups of collaborators.

2.2.3 Convergence of intranets and Groupware

An intranet also provides an ideal platform on which to deploy Groupware applications. Indeed most, if not all, Groupware applications can now be provided as part of an intranet (Radosevich 1996) and web-based systems now bring the power of Groupware to any desktop equipped with a web browser (Dennis *et al.* 1998). This has forced Groupware developers to make their Groupware products 'web-friendly' (Petreley 1996), and is leading to a lot of interest in web-based Groupware (Rose 1996; Bruno 1996). Similarly, intranets have taken on many of the features of 'traditional' Groupware such as a high degree of security and ease of managing databases. The cost of 'traditional' Groupware products has also fallen significantly since the ascent of intranets.

However, although web-based Groupware may encourage more organisations to consider using intranets to improve communications and to facilitate the building of virtual communities, as Dennis *et al.* (1998) point out, the technology alone will not necessarily cause people to communicate, nor can it create virtual communities.

Having reviewed the general IT literature and identified Groupware as being particularly relevant to a study on intranets/extranets, Section 2.3 reviews the IS literature on the relationship between IT implementation and the associated organisational issues that may arise. This section thus provides a theoretical basis for understanding the factors and conditions that may shape the form and function of intranets/extranets.

2.3 The role and effect of IT

The notion of the 'impact' of IT/IS is an issue that attracts considerable attention in the literature. The idea that information systems have both a social and a technical element has been recognised but as pointed out by Jones (1999: 287) 'this recognition has not been matched by the emergence of a coherent theoretical understanding of the nature of, and relationship between, these elements'. Indeed the relationship between information technology and organisational change is a central concern in the field of information systems (Markus and Robey 1988) and remains a source of controversy. Jones (1999) comments that traditionally this controversy has been seen as a struggle between technological determinism (where technology shapes the forms of society and organisations) and social determinism (where cultural and social structural patterns determine the way in which technology is used in organisations).

2.3.1 Technological determinism

Proponents of technological determinism in organisations (e.g. Rockart and Scott-Morton 1984) take the view that IT is a cause of organisational change and that the use of IT in an organisation and the subsequent changes that occur have a predictable cause and effect relationship. In terms of the effects of IT on organisations, Attewell and Rule (1984) point out that these effects are more complicated and diverse than that has traditionally been assumed. With the continued advance in technology and the corresponding impact being seen not only at the level of the organisation but also at the level of the industry, it is likely that the effects of IT will become not only more complicated and diverse, but even more difficult to manage.

Although, it is clear that IT can have wide ranging impacts on the industry level (Bakos and Brynjolfsson 1993), many business managers are still struggling to cope with the problem of managing the changing role within the organisation. Henderson and Venkatraman (1993: 5) point out that 'although there may be some consensus on the changing role of IT within organisations, managers are still confronted with basic questions such as: what are the implications of IT in my business operations? Today? In the future?'

Jurison (1996: 75) also reports that many senior managers are 'dissatisfied with their capabilities for evaluating IS impact on organisational performance'. He adds that despite the number of empirical studies that have been conducted, they have produced mixed or even conflicting results. In addition to suggesting that this may be due to the fact that the intervening effect of time was not being recognised explicitly, he suggests a further possible explanation for this may be:

> the complex interactions between technology and its organisational users in the implementation process can lead to outcomes that are not necessarily predictable. As a result it is difficult to make comparisons and develop consistent theories.

However, while the approach of technological determinism is useful in that it provides a perspective on IT and organisational change, it does not tell the whole story. It fails to capture sufficiently the nature of how technology affects organisations. The nature of causal influence on why and how technology affects organisational life is addressed by Markus and Robey (1988) who use the term 'technological imperative' to refer to the case where IT is viewed as a cause of organisational change (similar to the notion of technological determinism), and 'organisational imperative' to refer to the case where the motives and actions of the designers of IT are a cause of organisational change. They point out that:

while the technological imperative has a long history and makes some compelling claims, empirical research has generated contradictory findings on almost every dimension of hypothesized computer impact. Information systems have been found both to enrich and routinize jobs, both centralize and decentralize authority and produce no changes where changes were expected (Markus and Robey 1988: 585).

This point is echoed by Robey (1995) who adds that despite the availability of numerous studies, a consistent picture of the effects of technology on organisations does not appear. In addition, in some cases where the implementation and use of nearly identical technologies was performed, studies indicated contradictory outcomes. Horvath and Fulk (1994: 117) add that the literature 'presents a bewildering array of arguments, including some ill-defined and contradictory claims ... and information technologies are implicated in at least several different arguments about organisational change'.

To get a fuller picture of IT and organisational change it is necessary to look at aspects of social determinism and the organisational imperative.

2.3.2 Social determinism

Compared to technological determinism, the stance adopted by social determinism is an explicitly humanist one. It argues that technology or scientific knowledge is solely a product of human agency (Jones 1999). Taking this approach, 'the design, introduction, and use of information systems is to be understood in terms of the playing-out of socio-political forces, rather than of any inherent character of technology' (Jones 1999: 290). This does not mean that technology has no effect whatsoever but rather it does not necessarily lead to particular social effects (Gallie 1978). The perspective of social determinism is similar to the 'organisational imperative' considered by Markus and Robey (1988: 587). They point out that:

> whereas the technological imperative argues that information technology constrains or determines human and organizational behaviour, the organizational imperative assumes almost unlimited choice over technological options and almost unlimited control over the consequences.

2.3.3 Bridging the gap between the social and the technical

Complementing the technological imperative (where technology is the 'cause' of predictable change) and the organisational imperative (where people are the 'cause' of predictable change) is a third perspective considered by Markus and Robey (1988: 588). This third perspective, the emergent perspective, holds that 'the use and consequences of technology emerge unpredictably from complex social interactions'. Thus, organisational change emerges from an unpredictable interaction between IT and its organisational users. The emergent perspective is essentially an attempt to bridge the gap between the other two perspectives and seeks to acknowledge the interplay of the technical and the social factors in IT design and use. Other attempts to bridge this gap include:

- *Actor network theory* (e.g. Monteiro and Hanseth 1996; Walsham 1997) – actor network theory treats the social and the technical as inseparable and as Walsham (1997: 467) points out it 'argues that people and artefacts should be analyzed with the same conceptual apparatus'. It thus insists on the equality of treatment of the social and the technical elements.
- *Socio-technical systems theory* (e.g. Grint and Woolgar 1997) – in this approach the technical and social elements are seen as independent of each other and as Jones (1999: 291) points out, this theory 'argues that the effective design of technologically-based work processes requires the simultaneous optimisation of both elements'.
- *Structurational* (e.g. Orlikowski 1992) – this approach also recognises that there is a tight interplay between the social and the technical elements but argues that technology is 'interpretively flexible' and that there is a recursive relationship between users, technologies and the structural properties of the organisation.

However, Jones (1999) notes that none of these approaches are perfect and the debate over the relative merits of each will continue.

2.3.4   Communication technologies and organizational change

The use of communication technologies as a vehicle with which to bring about 'planned' organisational change is addressed by people such as Fulk and DeSanctis (1995), Marlow and O'Connor-Wilson (1997), Sproull and Kiesler (1991), Orlikowski *et al.* (1995). As Fulk and DeSanctis (1995: 337) point out:

> electronic communication technologies are enablers of changed forms by offering capabilities to overcome constraints on time and distance, key barriers around which organizational forms traditionally have been designed.

Electronic communication technologies can be viewed as 'occasions' for structuring, in that they offer opportunities to manipulate both the technology itself as well as the organisational contexts in which they are implemented and used (Barley 1986; Orlikowski *et al.* 1995). Features of new communication technologies such as the dramatic increase in speed of communication, unprecedented reduction in the costs of communications, increase in bandwidth (permitting multimedia communications), vastly expanded connectivity, and the integration of communications with computing technology, together enable communication of richer, more complex information than was previously possible and contribute to a large variety of changes in organisational form (Fulk and DeSanctis 1995).

In addressing the interplay between communications technology and organisational form, Fulk and DeSanctis (1995) describe key dimensions of intraorganisational and interorganisational forms that are linked to electronic communication technologies.

The two main interorganisational forms they address are referred to as interorganisational 'coupling' and strategic alliances, both of which are related to the degree of cooperation between the organisations involved. The main intraorganisational forms they address are as follows:

1. *Vertical control* – this refers to the degree to which hierarchical control in an organization is affected by communications technologies and how these technologies can be used to enable flattening of hierarchies.
2. *Horizontal coordination* – this refers to the use of the technology to facilitate activities such as electronic workflow (e.g. through electronic document sharing), concurrent engineering, and a movement towards a virtual organisation where people are not tied to any particular workspace and they can work away from the physical location of the organisation.
3. *Organization and unit size* – this refers to how large 'segmented organisations' can be replaced by 'leaner, integrated ones' with the assistance of communications and related technologies.
4. *New types of coupling* – this refers to cases where, taking advantage of the increased capabilities for both vertical and horizontal coordination, new types of coupling across organisational units is possible. Examples include spin-off entrepreneurial organisations for which the core organisation retains some ownership and control.
5. *Communication cultures* – this refers to cases where through the use of communication technologies the culture of communication in the organisation changes. For example, individuals 'learn to link' with others throughout the organisation, many of whom they may never

have met. This point is echoed by Nohria and Berkley (1994) who argue that major changes in social space are enabled by communication and information technology, particularly the Internet.

As intranets are a relatively new technology, it is useful to look at the history of other communications 'technology' and see what can be learned about what to expect. Sproull and Kiesler (1991: 4) in focusing on communications facilitated by e-mail, argue that the effects of communications can be seen at two levels:

1. First-level effects are the anticipated technical ones – the planned efficiency gains or productivity gains that justify an investment in new technology. They point out that 'conventional cost-displacement or value-added analysis often underlies the calculation of these gains' and that these analyses are fraught with enormous difficulties. They argue that 'cost estimates of new technologies typically underestimate implementation costs of training and conversion to new ways of working even when they do not underestimate installation costs . . . . These analyses have no way to recognise that the most important effects of a new technology may be not to let people do old things more efficiently but instead to do new things that were not possible or feasible with the old technology'.

2. Second-level effects of communication technologies come about primarily because new communication technology leads people to pay attention to different things, have contact with different people, and depend on one another differently. By change in attention they mean changes in how people spend their time and in what they think is important. They add that 'change in social contact patterns means changes in who people know and how they feel about them'. Finally they note that 'change in interdependence means change in what people do with and for each other and how these coupled functions are organised in norms, role, procedures, jobs, and departments. Social roles which codify patterns of attention and social interaction, change'.

They conclude that when technological change creates new social situations, traditional expectations and norms lose their power and 'people invent new ways of behaving' (Sproull and Kiesler 1991: 39). They also add that rules and policies for electronic communication differ from organisation to organisation and that 'some organisations explicitly forbid extracurricular messages, others do not' (Sproull and Kiesler 1991: 51).

This will obviously colour the effects that are likely to result from the use of such technologies in organisations.

The nature and extent of the effects that may occur will also be contingent on what Markus and Robey (1983) refer to as 'organisational validity'. This is the 'fit' or match between an information system and its organisational context of use. One of the key 'dimensions' of this validity concerns the distribution of power and the nature of the political environment within an organisation and the degree to which this may be affected by the implementation of a new information system.

2.3.5 Power and politics

It is widely regarded that the implementation of information systems in organisations is a political process (e.g. Hedberg *et al.* 1975; Keen 1981; Markus 1983; Bloomfield and Coombs 1992) and thus in attempting to understand the nature of the changes that may accompany the implementation and operation of an IT system it is necessary to consider the role of politics in shaping these changes. Morgan (1986) argues that we should view organisations as loose networks of people with divergent interests. Similarly, Bariff and Galbraith (1978: 15) observe that 'organisations may be viewed as shifting political coalitions competing for organisational resources'. Walsham (1993), in discussing organisations as political systems, points out that a crucial concept for this political metaphor of organisations is power. He notes (Walsham 1993: 39) that:

> power is the medium through which conflicts of interest are resolved.

Furthermore, he points out that power remains 'an elusive and problematic concept' despite the common usage which is made of the word and that the process of the exercise of power is also highly complex. This complexity is illustrated by the different treatments of the concept of power that appear in the literature. For example, Markus (1983) and Markus and Pfeffer (1983) treat power as an 'entity', something which you can possess, whereas Foucault (1980, 1983) and Knights and Roberts (1982) argue that power is not an object but rather should be viewed as a condition and outcome of relationships.

In addressing the conceptualisation of power in relation to the use of IT in organisations, Bloomfield and Coombs (1992) observe that there are four main approaches that can be used:

1. The first approach is referred to as a *'sovereign'* view of power. This is the notion mentioned above that power is an entity. They note

(Bloomfield and Coombs 1992: 462) that 'you either exercise power over others, or it is exercised over you'.

2. The second approach is based on the argument that power in organisations resides not in people but in systems and structures. In this view, the use of information systems in organisations tends to reinforce the power of already potent players.

3. The third approach avoids a consideration of sources of power and looks instead to the exercise of power, which is interpreted in terms of behavioural outcomes. They note (Bloomfield and Coombs 1992: 465) that this approach 'presupposes the notion of real interests because it is only against this assumption that user behaviour can be judged'. In other words, users of information systems will always act in their real interests unless prevented from doing so by the exercise of power by others in the organisation.

4. Their final approach to the conceptualisation of power relates to the view mentioned earlier that power is not a possession but a relationship.

The introduction of IS into an organisation both influences the exercise of power (Keen 1981; Bariff and Galbraith 1978) and is itself influenced by the exercise of power within an organisation (Markus 1983; Markus and Robey 1983; Knights and Murray 1992; Sayer 1998). Even the design of an information system can be an exercise of power (e.g. Markus and Pfeffer 1983) as can the actual use of the system (Markus and Bjørn-Andersen 1987). For example, Bariff and Galbraith (1978) point out that the ability of some individuals or groups within an organisation to control the administration and distribution of information provides perceived power over other individuals. They note that systems can be implemented with one of two goals in mind: improvement in current operations entailing minimal change in the existing power structure, or substantial change in the structure with the system as the vehicle of change. Boland (1997: 373) points out that this view stems from the '*fantasy*' that information is power and adds that:

> the fantasy that information is power inflates the role of the IS designer to include the creation and reallocation of power.

More importantly, he notes that the 'fantasy' that information is power distorts the idea of power relationships and that it 'reduces power from an interactive, relational phenomenon to a commodity that operates unidirectionally' (Boland 1997: 370).

While recognising the limitations of the maxim that 'information is power' (i.e. it 'reifies' power), as will be seen later in the case studies, it does provide a useful base on which to frame a discussion of the political issues associated with the implementation and operation of intranets and extranets. While intranets and extranets do permit access to large amounts of information, in general as noted by Markus (1983: 442):

> access to information is probably less important as a basis of power than is the ability to control access to information or to define what information will be kept and manipulated in what ways.

As noted by Walsham (1993: 41) 'the process of the exercise of power and the taking of political action is highly complex, both in theoretical terms and in attempting to observe it in practice'. He adds that the reason why it is difficult to observe it in practice is because 'people often attempt to conceal their motives for political action in order to protect what they perceive as their self-interest'. As will be seen in Chapter 8, the implementation of intranets and extranets permits a degree of 'openness' that may help to expose to a wider audience the exercise of power and the taking of political action.

2.4 Summary

The widespread interest and implementation in organisations of new technologies such as intranets and extranets and the opportunities they offer is likely to lead to a renewed interest in IT and IS research. Some of this research is likely to reuse and re-evaluate the models and frameworks that are extant in the literature. Indeed the approach taken in this research is to view intranets/extranets as the latest in a line of IT systems. However, as noted above, intranets also share characteristics with Groupware and thus intranets should also be viewed in the context of the literature relating to communications technologies.

2.4.1 Main themes

This section has presented a review of the literature concerned with the implementation and use of IT. It has served to identify a number of issues and potential measures that can be used both as a guide to data collection and as a framework for structuring the discussion of the results of this research. In terms of the 'traditional' IT literature the main themes are illustrated in Table 2.1. The table also includes some

Table 2.1   Main themes and potential measures related to the use of IT

Theme	Measures
Integration into corporate strategy	Degree of linkage between business objectives and IT objectives
	Degree of integration with existing IS/IT systems
Competitive advantage	Degree to which the advantage is sustainable
(i) Change in bargaining power	Change in 'search-related' costs
	Change in switching costs (suppliers)
	Change in switching costs (customers)
(ii) Change in comparative efficiency	Change in internal efficiency
	Change in interorganisational efficiency
Planning and implementation	Amount of time spent in the formal planning process
	Time lag between planning and implementation
	Facilitators and inhibitors to implementation
	The involvement of external expertise in planning and implementation
Evaluation	Benefits
	Time before benefits accrue
	Downsides
Groupware-related issues	Degree of integration and appropriation into use
	Degree of drifting (if any) that occurred
Role and effect of IT	Resultant changes in organisational forms
	Identification of factors which shape the form and function of IT in its organisational context
	Degree of influence on power and the exercise of power
	Degree of influence of existing social and power structures in the organisation

potential measures or criteria against which to assess the use of intranets/extranets.

The main themes with respect to the review of the Groupware literature that was presented earlier are also illustrated in Table 2.1. Appropriation refers to how the system is employed by users and the amount of 'care' given to the system. As discussed earlier, three forms of care were identified; perception (essentially refers to the case where the potential of the system is not being exploited), circumspection (refers to an evolving and richer use of the technology), and understanding (refers to the case where the system is 'taken for granted' and is thus fully appropriated).

As people in organisations experiment and learn from their use of Groupware, the role of the technology may also evolve as users 'discover' or 'invent' new applications and new ways of doing things. This 'evolution' of use away from what is intended originally is referred to as drifting, and as such is related to the types of changes that may occur around Groupware. As discussed earlier, the types of changes may be referred to as anticipated, emergent, or opportunistic.

Building on the notion of changes it is also useful to recap on Fulk and DeSanctis' (1995) key dimensions of changes in intraorganisational and interorganisational forms that are linked to electronic communication technologies. The intraorganisational dimensions refer to changes in forms of vertical control, horizontal coordination, organisation and unit size, new types of coupling, and communication cultures. The two key dimensions of changes in interorganisational forms are strategic alliances and interorganisational coupling. However, both of these are merely external instantiations of the intraorganisational forms and thus the five intraorganisational forms can be used to address both the internal and the external issues.

The final main theme discussed concerned the importance of considering the political issues associated with the implementation and operation of information systems. As was noted in the discussion, the implementation of an IS both affects and is affected by the nature of the political environment into which it is introduced. Therefore, it is necessary to examine to what extent the exercise of power in an organisation influences and is influenced by the implementation and operation of intranets and extranets.

In summary the themes identified in Table 2.1 identify the key issues relevant to an understanding of intranets/extranets.

2.4.2 Linking to the rest of the book

Having identified (as above) the key issues relevant to an understanding of intranets/extranets, these themes were used to derive the research schedule and to identify the questions asked during the data collection phase of the research. This is addressed in detail in Chapter 4. Furthermore, in order to situate the research findings in the literature, these themes will be used in Chapter 8 to structure a discussion of the findings from the case studies that are presented in Chapters 5, 6 and 7.

However, as noted in the introduction, a strong emerging theme from the case studies and the preliminary research was the potential role of intranets/extranets in facilitating aspects of knowledge management. Thus, in order to introduce the issues addressed by knowledge management and to provide a theoretical basis on which to discuss the findings, Chapter 3, which follows, presents a review of the literature in this area.

3
Knowledge Management

As noted in Chapter 1, interest in intranets and the Internet in general, is leading to an interest in the use of the technologies to facilitate various aspects of knowledge management. This issue emerged quite strongly both in the preliminary and main phase of this research, and as will be seen in the case studies, many of the issues that arose from the cases are related to issues of information and knowledge management. As will be seen later, an appreciation of these issues is important in helping to understand the political aspects that accompany the implementation and operation of intranets/extranets. Thus, in order to provide a theoretical basis on which to discuss these topics and to enhance further the understanding of the issues surrounding the use of intranets/extranets, this chapter presents a review of the literature relating to knowledge management.

The chapter begins with an explanation of the terminology associated with knowledge management and a clarification of the distinction between data, information, and knowledge is presented. This helps to set the context for a discussion of why knowledge management in a general sense is of interest to managers in organisations. Clarifying the terminology also helps to set the context for the subsequent discussion of different perspectives of knowledge and knowledge management.

3.1 What are data, information, knowledge?

There are numerous definitions of data, information and knowledge in the literature. As Davenport and Prusak (1998: 1) note:

> knowledge is neither data nor information, though it is related to both ... However basic it may sound, it is still important to emphasise

that data, information, and knowledge are not interchangeable concepts.

While it is recognised that there are differences between data, information and knowledge, unfortunately there are no generally accepted definitions and the boundaries between them depend on the author's perspective. Much confusion can occur by the interchangeable use of these terms. Furthermore, as Prusak (1998) notes, if knowledge is not something different from data or information, then there is nothing new or interesting in knowledge management.

3.1.1   Data

Defining data would appear to be relatively straightforward. According to Harris (1996), the lowest level of known facts is data; data have no intrinsic meaning. Similarly, Avison and Fitzgerald (1995: 12) note that 'data represent unstructured facts'. However, while there is no inherent meaning in data, data are important because they are the 'essential raw material for the creation of information' (Davenport and Prusak 1998: 3).

3.1.2   Data to information

When data are sorted, grouped, analysed, and interpreted, they become information (Harris 1996). Information is thus data organised into meaningful patterns (Marshall 1997). Information is quite simply an understanding of relationships between pieces of data (Bellinger 2001). Checkland and Holwell (1998: 89) argue that there is an intermediate stage between data and information. They use the term data to refer to the 'great mass of facts' and the term 'capta' to refer to the subset of data which we are interested in or to which we pay attention.

However, rather than viewing data, information, and indeed knowledge as being discrete, it is perhaps more beneficial to consider a continuum from data through to knowledge (Bellinger 2001), with the decision as to where a particular item resides being determined both on an individual level, and situationally, by its specific context. As pointed out by Marshall (1997: 94), 'one person's knowledge can be another person's information'. A similar perspective is taken by Davenport and Prusak (1998: 7) who point out that 'knowledge can also move down the value chain, returning to information and data'.

3.1.3   Information to knowledge

Perhaps the greatest confusion lies in distinguishing between information and knowledge, and many authors use the terms interchangeably. For example, Huber (1991: 89) in discussing the role of information and knowledge in organisational learning states that 'the words information and knowledge will be used interchangeably in this paper' but then goes on to give different definitions of the two terms; 'information when referring to data that give meaning by reducing ambiguity, equivocality, or uncertainty' and 'knowledge when referring to more complex products of learning, such as interpretations of information'.

The idea that interpretation and context are important when referring to information and knowledge is also discussed by Marshall (1997: 94) who adds that 'information is transformed into knowledge when a person reads, understands, interprets, and applies the information to a specific work function'. Similarly, from an information systems perspective, Jones (1995: 64) notes that:

> it is typical in the information systems literature to distinguish between data as symbols that represent, describe, or record states of the world; information as the purposeful interpretation of data; and knowledge as the retained understanding arising from interpretation.

Thus, one view of knowledge is that it is information combined with context, experience, interpretation, and reflection (Davenport *et al.* 1998). However, as knowledge is an interdisciplinary field incorporating many disciplines such as philosophy, economics, management, information technology, psychology, and artificial intelligence, it is not surprising that there are many views and definitions (Ponelis and Fairer-Wessels 1998).

From the perspective of knowledge management – and assuming for the moment that knowledge is capable of being managed in the conventional sense – what is important is not the precise words used to define knowledge but rather an appreciation of the range of practical issues embraced by the terms (KPMG 1998c). Some of the most important characteristics that set knowledge apart from other organisational resources, as identified by Wiig *et al.* (1997: 16), include the following:

* knowledge is intangible and difficult to measure
* knowledge is volatile, that is, it can 'disappear' overnight
* knowledge is not 'consumed' in a process, it sometimes increases through use.

Thus, as noted by Cropley (1998), a key aspect of knowledge is that it is dynamic and thrives on being supplemented, adapted and applied iteratively; knowledge which is controlled and fixed ossifies.

3.2   Interest in knowledge management

The level of interest in knowledge management has been building for several years (Skyrme 1997a; Cropley 1998) and this is partly because of the recognition that knowledge has become increasingly important to an individual firm's success (Cole 1998). As pointed out by KPMG (1998c: i):

> we are in an era where the traditional pillars of economic power – capital, land, plant and labour – are no longer the main determinants of business success. Instead, an increasing number of organisations depend for their value on the development, use and distribution of knowledge-based competencies.

Knowledge is increasingly regarded as the primary source of sustainable competitive advantage (e.g. Pralahad and Hamel 1992; Grant 1996).

Wiig (1997) notes that systematic management of knowledge takes on new importance with the current economic reality where knowledge is a differentiating competitive factor for individuals, corporations and nations. He concludes that in the future, knowledge management will become a routine activity for all organisations. Similarly, Stein (1995: 32) notes that:

> knowledge is a new source of competitive advantage. A better understanding of the memory processes of knowledge acquisition, retention, maintenance, and retrieval will offer new ways for organisations to profit from organisational knowledge.

However, knowledge management has always been of interest to managers in the sense that 'organisations' have desired to capture and document business processes, for example as part of Total Quality management (TQM) programmes (Gundry and Metes 1998) and also in the sense that innovative 'organisations' in particular have long appreciated the value of knowledge to enhance their products and services (Skyrme 1997b). So why is knowledge management receiving so much attention now? Is it just the latest fad? Is it simply the thing that managers feel they need to do now that they have 'done' TQM and BPR?

Knowledge management is certainly the latest in a series of business trends and as tends to happen in such cases, some 'relabelling' of existing activities takes place and many activities are loosely called knowledge management. Cropley (1998) notes that while some of these may be truly new ways of regarding information and knowledge, others are merely name changes or attempts to enhance the value and status of existing activities. As pointed out by Ruggles (1998), knowledge management is a term which has now come to be used to describe everything from efforts at organisational learning to database management tools. However, knowledge management is also concerned with establishing an environment in which knowledge can evolve. As noted by Schultze (1999), concepts like organisational learning, organisational memory, information sharing, and collaborative work are closely related to knowledge management.

If the time has come to take up the challenges of knowledge management, then as pointed out by Cropley (1998: 28):

> everyone trying to do so should be aware that this is a dangerous world, far more complex than anything met by the average business information worker in the past.

3.3 Perspectives of knowledge

It is clear from the literature that knowledge can be thought of in many ways, and indeed there are a number of different types of knowledge discussed (Teece 1998). From a knowledge management perspective, it is useful to be able to identify and categorise types of knowledge as it may help to indicate which of the categories are more amenable to management than others (Ponelis and Fairer-Wessels 1998). Nonaka (1991: 98) discusses two very different types of knowledge, explicit and tacit. He describes explicit knowledge as being 'formal and systematic'. Nonaka and Takeuchi (1995) add that explicit knowledge can be articulated in formal language including grammatical statements, mathematical expressions, specifications, manuals, and so forth. Explicit knowledge is articulated knowledge – knowledge which has been formalised by way of speech, text, and visual graphics for example (Doyle and du Toit 1998). Thus explicit knowledge can be easily communicated and shared, in product specifications or a scientific formula or a computer program (Nonaka 1991).

Tacit knowledge, on the other hand, is 'highly personal. It is hard to formalise and, therefore, difficult to communicate to others' (Nonaka 1991: 98). As Polanyi (1997: 136) notes 'we can know more than we can tell'. Nonaka (1991: 98) adds that tacit knowledge consists 'partly of technical skills – the kind of informal, hard-to-pin-down skills captured in the term "know-how" '. Distance, both physical separation and time, renders sharing the tacit dimensions of knowledge difficult, although technology may offer a partial solution (Leonard and Sensiper 1998). If tacit knowledge is difficult to reproduce or formalise in a document or a database then perhaps, in an organisational context, the 'codification' process could be based on identifying someone with the knowledge, directing the seeker to it, and encouraging or facilitating them to interact (Davenport and Prusak 1998). There is evidence that intranets are being used to fulfil this role (Campalans *et al.* 1997; Wiig 1997; KPMG 1998a).

Although the distinction between tacit knowledge and explicit knowledge is useful in helping to identify and understand which aspects of knowledge could be managed, it is also informative to return to the notion of knowledge as being part of a continuum. As pointed out by Polanyi (1966: 4), all knowledge has tacit dimensions. Thus at one extreme, knowledge is almost completely explicit, codified, structured and accessible to others. At the other extreme, knowledge is almost completely tacit, that is, semiconscious and unconscious knowledge held in people's heads. Most knowledge exists in between the extremes (Leonard and Sensiper 1998).

Another way of looking at this 'dual' aspect of knowledge is to consider knowledge as composed of elements of 'knowing how' and 'knowing what' (Polanyi 1997), where the 'knowing how' represents the tacit dimension and tends to be more intellectual, whereas the 'knowing what' represents the explicit dimension and tends to be more practical. As Polanyi (1997: 137) adds, 'these two aspects of knowing have similar structure and neither is ever present without the other'. As discussed by Sveiby (1998), this essentially means that knowledge can be viewed as being both 'static' (the knowing what) and 'dynamic' (the knowing how), both of these dimensions are complementary. Tsoukas (1996: 14) contends that one cannot split tacit from explicit knowledge as 'the two are inseparably related'.

The above perspectives of knowledge essentially portray knowledge as some form of entity that can be possessed and exchanged. Tsoukas (1996: 13) refers to such treatments of knowledge as being 'primarily taxonomic in character' and as noted by Hayes and Walsham (2000), this tends to be the dominant approach in the knowledge work literature. There is also a less dominant relational approach which, as Hayes and Walsham (2000) point out, portrays knowledge as being provisional and context bound. For example, Tsoukas (1996) contends that knowledge cannot be separated from its context and argues that rather than focusing on the classification of forms of organisational knowledge, firms should actually be viewed as being distributed knowledge systems.

He points out (Tsoukas 1996: 13) that taking this approach allows knowledge to be understood 'in a much broader sense'. This view also obviates the need to classify knowledge into conceptual categories and thus 'avoids the dichotomies inherent in the typologies of organisational knowledge' (Tsoukas 1996: 14). Boland and Tenkasi (1995: 351) take a similar relational view in that they see organisations as being characterised by a process of distributed cognition where multiple communities with specialised expertise 'interact to create the patterns of sense making and behaviour displayed by the organisation as a whole'.

Similarly, Blackler (1993: 863) offers a theory of organisations as 'activity systems' which he contends 'reveals the tentative nature of knowledge and its action orientation'. Blackler (1995: 1021) develops this idea further and suggests that:

> attention should be focused on the systems through which people in an organisation achieve their knowledge (or more appropriately, knowing), on the changes that are occurring within such systems and on the processes through which new knowledge may be generated.

A final perspective of knowledge is provided by Alvesson (1993) who points out that to attempt to define knowledge in a non-abstract and non-sweeping way is very difficult and that organisations lay claim to knowledge rather than actually possess knowledge.

An awareness of these different perspectives of knowledge is important not only in understanding which elements of knowledge lend themselves to management but also in looking at the different approaches that could be taken to managing knowledge.

Having looked at different perspectives of knowledge, it is now necessary to examine what is actually meant by 'knowledge management'.

3.4 What is knowledge management?

Just as there are many definitions and interpretations of knowledge, there are also numerous definitions of knowledge management. As noted by Wiig (1997), to date, no general approach to managing knowledge has been commonly accepted – although several isolated, and at times diverging, notions are being advanced. Malhotra (1998) observes that the academic notions of knowledge and its management are split between the various camps of psychologists, technologists and organisation theorists, and that the 'trade' press or practitioners follow either

a techno-centric approach (looking at how various IT systems can facilitate knowledge management) or they take a human-resource oriented
approach (for example, looking at the cultural issues that are relevant to
knowledge management).

Ruggles (1998) points out that knowledge management is a relatively
new set of ideas for the general business community and that managers
when faced with a new challenge tend to approach it with tools with
which they are already familiar. Thus, with knowledge management
seeming initially to be a problem related to content management, these
tools tend to be technological, intranets and/or Groupware for example.
However, he notes that the nature of the 'challenge' of knowledge management is much more about the interrelationship of content, context,
and people, and thus 'it is inevitable that the technology will not be
enough' (Ruggles 1998: 88).

A fairly simple definition of knowledge management is given by
Coleman (1997a: 1) who notes that 'knowledge management is composed of business and technical strategies that make the right information available to the right people at the right time'. Similarly, Ruggles
(1998: 80) points out that:

> knowledge management is an approach to adding or creating value
> by more actively leveraging the know-how, experience, and judgement
> resident within and, in many cases, outside of an organisation.

Campalans *et al.* (1997: 29) suggest that knowledge management is 'an
exercise or process for capturing an organisation's intellectual assets,
which are critical to maintaining competitive advantage and managing
day-to-day operations'. They add that 'knowledge management also
encompasses the processes for sharing intellectual assets, as well as the
development of a technology platform – either Groupware of an intranet –
for sharing those assets'.

The notion that knowledge management refers to the harnessing of
an organisation's intellectual capital is also discussed by Wiig (1997)
and Stewart (1998). Marshall (1997: 93) adds that 'knowledge management theory discusses accessing and using all information within an
institution, enabling individuals to apply pertinent information to
what they already know, in order to create knowledge'. This is perhaps
getting nearer to a meaningful approach to knowledge management in
that it recognises the role of people in the process of knowledge management. As pointed out by Malhotra (1998), knowledge management
embodies organisational processes that seek synergistic combinations of

the data and information processing capacities of IT and the creative and innovative capacities of human beings.

3.4.1 Contradictions in the knowledge management literature

As discussed earlier, there are many definitions of knowledge and many interpretations of what is involved in knowledge management. This not only leads to confusion but also gives rise to a number of contradictions. A recent paper by Schultze (1999) categorises the research in knowledge management according to assumptions about knowledge and the nature of social order. She points out that a key to understanding knowledge management and the contradictions within this area of research is the definition of knowledge and the work of creating, transferring, and using it. She uses a framework (developed by Burrel and Morgan 1979) to provide a theoretical structuring for exploring these apparent contradictions. Of interest here is that she explores knowledge management research from the perspectives of the functionalist paradigm and the interpretative paradigm. Her views of this are presented below.

Knowledge management from the functionalist perspective

In the knowledge management arena the functionalist assumption that facts about the world are 'just' waiting to be discovered, translates into the notion that knowledge has an 'object-like' existence. This means that it can be captured, manipulated, transferred, and protected (Schultze 1999). From the perspective of the functionalist researcher, much time is spent categorising and classifying this object according to criteria such as location (e.g. individual knowledge, organisational knowledge), form (e.g. explicit or tacit knowledge), applicability (universal or local knowledge), and content (e.g. know-what, know-how, practical knowledge). Thus, from the functionalist perspective, the knowledge management challenge lies in the creation, manipulation, storage, transfer, and protection of the object. This involves the conversion of the knowledge object from one form to another, especially from its tacit and individually-held state into an explicit and sharable state.

However, there are contradictions inherent in this perspective. In particular, functionalists claim to act on actuality, that is on the way things work, but their taxonomies of knowledge are established *a priori* and are theoretical in nature. For instance, 'dualisms like tacit and explicit knowledge that set up the possibility of conversion from one form to another ignore the interdependence and mutually-constitutive relationship between tacit and explicit knowledge. The different types of knowledge are not only difficult to discern empirically . . . but also are not reflective of reality' (Schultze 1999: 162). The notion of knowledge as a continuum is not recognised from the functionalist's perspective.

Knowledge management from the interpretivist perspective

In the knowledge management arena, the interpretivist's view that the purpose of social science is to interpret the meanings of social actions and that reality is socially constructed, translates into a view of knowledge as a 'continuous accomplishment', that is a process rather than an object. Organisations are seen as streams of knowledge and streams of distributed cognition, where distributed cognition refers to 'a process in which individuals act autonomously yet with an understanding of their interdependence with others' (Schultze 1999: 163). From the interpretivist perspective, the knowledge management challenge is 'to coordinate purposeful individuals whose actions stem from their unique interpretation of situated circumstances' (Schultze 1999: 164). Thus individual actors need to take their interdependency with others into account both in making interpretations and in taking action. Given the dynamic nature of the socially constructed world and the incompleteness of knowledge, 'the challenge of knowledge management is to facilitate the continuous process of creating and recreating the appreciation for the interdependence between individual actors that need to act as a collective' (Schultze 1999: 164). Knowledge management solutions rest in the development of languages or communication genres (Yates and Orlikowski 1992) that guide an individual's interpretation of communicative acts. As Schultze (1999: 164) notes:

> developing genres of communication is equivalent to developing a language that offers members of a community dynamic affordances to express themselves in a way that they will be understood, and to interpret the messages and action of others in a way that is consistent with their intentions.

However, there are also some contradictions inherent in the interpretive perspective. Firstly, it assumes people are capable of being self-reflexive and that they are willing to be open. This perspective further assumes that people trust knowledge management processes and the technology that supports them. These assumptions 'are associated with the notion that knowledge and understanding are "good" or at least neutral' (Schultze 1999: 165). As Schultze (1999: 165) points out this might be true in the context of scientific inquiry where knowledge is openly shared but this assumption about knowledge 'does not hold in a competitive business environment in which knowledge is frequently associated with power and competitive advantage'.

3.4.2 Process view of knowledge management

Another commonly occurring thread in the knowledge management literature is that of taking a process-based perspective of knowledge focused activities. For example, Coleman (1997a) suggests that knowledge management revolves around the following four processes:

1. Gathering – process of bringing information and data into the system.
2. Organizing – process of associating items to subjects, giving them a context, making them easier to find.
3. Refining – process of adding value by discovering relationships, abstracting, synthesis and sharing.
4. Disseminating – process of getting knowledge to those who can use it.

Similarly, Gundry and Metes (1998) propose that the knowledge management process also involves four categories which they refer to as; capture, organisation and storage, distribution or sharing, and application or leverage. Other authors also propose various numbers of processes, with slightly differing names. For example:

- Ruggles (1998) proposes eight processes: generating new knowledge; accessing knowledge from outside sources; accessible knowledge in decision making; embedding knowledge in processes, products, and/ or services; representing knowledge in documents, databases, and software; facilitating knowledge growth through culture and incentives; transferring existing knowledge into other parts of the organisation; and measuring the value of knowledge assets and/or impact of knowledge management.
- Schultze (1999) proposes five processes: generation; organisation; storage; transfer; and use.
- Warren (1998) proposes four processes: collecting; storing; analysing; and making accessible.
- Skyrme (1997b) proposes five processes: creating knowledge; gathering knowledge; organising knowledge; diffusion; use and exploitation of knowledge.

Examination of all these various different suggestions for the processes of knowledge management reveals that there are four 'core' processes that encompass the above. These 'core' processes are:

1. knowledge creation
2. knowledge storage
3. knowledge transfer
4. knowledge use.

Each of these processes is discussed in detail below. It should be noted that these processes are not discrete and there is a certain degree of overlap between them.

3.5   Knowledge creation

As seems to be the case in most aspects of knowledge management, there are different perceptions of what is meant by knowledge creation. In simple terms, knowledge creation can be defined as 'the process of adding value to information, which in turn was created by adding value to data' (Ponelis and Fairer-Wessels 1998: 5). However, this fails to take account of different types of knowledge as discussed above.

The other perspective approaches knowledge creation from the organisational learning point of view and argues that knowledge creation is a key component of the organisational learning process. These two perspectives are discussed below.

3.5.1   Interaction between tacit and explicit knowledge

Perhaps, the key work in the area of knowledge creation is done by Nonaka and Takeuchi (1995), who note that organisational knowledge creation is a continuous and dynamic interaction between tacit and explicit knowledge. Thus, knowledge creation is a dynamic and inter-active process. In a seminal paper, Nonaka (1994) points out that the distinction between tacit and explicit knowledge suggests four basic patterns for creating knowledge in any organisation.

These four patterns are explained as follows:

1. From Tacit to Tacit – sharing tacit knowledge directly with another, referred to as *socialisation*. This is where individuals acquire knowledge directly from others.
2. From Explicit to Explicit – combining discrete pieces of explicit knowledge into a new whole, referred to as *combination*.
3. From Tacit to Explicit – articulating the foundations of the tacit knowledge through dialogue, referred to as *externalisation*. However, as noted by Nonaka (1991), to convert tacit knowledge into explicit

knowledge means finding a way to express the inexpressible. The nature of tacit knowledge renders it highly personal and hard to formalise and to communicate (Malhotra 1997).
4. From Explicit to Tacit – using new explicit knowledge to broaden, extend and reframe one's tacit knowledge, referred to as *internalisation*.

In the 'knowledge creating company', these four patterns exist in dynamic interaction in what Nonaka and Takeuchi (1995) refer to as a spiral of knowledge. Tacit and explicit knowledge feed each other in a continual process of knowledge creation (Cohen 1998a).

Nonaka (1994: 16–17) notes there are two dimensions of knowledge creation:

1. 'One dimension of the knowledge creation process can be drawn from a distinction between two types of knowledge – tacit knowledge and explicit knowledge' – this is essentially the epistemological dimension.
2. 'At a fundamental level knowledge is created by individuals. An organisation cannot create knowledge without individuals. Organisational knowledge creation, therefore, should be understood in terms of a process that "organisationally" amplifies the knowledge created by individuals, and crystallises it as a part of the knowledge network of organisation'. This is the ontological dimension.

The spiral model of knowledge creation referred to above thus embodies the relationship between the epistemological and ontological dimensions of knowledge creation (Nonaka 1994).

Davenport and Prusak (1998) argue that there are five modes of knowledge generation or acquisition of knowledge in an organisation:

1. Acquisition – acquired knowledge does not have to be newly created, only new to the organisation.
2. Dedicated resources – for example, R&D departments whose specific purpose is to generate knowledge.
3. Fusion – 'knowledge generation through fusion purposely introduces complexity and even conflict to create new synergy. It brings together people with different perspectives to work on a problem or project, forcing them to come up with a joint answer' (Davenport and Prusak 1998: 60). Leonard-Barton (1995: 63) argues that innovation occurs 'at the boundaries between mind-sets', but the mind-sets must connect for boundaries to exist. Nonaka and Takeuchi (1995)

call this overlapping knowledge 'redundancy' and identify it as a necessary condition for knowledge creation.
4.   Adaptation – use crises (either real or instilled) in the environment to act as catalysts for knowledge generation.
5.   Knowledge networking – knowledge is also generated by informal, self-organising networks within organisations that may over time become more formalised.

3.5.2   Knowledge creation and organisational learning

Knowledge creation and acquisition are very closely linked with organisational learning. As noted by Huber (1991), knowledge acquisition is one of the four constructs related to organisational learning. The other three constructs being: information distribution; information interpretation; and organisational memory (this is the means by which knowledge is stored for future use, and is discussed below).

Jones (1995) observes that organisational learning is actually a metaphor rather than a reference to a 'collective mind' and thus organisational learning describes the process of acquisition of knowledge rather than the performance of particular cognitive tasks. This point is echoed by Argyris and Schon (1978: 11) who point out that terms such as organisational action, organisational behaviour, organisational intelligence and memory are also metaphors and that 'organisations do not literally remember, think, or learn'.

Jones (1995) notes that the literature on organisational learning reveals much ambiguity and numerous different perspectives on the nature of this phenomenon. Huber (1991: 89) asserts that a very broad view should be taken and that any time the participants in an organisation acquire any knowledge, some learning has occurred, regardless of whether that knowledge was actually put to use. He points out that 'learning need not result in observable changes in behaviour'. Thus, taking a behavioural perspective, he notes that 'an entity learns if, through its processing of information, the range of its potential behaviour is changed'.

At the other end of the scale, Weick (1991: 117) notes that 'stimulus-response' definitions of organisational learning have been proposed, whereby learning can be presumed to occur *only* if an organisation responds differently to the same stimulus when it occurs on different occasions. He adds that 'the defining property of learning is the combination of same stimulus and different response. If this combination is difficult to observe or difficult to create, then an inference of learning is difficult to sustain'. However, the practicality of such definitions is limited because, as Weick (1991: 117) notes, 'identical stimuli rarely, if ever, occur in "real world" situations'. He thus argues that either organisations do not learn or that organisations learn in non-traditional or novel ways.

Gill (1995) observes that a common compromise between the two extremes is to view organisational learning as coming in two forms:

1. Learning which does not require significant organisational restructuring or modification of organisational norms.
2. Learning that requires significant modification of organisational structure/strategy/norms.

Argyris and Schon (1978) suggest that the norms, strategies, and assumptions, which are actually exhibited by an organisation together constitute a 'theory-in-use'. This leads authors such as Gill (1995) to use organisational learning to mean the processes through which an organisation's theory-in-use is changed over time.

Argyris and Schon (1978: 18) refer to the above forms of organisational learning as single-loop and double-loop learning, respectively. Single-loop learning refers to 'the case when members of the organisation respond to changes in the internal and external environments by detecting errors (in the organisation's theory-in-use) which they then correct so as to maintain the central features of organisational theory-in-use'. There is a single feed-back loop which connects detected outcomes of action to organisational strategies and assumptions which are modified so as to keep organisational performance within the range set by organisational norms. The norms themselves – for example, for product quality, sales, or task performance – remain unchanged. Single-loop learning is concerned primarily with effectiveness, that is 'with how best to achieve existing goals and objectives and how best to keep organisational performance within the range specified by existing norms' (Argyris and Schon 1978: 21). On the other hand, double-loop learning refers to the case where error correction requires an organisational learning cycle in which organisational norms themselves are modified.

However, it is clear that organisational learning is not the same thing as individual learning, even when the individuals who learn are members of the organisation. As noted by Argyris and Schon (1978: 19), if individual organisation member's 'discoveries, inventions and evaluations' are not encoded in the 'individuals images and the shared maps of organisational theory-in-use', then the individual will have learned but the organisation will not. Hence, there is no organisational learning without individual learning. Thus, individual learning is a necessary but insufficient condition for organisational learning.

Organisational learning is clearly an important issue, of interest both to researchers and managers. Levine and Monarch (1998) recommend that for organisational learning to become part of daily work, collaborative technology must be integrated with evolving technical and business processes. Nonaka (1994) adds to this by emphasising that only human beings can take the central role in knowledge creation. He argues that computers are merely tools, however great their information-processing capabilities may be.

As will be seen later in the case studies the use of intranets/extranets can greatly enhance knowledge creation by virtue of the fact that they facilitate access to and sharing of large quantities of information.

Having reviewed knowledge creation, the next section moves onto to explore the issues related to knowledge storage. Again, as will be seen in the case studies this issue is highly relevant to an understanding of intranets/extranets.

3.6   Knowledge storage

While there is a relatively large amount of literature on concepts such as organisational learning, there is a dearth of material addressing how organisations store the knowledge they have acquired through organisational learning . As noted by Walsh and Ungson (1991), the current representations of organisational memory are fragmented and under-developed. Also, as noted by Jennex *et al.* (1998), there is no one agreed definition. For example, Walsh and Ungson (1991) view organisational memory as being abstract and supported by physical memory aids such as databases, whereas Huber (1991) views it as concrete and including computerised records and files. Jones (1995) observes that organisational memory helps to explain the way in which the behaviour of individuals may be influenced by stored information even when the original individuals or the stimulus for the interpretation is no longer present. Organisational memory is the means by which knowledge from the past exerts influence on present organisational activities (Stein and Zwass 1995). Organisational memory is considered distinct from individual memory just as organisational learning is distinct from individual learning as discussed earlier. As stated by Takeuchi (quoted in Cohen 1998a: 23), 'the natural place for knowledge to reside is in the individual. The important question is how to convert individual knowledge to organisational knowledge'. Davenport *et al.* (1998) suggest that to achieve this, organisations usually use some form of 'community-based' electronic discussions. This point is clarified by Brown (1998) who adds that although knowledge is often thought of as belonging to individuals, a large amount of knowledge is also both produced and held collectively. He notes that 'such knowledge is readily generated when people work together in the tightly knit groups known as "communities of practice" ' (Brown 1998: 91). Information or knowledge stored by such groups represents an instance of collective memory, where collective memory refers to the social process of articulating, exchanging, and sharing information leading to shared interpretations (Stein and Zwass 1995).

3.6.1 Why is organizational memory important?

Walsh and Ungson (1991) point out that organisational memory plays three important roles within organisations:

1. First, it plays an *informational role*. The information content that is housed in an organisation's memory 'facilities' can contribute to decision making. However, authors such as Prusak (1998), Stein and Zwass (1995) caution against retrieving 'best practices' or 'standard' responses for application to situations that may not meet the current environmental demands placed on the organisation.
2. Second, organisational memory fulfils a *control function*. It can reduce costs associated with the implementation of a new decision.
3. Third, organisational memory can play a *political role*. 'Control of information creates a source of dependence with which individuals or groups in power are able to influence the actions of others. The filtering of particular information from memory that supports a particular agenda can serve as a means to enhance and sustain power' (Walsh and Ungson 1991: 73–4).

Huber (1991) points out that problems caused by poor organisational memory can mean that non-anticipation of future needs for certain information can mean that much potentially useful information does not get stored. Levitt and March (1988) add that the costs associated with recording 'non-essential' knowledge are often prohibitive. Another problem noted is that organisational members with information needs often are not aware of the existence or whereabouts of information stored by other members of the organisation. Gilbert *et al.* (1999) reveal that even with the communication capabilities of today's IT systems, this problem still exists.

While papers such as Stein (1995) and Stein and Zwass (1995) provide useful perspectives of some of the processes associated with organisational memory, Walsh and Ungson (1991) seek to explore the implications of a functional conceptualisation of organisational memory. Their analysis is based on two key assumptions. First, they assume that organisations functionally resemble information processing systems as discussed by Galbraith (1974) amongst others and thus they exhibit memory that is similar in function to the memory of individuals. Information can be received by sensors, processed, stored in, and retrieved from organisational memory. The second assumption extends the first by also depicting organisations as interpretive systems, as discussed by Daft and Weick (1984). This assumption implies that varieties in organisational interpretation result from the differences in the ways managers understand and choose to behave in the context of the organisational environment. As Walsh and Ungson (1991: 60) point out, 'this particular concept of organisations implies the existence and use of some form of memory'.

All of these constructs are actually encompassed by the typology of organisational memory presented by Walsh and Ungson (1991) who posit the existence of five retention facilities or 'storage' bins, as follows:

1. Individuals – members of an organisation will retain knowledge from the past that can be applied to the current organisational environment. As discussed earlier, this knowledge is in two forms, explicit knowledge and tacit knowledge.
2. Culture – Schein (1984) defines organisational culture as a learned way of perceiving, thinking, and feeling about problems that is transmitted to members in the organisation. Culture embodies past experience that can be useful for dealing with the future. It is, therefore, one of organisational memory's retention facilities.
3. Transformation – knowledge retained in transformations is regarded as 'the logic that guides the transformation of an input (whether it is a raw material, a new recruit, or an insurance claim) into an output (be it a finished product, a company veteran, or an insurance payment)' (Walsh and Ungson 1991: 65). Transformations can thus be regarded as procedures, processes and rules that govern the organisation.
4. Structures – as noted by Walsh and Ungson (1991), organisational structure must be considered in light of its implications for individual role behaviour and its link with the environment. The concept of role provides one link between individual and organisational memories.

For example, interaction between members in an organisation is conditioned by mutual expectations associated with their individual roles.

5. Ecology – the actual physical structure or workplace ecology of an organisation embodies and thus reveals a good deal of information about the organisation. In particular, the physical setting often reflects the status hierarchy in an organisation. For example, the trend in large organisations towards large open plan offices rather than individual offices may reflect an attempt at encouraging more open sharing of information and knowledge.

In this book, knowledge acquisition is treated as being more than just a component of organisational memory. While it is recognised that there is an overlap between knowledge acquisition and organisational memory, not all of the knowledge acquired necessarily end up in one of the five retention facilities discussed above. For example, all knowledge about an organisation is not necessarily stored within the organisation itself. Walsh and Ungson (1991) introduce the construct of external archives to refer to the fact that 'the organisation itself is not the sole repository of its past' (Walsh and Ungson 1991: 66). External archives do retain information about an organisation's past, even though they are not part of an organisation's memory as such.

While the above structure of organisational memory provides a useful conceptualisation, it fails to recognise adequately the role of the information systems constituent in organisational memory. As noted by Walsh and Ungson (1991: 63), this framework allows for the role of information systems 'only by noting that individuals and organisations keep records and files as a memory aid'. Huber (1990) postulates that the availability of advanced information technologies and related procedures will lead to the development and use of databases and expert systems as components of organisational memory. Modern IT, such as intranets and the WWW have made it possible for the average person to acquire information on almost any topic (Harris 1996), and while recognising that technology is not a panacea, storing information and knowledge in electronic formats means that, at the very least, searching for it becomes easier. The use of knowledge 'maps' to locate, in an organisation, knowledge or individuals with knowledge is being facilitated by tools such as Lotus Notes and intranets (Davenport and Prusak 1998). Modern communications systems allow what people write and send to each other to be stored, and that 'material' thus stored becomes a rich base from which people can acquire knowledge (Gundry and Metes 1998). As observed by Malhotra (1996), the use of Groupware tools, intranets, e-mail, and bulletin boards can facilitate the processes of information distribution and information interpretation, and the archives of these communications can provide elements of the organisational memory. And as technology becomes more powerful, so exploitation of knowledge becomes easier still (KPMG 1998b). Finally, with the growing interest in knowledge as a competitive differentiator and the increasing sophistication, and falling costs, of IT, the need to recognise and develop the information systems aspect of organisational memory is likely to grow stronger (Stein and Zwass 1995).

3.7   Knowledge transfer

Knowledge transfer encompasses two aspects. Firstly, it involves the transfer of information and knowledge as part of the processes of creating and storing knowledge, as discussed earlier. Secondly, it is also a constituent of the retrieval of information and knowledge from organisational memory so that it may be used by members of the organisation. Coleman (1997b: 1) defines knowledge retrieval as 'the ability to search, browse, and access the explicit, relevant knowledge assets of an organisation'.

Retrieving information from organisational memory is typically triggered by problems, cues in the environment, and new projects that require information for the purposes of decision-making. Stein (1995) states that an individual is motivated to retrieve information if:

1. The enquirer has knowledge that the required information exists. However, as observed by Huber (1991), 'organisations' often do not know what 'they' know. He adds that how those who possess non-routine information and those who need the information find each other is relatively unstudied.
2. The enquirer values that information and believes that it has a bearing on the current situation.
3. The enquirer has the ability to search, locate and decode the desired information. However, Huber (1991: 100) points out that 'except for their systems that routinely index and store "hard information", organisations tend to have only weak systems for finding where a certain item of information is known to the organisation'.
4. The cost of locating the information is less than that of recomputing the solution from scratch.

Walsh and Ungson (1991) note that the retrieval of information from memory can vary along a continuum from 'automatic' to 'controlled'.

'Automatic retrieval' addresses cases where information is drawn easily and intuitively, partly as a function of the execution of organisational procedures or business processes. Retrieving information in a 'controlled manner' and the ease with which this may be done varies across the five retention facilities of organisational memory identified above. For example, individuals may retrieve information purposefully and consciously by making an analogy to a past decision and by recalling their experiences and decisions, whereas for some firms, controlled retrieval from organisational culture will be difficult if not impossible, due to the fact that organisational members may not be aware of the information contained in such cultural 'icons' as historical sagas, stories, and even gossip. The retrieval of information from the retention facilities of transformations, structures and ecology is largely automatic.

The transfer of information and knowledge as part of the processes of creating and storing knowledge relies to a large extent on how willing people are to share their knowledge. While the knowledge creation spiral (where tacit and explicit knowledge feed each other in a continual process of knowledge creation) is useful from a theoretical perspective, it assumes that information and knowledge is shared willingly in organisations. However, Marshall (1997) notes that many individuals in organisations are simply not interested in sharing information and that having recognised that 'information is power' they want to keep 'their' information and to dole it out only as they see fit.

As observed by Martiny (1998), there are individuals in every organisation who want to share and communicate knowledge and those whose preference is to keep their knowledge as a 'private' asset. Professionals, for example, are often reluctant to share their tacit knowledge which has been gained as the result of a long apprenticeship and life-time career. Leonard and Sensiper (1998: 113) observe that in organisations where expertise is highly regarded, but mentoring and assisting others is not, then 'rational people may be unlikely to surrender the power they gain from being an important knowledge source'.

Given the amount of organisational downsizing that has occurred in the past decade, Davenport *et al.* (1998) note that it is not uncommon to find negative cultural aspects with respect to knowledge and that as individuals may believe their knowledge is critical to maintaining their value as employees, they may be reluctant to share their knowledge with others. However, this issue was identified long before the recent wave of downsizing. For example, Thibaut and Kelly (1959) noted that giving away knowledge eventually causes the possessor to lose his or her unique value relative to what others know.

The conventional view thus appears to be that the barriers to knowledge sharing are personal and cultural and are centred around this unwillingness of individuals to share knowledge. However, research by EFQM (1997) indicates that the majority of organisations facilitate knowledge sharing on an occasional basis rather than as a continuous part of the way they manage the business and also that many organisations may be too lean to actually allow knowledge sharing to happen. KPMG (1998b: 3) note that in a survey '49 per cent of respondents said that people wanted to share knowledge but do not have the time'. While a certain proportion of this figure may be due to respondents not wanting to identify themselves as knowledge 'hoarders', it does indicate that there is often a not insignificant personal cost to sharing information and knowledge. However, Constant *et al.* (1994: 406) argue that even though personal costs may result from sharing expertise, it may produce significant personal benefits to the information provider because 'it permits self-expression and demonstrates self-consistency'.

Certainly most managers will acknowledge that getting knowledge to move around organisations can be difficult. In general, however, as noted by Brown (1998), such problems are reduced to issues of information flow, and a great deal of 'hope' is being placed on the role that intranets can play in facilitating greater access to organisational information and making it easier for individuals to share knowledge. Cohen (1998b: 53) notes that 'this may be the first real technology that encourages true organisational learning. It opens up a business and creates a knowledge sharing, rather than a knowledge hoarding, culture'. He adds that this is a result of the fact that at the core of web-based technology is the fluidity of information and that employees can now access information that once was only available to a few key people. Similarly, Teece (1998: 60) adds that such technology 'challenges existing organisation boundaries, divisions, and hierarchies'.

However, Campalans *et al.* (1997) point out that managers in an organisation attempting to embrace the benefits that intranets as 'knowledge sharing' tools can bring will require a concerted change management programme to bring about the necessary widespread changes in culture and behaviour. Constant *et al.* (1994) add that employees may or may not be willing to share information as widely as technology makes possible or as much as managers might desire. Leonard (1998) points out that technology alone will not make a person with expertise share it with others. As noted by Davenport and Prusak (1998: 142), 'technology alone won't get an employee who is uninterested in seeking knowledge to hop onto a keyboard and start searching or browsing' or indeed sharing information and knowledge. They conclude that the mere presence of technology will not create a learning organisation or a knowledge creating company.

Having addressed the issues of knowledge creation, storage, and transfer, the final 'core' process is knowledge use. This is discussed in the next section.

3.8 Knowledge use

Facilitating the transfer of knowledge or even transferring knowledge is no guarantee that such knowledge will actually be used. When knowledge is transferred from one person to another, the knowledge is drawn into the receiver's context (Bohm 1994; Gick and Holyoak 1987). The new knowledge is interpreted according to the receiver's context and experience. If the receiver does not have an appropriate background for interpreting the new knowledge, the new knowledge will not be interpreted correctly and the knowledge will have little or no value. Access to knowledge is a necessary condition for knowledge use but is not sufficient to ensure that the knowledge will be used (Davenport and Prusak 1998). Whether the knowledge transferred will be considered meaningful by those who receive it will depend on whether they are familiar with the way in which the knowledge has been 'codified' as well as the different contexts in which it is used (Teece 1998). Hypertext and hypermedia technologies can assist in richly embedding knowledge in context (Stein and Zwass 1995).

Miles *et al.* (1998) observe that although the importance of knowledge and the means by which it is utilised to add economic value varies from industry to industry and also between firms within industries, there is as yet little recognition of these differences either in the way organisations are governed or in the basic tools, ratios, and time frames applied to the measurement of the effectiveness of such knowledge. They add that knowledge is not easily accounted for within traditional systems (which track the use of economic capital such as money and physical assets and measure the economic returns accruing). Thus, 'when managers are not able to see direct cause and effect, they are less confident in decisions that might affect them and they may revert to decisions that are more easily justified by the "bottom line", no matter how illusory such a justification might be' (Miles *et al.* 1998: 282). Alternatively, managers may seek to develop direct measures of knowledge. Prusak (1998: 273) terms this approach one of the 'eleven deadliest sins of knowledge management' and argues that rather than seeking to measure knowledge directly, its effectiveness should be judged by its outcomes, activities, and consequences.

Having discussed the four core processes of knowledge management, the final section of this chapter draws together the key issues and describes the framework that will be used to structure the analysis and discussion of the findings from the three case studies.

3.9   Summary

This chapter presented a view of the literature identifying and addressing various issues related to knowledge management. Beginning with an explanation of why knowledge management is important to managers in organisations, the review moved on to present views of the different 'types' of knowledge discussed in the literature. Explicit knowledge and tacit knowledge are perhaps the two main types prevalent in the literature but problems in separating the 'knowing what' from the 'knowing how' can be overcome by adopting the view of knowledge as a continuum. At one end of this continuum knowledge is almost completely explicit, whereas at the other end it is almost completely tacit. Most knowledge actually lies somewhere in between the extremes and thus knowledge can be treated as having both tacit and explicit components, and both of these 'dimensions' are complementary.

Knowledge management as a 'concept' and as a 'practice' is then addressed. It is recognised that the practice of knowledge management involves more than just using appropriate technologies (be they intranets, Groupware, expert systems or sophisticated databases) but is also reliant upon the role played by people in the organisation in terms of creating, sharing and using knowledge.

3.9.1   Main themes

The process of knowledge management can be represented by four core processes of knowledge creation, knowledge transfer, knowledge storage, and knowledge use. These processes essentially represent a cycle of knowledge in the organisation, as illustrated in Figure 3.1.

It is worth noting that this creation/storage/transfer/use approach is very much a 'physical commodity' metaphor and as such tends to divorce knowledge from its organisational context. This approach thus 'sidesteps' the complex interactions that occur as a result of the mutual interdependency between organisational actors and their understanding and use of organisational knowledge. However, this approach does have advantages in that it lends itself to recognising and making use of the

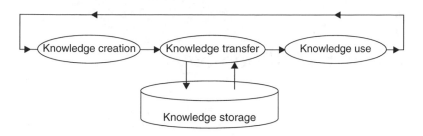

Figure 3.1 The knowledge cycle.

information systems aspect of knowledge management and the role that technology can play in facilitating the process. Furthermore, just as attempting to observe the exercise of power in practice is complicated by the fact that people often attempt to conceal their motives for political action (Walsham 1993), so the attempt to observe the 'practice' of knowledge management is complicated by the fact that employees attempt to conceal their personal interest motives for not sharing 'their' knowledge with others in the organisation. Separating knowledge from its organisational context helps to address this problem.

In summary, the main themes related to knowledge management (i.e. the four 'core' processes as identified above) are relevant to an understanding of intranets/extranets. As will be seen in Chapters 5, 6, and 7, the core processes of knowledge creation, storage, transfer and use are evident in each of the case studies, but to different degrees.

3.9.2 Linking to the rest of the book

Just as the themes extracted from the literature review in Chapter 2 were used in deriving the research schedule and in identifying relevant questions for the data collection process, so too were the themes of knowledge creation, storage, transfer and use. Again, this is detailed in Chapter 4 where the linkages between the research questions and the literature reviews presented here and in Chapter 2 are made explicit.

Finally, the discussion of the findings from the case studies in terms of knowledge management is also structured according to the four 'core' processes identified above. This helps to situate the findings in the literature and is presented in Chapter 8.

However, prior to this discussion, it is necessary to present the case studies and the details of the methodology used in the research for this book. The research methodology is thus presented in the Chapter 4, following which are the three case study chapters.

4
Research Methodology

This chapter presents the approach and methodology used in conducting the research for this book. It includes an outline of the research philosophy adopted together with a justification of why the case study approach is appropriate for research of this nature. Finally, it presents some background information on the case studies that are presented in Chapters 5, 6 and 7.

4.1 The research approach

The starting point for this research was an interest in the use of intranets/extranets in organisations and the potential of such technology to facilitate collaboration and the sharing of information both within and between organisations. Of particular interest was the identification and examination of the issues that arose as a result of the introduction of intranets/extranets. The main research question could thus be stated as follows:

> What issues accompany the implementation and operation of intranets and extranets?

In order to refine the main research question and to be able to select the appropriate methodology and research design, it was felt useful to conduct a short phase of preliminary research into how intranets and extranets were being used.

Based on this preliminary research, two clear motives for the use of intranets/extranets were quite evident. The first of these motives was the use of the technology to improve the efficiency of current methods of sharing information, and the second motive was the use of the technology to facilitate new ways of sharing information. For example, for some companies the emphasis was on using an extranet to improve the efficiency of the existing links with other organisations. For others, the emphasis was on using an extranet to facilitate new ways of sharing information with other organisations. Similarly, with the use of intranets, companies were using the technology to improve the efficiency of sharing information within the organisation. Other companies, having already made use of the technology to begin to improve the efficiency of existing ways of sharing information within the organisation were exploring the use of the technology to facilitate new ways of sharing information.

The commercial literature also identifies a number of specific benefits of intranets, which may help to add to the classification of reasons why (and how) intranets/extranets are being used. Such benefits include:

- The ability to distribute and share large amounts of information electronically rather than having to print and distribute numerous copies of such information on paper. Early examples of companies claiming benefits from using intranets in this way include: Eli Lilly & Co., whose intranet contains more than 12 000 pages of information and is available to over 25 000 users worldwide (Datamonitor 1998a); Bull Information Systems, who use their intranet to distribute to around 21 000 employees a company monthly news brief prepared specially by the Chief Executive Officer (CEO) (Datamonitor 1999); and the ASDA Group, who use an intranet to distribute information in the form of company-wide bulletin boards, to around 75 000 people across 220 stores plus another 1000 users at head office (Datamonitor 1999).
- Using intranets/extranets to distribute information has further benefits in that such information can be quickly and easily updated, obviating the need to reprint large volumes of paper where errors have been made, for example, in the case of sales and marketing information. Even in the case of less time-sensitive information such as that contained in operating manuals and service guides, rather than waiting until the next scheduled printing and distribution on paper, the use of intranets/extranets can mean that such information can be updated almost immediately and thus reduce the possibility of confusion that may arise due to the distribution of inaccurate or out-of-date information. Early examples of companies claiming benefits from using intranets in this way include: Genentech Inc., whose intranet serves as an online employee handbook available to its 2400 employees (Datamonitor 1998a); Anglian Water who use their

intranet for the provision of management information, including 120 business performance metrics, to over 4000 users (Datamonitor 1999); and Audi AG in Germany who use their extranet to support the distribution of engineering data to around 400–500 suppliers, development companies and other partners (Datamonitor 1999).

- Due to the global 'reach' of the Internet and the relative ease and low cost of using intranets/extranets for the distribution and/or sharing of information means that there are many opportunities now open to managers for facilitating new ways of sharing information both within their organisation and with other organisations. Early examples of companies claiming benefits from using intranets in this way include: Roche Laboratories, whose extranet (RocheNet) provides access to pharmaceutical information for up to one million doctors (Datamonitor 1998a); and Charles Schwab, who by the end of 1997 had an estimated 1.2 million online accounts worth about US$80 billion (Datamonitor 1998b).

The ubiquity of the Internet can mean that employees distributed around the world can retrieve information from their organisation's intranet literally at the click of a button rather than having to wait for information to be posted or faxed by a colleague. Similarly, a customer can easily retrieve information from a supplier located on the other side of the world. In addition, information on the intranet is available 24 hours a day and thus, for example, employees working in different time zones can publish information on the intranet ready for use by colleagues in other countries who may be beginning their shift just as the publisher of the information is about to go home. Similarly, this has benefits in reducing temporal barriers to inter-organisational coordination. Hence, the use of intranets can be seen to reduce the spatial and temporal barriers to communications and may increase the opportunities for facilitating new ways of sharing information both within an organisation and with other organisations such as suppliers and key customers.

Thus, the two motives cited above for why managers in organisations are deploying intranets/extranets can therefore be seen to actually comprise a number of different specific benefits. It may be argued that in practice these benefits constitute sub-categories of the two 'meta-benefits' of improving efficiency and facilitating new ways of sharing information. For example, using intranets as a substitute for distributing large volumes of paper and to keep information up to date can be seen to improve efficiency. Similarly, using intranets to overcome spatial temporal barriers to communication may been seen as facilitating

Table 4.1 Four aspects of the use of internet technologies

	Internal use – Intranet	External use – Extranet
Improving efficiency	Improving efficiency of current ways of sharing information within an organisation	Improving efficiency of existing links with other organisations
Facilitating new ways of sharing information	Facilitating new ways of sharing information within an organisation	Facilitating new ways of sharing information with other organisations

new opportunities for information sharing. These aspects of the use of intranets and extranets and the motivations that managers in the organisations gave for their use of such technologies are summarised in Table 4.1. This table thus shows the initial reasons for the use of intranets and extranets (or more generically Internet technologies) and as will be discussed later this was used as an aid in identifying and selecting case study companies that represented each of the 'four cells' in the table.

Moreover, further justification for the use of such a table is corroborated by Riggins and Rhee (1998) who in exploring the use of intranets and extranets in electronic commerce, indicate that intranets/extranets can enhance coordination between internal business units and existing trading partners and can also facilitate new channels of information exchange.

The choice of research methodology is discussed in the next section.

4.1.1 Choice of research methodology

There are several different approaches that can be taken to business and management research. These approaches include field experiments, surveys, case studies, action research, longitudinal research and forecasting/futures research (Remenyi 1995). In recent years there has also been an increase in the use of ethnographic approaches to research in this area, particularly when examining computer supported cooperative working systems (CSCW) (Hughes *et al.* 1994; Shapiro 1994; Pycock 1995, Russell 1996).

In terms of conducting research in the area of the strategic use of IT to facilitate and support collaboration, the main approach that has been used in the past is that of case studies (Bonoma 1985). For example, Konsynski (1993b) considers the relevance of the case study approach in studies that attempt to evaluate the business value of investments in information technology. He points out that (Konsynski 1993b: 23):

> the case study approach, when well executed offers a rich base for the application of multiple lenses or multiple paradigms (patterns of explanation) in addressing a research enquiry. This approach can permit the identification and examination of assumptions that often go unchallenged in other forms of inquiry.

The appropriateness of the case study approach to this research is also noted by Nandhakumar (1996), who argues for the use of in-depth study to challenge assumptions concerning success factors in executive information systems. Furthermore, in researching the use of complex IT systems involving many players, Benbasat *et al.* (1987), Walsham (1995), Clark and Stoddard (1996) argue the need for rich descriptions in trying to understand what is actually happening. Such richness can only be obtained through a case study approach.

Also as pointed out by Eisenhardt (1989), case study research can be especially powerful when the research design involves multiple case studies examining a single issue from different perspectives, as is the case with this research. However, it is worth remembering that the richness of the case study approach is 'matched by the opportunity to introduce bias' (Konsynski 1993b: 23). Therefore, there is a need to ensure that the research design and analysis is such that any bias is identified and taken into account.

The purpose of the research presented in this book is to explore how companies are making use of intranets and extranets. Bearing in mind that this is an area where there has been very little in-depth research, it was not possible to identify a definitive set of variables that could be used to design a quantitative approach to the research, thus necessitating a qualitative approach to the research. The research may be characterised as exploratory in that the research was not driven by any *a priori* conceptual framework. Furthermore, in trying to understand how intranets/extranets are being used, the required data are qualitative in nature, for example, perspectives on the role of intranets/extranets.

Bearing in mind that this research is exploratory and that it investigated the use of Internet technologies from different perspectives (an internal focus as in intranets, and an external focus as in extranets), coupled with a desire to build rich descriptions of the issues that surround the use of intranets/extranets, the case study approach was thus chosen as being the most appropriate. However, the case study approach to research design still leaves one the option of adopting either a positivist approach to the case study (e.g. as discussed by Yin 1994) or an interpretive approach to the case study (e.g. as discussed by Walsham 1993).

For this work, concepts and questions were only loosely defined at the start, these being derived from a combination of the preliminary research and the main themes extracted from the literature reviews. The understanding of these firmed up as the study and data collection proceeded. Thus, while it was possible to outline a general research strategy before data collection began, this strategy evolved as data collection and analysis proceeded. However, in these types of studies, it is not assumed at the start that the researcher knows all the appropriate questions to ask – indeed, part of the reason for using a qualitative research strategy is precisely because one wants to find the issues of significance to the people one is researching. The epistemological stance of the research is thus interpretive and comprises three in-depth case studies as described later.

4.1.2   Research design and methodology

As outlined earlier, the general research question to be addressed is *what issues accompany the implementation and operation of intranets and extranets?*

This section outlines the objectives of answering this question and also presents the details of the research design that was employed. The main output sought from this research was a description and analysis, based on the data collected, of the use of, and issues surrounding the use of, intranets/extranets.

Three case studies

Table 4.1 illustrated four aspects of the use of intranets/extranets. However, although there are two aspects to the use of intranets, the preliminary research indicated that companies' use of intranets was likely to evolve to encompass both aspects and thus the investigation of the 'internal' use of intranets was performed via a single case study.

In exploring the use of extranets, the preliminary research indicated that while it may be likely that a company's use of an intranet may evolve to encompass both aspects of use, this was not necessarily the case with the two aspects of the use of extranets. Thus, it was felt beneficial to explore each of the aspects of the use of extranets via individual case studies.

The data collection method employed was thus three in-depth case studies (discussed below), each of which focused primarily on one of the aspects of the use of intranets identified earlier. In addition to addressing the issues of concern, the use of a multiple case design is particularly desirable as it will allow for cross-case analysis (Yin 1994).

Guiding the data collection – making use of the literature

Although, the epistemological stance of this research is interpretive, it was useful to have some initial questions in order to guide the data collection as recommended by Yin (1994) and Eisenhardt (1989). The use of theory as an initial guide to data collection is not inconsistent with an interpretive approach, and can actually provide a valuable initial guide (Walsham 1995). The main themes from the literature reviews presented in Chapters 2 and 3 were used to derive a set of questions that helped to guide the data collection. This set of questions is illustrated in Table 4.2, along with the main research question.

Although the contribution of IT/IS to competitive advantage was identified in Chapter 2 as a theme relevant to the study of intranets/ extranets, and thus was initially included as a theme in Table 4.2, it was not possible to collect data that were robust enough to support a grounded discussion of this issue. Therefore, this theme has been excluded both from Table 4.2 and from the discussion in Chapter 8.

Data collection methods

The main method of data collection used in this research was semi-structured interviews. In all three cases, internal and external documents relating to the selected organisation's use of intranets/extranets were also used. The goal of the data collection was to obtain a rich set of data on the use of intranets/extranets in the context of the three case studies. In line with the questions presented in Table 4.2, interviewees were asked, for example, to provide data on and to discuss their use of the respective intranet/extranet, their perspective of the benefits and downsides of the system, their view of the importance or otherwise of the systems, and their view of how well the systems 'fitted' with the 'normal' way of performing tasks in the respective organisation.

In terms of deciding when to cease the data collection process, the key factor that aided in making this decision was whether any new issues were being identified by interviewees. With the range of roles being addressed in each individual case study and the fact that the actual questions being asked in the interviews were often modified to take account of responses from previous interviewees, it was felt that when a stage had been reached where no new issues were arising then there was a 'critical mass' of data sufficient to paint a realistic picture of the case study. While further interviews after the 'critical mass' stage

Table 4.2 Using themes from the literature to derive research questions

Main research question	What issues are raised by the implementation and operation of intranets and extranets?
Themes from the IT/IS literature	
Integration into corporate strategy	To what extent are intranets/extranets integrated into corporate strategy? To what extent are they integrated into other systems?
Planning and implementation	What are the planning and implementation issues that arise with the use of intranets/extranets?
Evaluation of IT	What benefits and downsides accrue from the implementation and operation of intranets/extranets?
Groupware related 'issues'	To what extent has the intranet/extranet been appropriated into use in the organisation? To what extent, if any, did 'drifting' occur?
Role and effect of IT	What role is 'played' by intranets and extranets? What changes in organisational form are associated with the implementation and operation of intranets/extranets? What are the political issues associated with the implementation and use of intranets/extranets?
Themes from the knowledge management literature	
Knowledge creation, storage, transfer, use	What role do intranets/extranets play in facilitating and/or supporting aspects of knowledge creation, storage, transfer, and use?

would have added more data it was felt that they would not have contributed to a greater understanding. As noted by Van Maanen (1979) longer periods of field research do not necessarily lead to greater insight.

4.2 Overview of the case studies

The three case studies, together with the pseudonyms of the chosen companies that form the basis for each case are illustrated in Table 4.3. Outline details on each case are given.

Table 4.3   The three case studies

	Internal use – intranet	External use – extranet
Improving efficiency	Improving efficiency of current ways of sharing information within an organisation	Improving efficiency of existing links with other organisations **Neotany UK** (HQ in London)
Facilitating new ways of sharing information	Facilitating new ways of sharing information within an organisation **Core Technologies (CoreTech)** (HQ in London)	Facilitating new ways of sharing information with other organisations **ATI (formerly The Advanced Technologies Institute)** (based in Birmingham)

It should be noted that the 'allocation' of companies to the cells in the table is based on the initial view of the motivation in each company for their respective use of intranet/extranet. As will be seen later, in the light of the case study data, the limitations of this framework became apparent as the research unfolded. This will be discussed in Section 9.1. However, at this stage in the book the table serves a useful purpose in that it shows the initial view of the motivation for using intranet/extranet and thus helped in the selection of the case study companies.

Although each of the companies chosen had implemented an intranet/extranet, they each had a different primary focus. It is this issue that makes the multiple case design interesting. The three companies and the three aspects of the use of intranets/extranets were deliberately chosen because of this difference. This approach was anticipated to lead to both complementary and contradictory results on the use of the technology. This selection of the above companies for case studies is in line with the recommendations made by Yin (1994: 46), in which he proposes that the two key criteria for selecting potential case study sites are as follows:

1. First, sites where similar results are predicted may be used as 'literal' replications.
2. Second, sites may be chosen for 'theoretical' replication. That is, chosen such that contradictory results are predicted.

4.2.1   Background information on each case study

This section presents a brief overview of the three case studies. The full case reports are presented in Chapters 5, 6 and 7.

Use of an intranet – Core Technologies (CoreTech)

This case study investigates the use of intranet technology in a UK-based company of 120 000 employees. The company operates in a number of industries but mainly software, multimedia and IT systems. There were two key reasons that led the company to experiment with and deploy an intranet. Primarily, managers in the company were facing the problem of increased levels of competition and identified a need to reduce the cost base of the organisation through improved efficiencies. There were also problems of information transmission and storage resulting from paper 'overload'. Following trials in 1994 and 1995 of intranet technology, and forecasts of large cost savings, managers decided subsequently to roll out an intranet across the company. Data from this case study are presented in Chapter 5.

Using an extranet to facilitate new ways of sharing information with other organisations – ATI

ATI is one of the world's leading authorities on all specialist materials technologies and supplies information on all forms of these technologies to a worldwide customer base. ATI's information and knowledge is disseminated through written reports, 'word of mouth', training courses and other information channels. Increasing demand for ATI information and knowledge led to the development of an extranet system that gives customers access to information on-line. Via the use of this extranet, ATI are attempting to change the way that the needs of customers are addressed. Data from this case study are presented in Chapter 6.

Using an extranet to improve efficiency of existing links with other organisations – Neotany

In April 1997, Neotany, United Kingdom installed an extranet connecting Neotany HQ with its dealerships (which number approximately 300) throughout the United Kingdom and Ireland. Previously, Neotany spent over £100 000 a year just printing and distributing monthly price lists to its dealers. Now with the use of an extranet, prices, product information, and even the paint catalogue are all held centrally, but instantly available to every dealer. Data from this case study are presented in Chapter 7.

4.3 Data collection and analysis

There were a number of stages in the data collection and analysis processes. The key elements that were conducted were as follows:

- development of guiding questions
- selection of case studies
- execution of case studies
- write up individual case reports
- categorisation of themes from the case studies
- identification of patterns – both within and across cases
- drew conclusions.

These stages are based on the recommendations of Yin (1994) and Miles and Huberman (1984).

A key characteristic of a lot of issues that arose from the case studies was that they were related to various aspects of knowledge management. Also, as noted in Chapter 3 the growth in interest in intranets is leading to a growth in interest in knowledge management and in the research reported here, knowledge management emerged as an important theme. Thus, in order to enhance the understanding of intranets/extranets and to more appropriately situate the results of the research in the literature, a review of the knowledge management literature was conducted after the initial data collection had begun.

There were a number of stages used in the analysis of data collected. First, an initial read through of the data collected identified clusters of related concepts. The data were then sorted and coded to an initial total of 82 nodes. An iterative process of refinement and recoding of data resulted in the identification of a coherent set of key issues that captured the similarities and differences in issues from the three cases. This set of issues included benefits, downsides, aspects of use, relationships, effects on people's roles, and issues relating to the ownership of information. These issues are used to structure the presentation of the data from the three case studies. Having a 'common' structure in the three cases also allows comparison across the cases.

4.4   Summary

This chapter presented the methodology and approach used in conducting this research. It also presented the evolution of the research together with an outline of the research philosophy and research design adopted. Finally, it presented some background information on the case studies that are presented in Chapters 5, 6 and 7.

5
Case Study – Software and IT Company

This chapter presents the first of the three case studies. The initial focus for this particular case study was on the use of an intranet and was concerned with investigating the issues that arose as a result of using the intranet both to improve the efficiency of ways of sharing information and the facilitation of new ways of sharing information within the organisation. Table 5.1 illustrates how this case study sits in relation to the case studies presented in Chapters 6 and 7. As mentioned in Chapter 4, when discussing the research methodology, the purpose of the table is just to show the initial objective for deployment of the intranet in each of the three case studies. As will be seen, a wide range of issues arose during the case study and the limitations of this table will be discussed in Chapter 9. Nevertheless, the table serves as a useful starting point.

The data in this chapter are presented under a number of headings. Section 5.1 presents background data on the company and identifies problems and issues that the company was facing prior to implementing an intranet. The origin and implementation of the intranet is then described and an overview of the applications and facilities of the system is presented, following which, data are presented on the changes to the flow of information in the company and the effects on communications patterns. The post-implementation outcomes are then addressed and are categorised under the headings of benefits, downsides and other issues related to the use of the intranet such as effects on relationships and the use of discussion forums. Finally, Section 5.5 presents views on the role of the intranet. The chapter concludes with a brief summary.

Table 5.1   The CoreTech case study in relation to the other two cases

	Internal use – intranet	External use – extranet
Improving efficiency	*Improving efficiency of current ways of sharing information within an organisation*	Improving efficiency of existing links with other organisations Neotany UK (HQ in London)
Facilitating new ways of sharing information	*Facilitating new ways of sharing information within an organisation* *Core Technologies* *(CoreTech)* *(HQ in London)*	Facilitating new ways of sharing information with other organisations ATI (based in Birmingham)

5.1   Background

This case study is centred on the use of an intranet within a large software and IT-solutions organisation. The company in question, referred to as Core Technologies (CoreTech), is based mainly in the United Kingdom but also participates in a number of joint ventures in Europe and the Far East.

The employee base in the United Kingdom numbers around 120 000 with a further 5000 employed in the joint ventures outside the United Kingdom. The company operates in a number of industries but mainly software, multimedia and the provision of IT systems. Organisationally, the company operates as a group of semi-autonomous divisions, each of which is headed up by a managing director. The company has rather a hierarchical and bureaucratic structure with many levels, as illustrated in Figure 5.1. The figure also shows the location in the hierarchy of the main roles of people in the case study. A brief explanation of these roles is given in Table 5.2.

5.2   Prior to the intranet

Prior to the development of the intranet, the majority of general company information (covering areas such as briefings on company strategy and company news and events) to be communicated throughout the organisation flowed vertically down the hierarchy, with each manager relaying the information to their direct reports who in turn passed the information on to their direct reports. Towards the bottom of the hierarchy, typically at the level of group or team leaders, the information would often be disseminated verbally in team meetings. Some types of

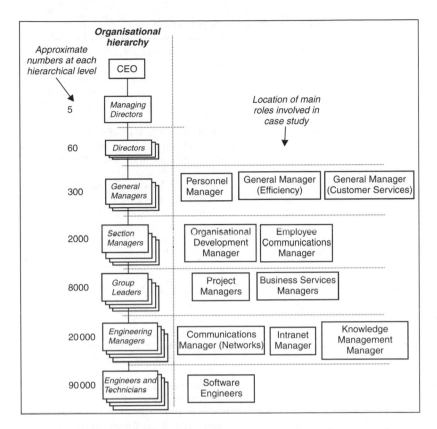

Figure 5.1   Organizational hierarchy and location of roles in the case study.

information, for example, *Job News*, a weekly list of internal job vacancies, would be sent to section managers or group leaders, for onward circulation. It was not uncommon for this to take up to two months before being seen by each team member, by which time the closing date for applying for the jobs had long since passed.

Sometimes, certain types of information would also be sent directly, in paper form, to every employee. Typical examples of such types of information would be 'personal' messages from the CEO, or a managing director, expressing 'thanks' for recent improvements in business performance. Other examples of information sent directly, on paper, included updates to the safety manual and various in-house glossy magazines.

If an employee had a query on a briefing or other information that was relayed down the hierarchy, he would first address it to his line

Table 5.2   Main roles of key people in the case study

Personnel Manager (Employee Communications)	Carries overall responsibility for the internal communications process in the Communications Engineering division of CoreTech. This division is the largest in CoreTech and comprises around 60 000 employees
General Manager (Efficiency)	One level below that of director, carries senior level responsibility for improving the efficiency of current business processes
General Manager (Customer Services)	Carries senior level responsibility for managing the delivery of products and services to end customers
Organisational Development Manager	Involves the investigation and deployment of HR processes associated with managing change in the organisation
Employee Communications Manager	Associated with managing the process of preparing internal communications typically conveying briefings or messages from senior management
Business Services Manager	Involves responsibility for the QMS (quality management system) and the development of management systems
Communications Manager (Networks)	Associated with the management of CoreTech's internal IT networks and keeping CoreTech employees in certain units informed of changes, updates, and maintenance of such systems
Intranet Manager	Assumes responsibility for the overall management of the CoreTech intranet
Knowledge Management Manager	Located in the Global division of CoreTech, is associated with 'managing and propagating the message of knowledge management'

manager, who if unable to resolve the query, would pass it up to his line manager in turn. Eventually, someone sufficiently high up in the hierarchy to be able to resolve the query would respond, and the response would again travel back down the hierarchy to the originator. Similarly, if an employee required information, for example, on his terms and conditions of employment, he was required to raise it first with his line manager who would then contact the appropriate person in the Personnel Department, obtain the necessary information, and then relay it back to the employee. It was not uncommon for many weeks to pass before a reply to the original query was received.

5.2.1 Directories of employees

Because of the sheer size of the organisation, finding information on other employees or on other parts of the organisation was not an easy task. It often entailed referring to a series of internal telephone directories or organisational charts, which were usually out of date by the time they were printed. Also, because of the costs involved in printing and distributing copies of the directories, updates were only printed once a year. The difficulty associated with gaining an awareness of what other people in the organisation were doing, or even knowing who they were, was not conducive to cross-divisional working and was also a barrier to the sharing of information.

In some parts of the organisation, there were basic electronic directories of employees, mainly consisting of lists of employees work addresses and their telephone numbers. However, access to these systems was restricted to people in the Personnel Department and Employee Communications. Also because changes to the entries had to be submitted on paper and suitably authorised by a line manager, there were often delays in the process of updating entries and thus even the electronic directories were often out of date.

5.2.2 Quality management system

In the early 1990s the company, like many others at the time, introduced a quality management system (QMS) which involved documenting work practices and procedures. This was paper based and while there were certain parts of the QMS that applied company-wide, there were often additional parts that detailed work processes and procedures which were specific to certain sections or work areas. The end result of this was that in some areas the QMS manual often ran to several hundred pages. While the company-wide parts were only updated approximately twice a year, it was not uncommon for the work-area specific parts to be updated on a monthly basis, sometimes even more than once a month. Because of the large volume of paper that resulted from this, not only was it very expensive in terms of printing and distributing the updates, but the time taken for individual employees to insert the updates and remove the old pages from their personal copy of the QMS meant that very often they just did not bother to update. A project manager commented that when he received updates to the QMS, he simply placed them in a drawer and that the only time he would actually update his QMS manual was the day prior to a Quality Audit. The purpose of such audits being to ensure that employees were conforming to the procedures

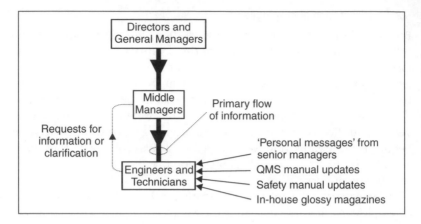

Figure 5.2   Illustration of main vertical flows of information prior to the intranet.

as defined in the QMS. Also the sheer volume of information in the QMS, coupled with the time and effort required keeping it up to date, often meant that people did not actually follow the procedures as defined in the QMS.

Figure 5.2 summarises and illustrates the main vertical flows of general company information prior to the intranet. As mentioned earlier, such information typically consisted of briefings on company strategy, company news and events, and also as illustrated in the figure updates to the QMS and safety manuals.

5.2.3   Horizontal flows of information

In addition to the information flowing vertically down the hierarchy, there were also large amounts of information flowing horizontally, typically between project team members and group members. Such information consisted typically of project briefings and project reports written by immediate colleagues. One of the requirements of the QMS, as discussed above, was that every project team member should receive a personal copy of every report written by other team members, in addition to a copy being placed in the project's report file. Despite the fact that the reports were generated electronically, the QMS required that all reports were distributed in paper format. With a typical team size of say ten members, each producing an average of at least two documents per year, resulting in at least 200 actual documents, it is relatively easy to see just how much information on paper was flowing just within teams.

It is probably fair to say that the overall amount of information on paper flowing horizontally in the organisation at least matched the overall amount of information on paper that flowed vertically in the organisation.

5.3 The origin and implementation of the intranet

Around the beginning of the 1990s, managers in the organisation, faced with the problem of increased levels of competition in all areas of business, identified a need to reduce the cost base of the organisation through improved efficiencies. It was also recognised that the company was suffering from problems, as identified earlier, of chronic paper overload. In 1994, a document-management-system project (known as CoaT – office automation in Core Technologies) was initiated. This project was tasked with identifying ways of 'taking paper from the business' and started the process of rolling out e-mail across the organisation. In the same year, people in the company began experimenting with intranet technology along with other proprietary technologies for on-line documentation systems. At the company's R&D facility, researchers were also experimenting with intranet technologies.

The CoreTech intranet manager commented that even before the decision was taken to deploy an intranet across the organisation, there were some 'early adopters' in the organisation already experimenting with the technology. She added that:

> CoreTech's intranet grew up pretty much like the Internet. We had early adopters and it grew from the bottom, not from the top. It grew because people wanted it and were using it.

The key early adopters were people at CoreTech Laboratories (the company's main R&D facility comprising approximately 3500 employees and commonly referred to as CoreTech Labs) and the CoreTech Corporate Relations Unit (CRU). The intranet manager, who works in the CRU, explained that at the beginning it was not possible to prove what the benefits of an intranet might be to the CRU or even the company as a whole, but there was a belief that there were benefits and the early experiments proved this to be the case. The reason that an intranet grew up at CoreTech Labs was partly because the type of work that people were doing there meant that they had access to the Internet and partly because a key element of their role was to experiment with and develop new technologies.

In 1995, following successful trials of intranet technology, senior managers decided that the deployment of an intranet would be managed and implemented as part of the CoaT programme. Following this decision, intranet connections in the 1995–6 financial year grew from virtually none at the beginning of the year to 15 000 by the end of the year. Usage of the web facilities grew at 100 per cent per month for much of the year. The number of employees connected to the intranet grew to an estimated 55 000 by the summer of 1997. By the end of 1998, the number of employees connected had risen to approximately 80 000.

5.3.1   Implementation

The CoreTech intranet was implemented as part of the CoaT office automation programme, which had already gone through all the various formal planning stages in CoreTech required for such a company-wide programme. The early implementation of the intranet thus neatly bypassed the normal formal planning processes and thus did not have to acquire the approval of various committees whose roles involved the assessing, evaluation and approval (or otherwise) of the implementation of new IT systems in CoreTech. In the early stages, there was actually little to plan since the implementation actually required no additional hardware, but merely the installation of a browser (which was free) and web server software (which in the early stages was also free). Also, in the early stages the growth of the intranet was very much organic rather than being driven by a formal implementation plan.

In the latter stages as the importance of the intranet began to grow and its potential began to be recognised by senior managers then investment was made in hardware and software specifically in order to support the intranet. However, by that stage, the benefits of the intranet had already been proven to many in CoreTech and it became relatively easy to justify and support the further development of the intranet.

5.3.2   Intranet applications and facilities

The intranet provides a facility where people in CoreTech can publish information electronically on internal web pages. The information on the intranet is accessible only within CoreTech. It is also accessible by anyone in the company who has access to the intranet. Examples of the type of information available on the intranet include CoreTech Standards (internal working practice documents), the QMS including all the various work-area specific information, on-line organisational charts, information on company strategy, company news, and personnel information.

It also contains information on the work being conducted within individual sections and often includes details of current projects, results of previous projects, and sometimes 'homepages' of individuals involved in the projects. Information from Directors and senior managers is available from their individual homepages.

At the time of conducting the case study, the intranet manager estimated that there were over one million pages of information on the intranet. Furthermore, it is now recognised and acknowledged by employees that the electronic version of information is always the current version. So, for example, if people are not sure if they have got the most current version of a document, they can always go to the intranet to check, and retrieve the latest version if appropriate.

There are also many software applications that run on the intranet. The most used application is known as the *Desktop Directory* which is a searchable database of all employees in the organisation. In addition to allowing employees to search by name, it also allows searches by job title, location, and work area. Updates to directory entries can be requested by telephone and the update is performed the same day. There are also parts of the directory entry that users can modify themselves on-line. This includes changes to their 'whereabouts', essentially an on-line diary illustrating their location for the following four weeks. Also, on their directory entry people can include up to four intranet addresses. These typically point to the individual's homepage on the intranet, their project's homepage or homepages, and their section homepage. At the time of conducting the case study, the Desktop Directory homepage on the intranet was typically getting over 100 000 'hits' per day.

Managers in the CRU unit responsible for the intranet are very pleased with its widespread use. Prior to this case study, they conducted a survey among users of the intranet. This survey indicated that 69 per cent of people used the system at least once a day and 76 per cent of users agreed that its use was growing. Also, 78 per cent of those surveyed agreed that it helped people to work more efficiently.

5.3.3 Information flow and effects on communication patterns

Figure 5.3 illustrates the main flow of information with the intranet in place. Perhaps the most significant change is that all employees who have access to the intranet have equal access to whatever information they choose. They no longer have to wait for the information to be relayed down the hierarchy as was the case previously. This also means that middle managers no longer have control over what information their subordinates receive. Also in terms of the horizontal flow of information between team members, project reports are now published on the intranet rather than on paper. Team members can thus access such reports on-line rather than having their own personal copy on paper.

Furthermore, as will be discussed later, many senior managers request feedback via their homepages and employees can actually do this directly, without having to go via their line manager. As Figure 5.3 shows, the intranet is now *the* source of information in the organisation, and new information is added continuously. Such information includes general company information such as 'personal' messages from senior managers, general company briefings, in addition to project reports and technical information shared amongst team members. The consequences of the changes in the flow of information are identified below.

The use of the intranet facilitates a much faster flow of information than was previously the case. For example, the personnel manager described a recent situation when CoreTech was involved in merger talks with another organisation, and explained how the intranet allowed senior managers to keep employees up to date with what was happening by disseminating information very quickly. He added:

> it was allowing people to share in where the company was going and to share in where the company was going fairly swiftly after the decisions had been made, decisions were being made in the morning and the information was coming out either that afternoon or the next

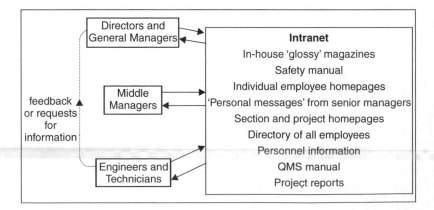

Figure 5.3 Main flow of information following the implementation of the intranet.

morning on the intranet. So people were getting to know very, very quickly and I think they felt part of the company and that was information management at its best, it was the impact of IT at its best, it was the opening up of where the company was.

The intranet manager commented that for many employees the use of the intranet has reached a stage where it is now becoming critical that employees have access. She added that:

it is definitely becoming the nerve system of the company. It is no longer nice to have, it is an essential; and that's how people are seeing it, 'this is not a nice-to-have on the desktop, this is essential for me to do my job'.

She commented that users get annoyed and frustrated when the system is not available for reasons such as maintenance or upgrades.

5.4 Post-implementation outcomes

This section presents data on the outcomes that followed the implementation of the intranet. The main issues to be addressed are the benefits, downsides, and different aspects of the use of the system.

5.4.1 Benefits

The benefits that CoreTech accrue from the use of an intranet can be divided into tangible benefits, where it is possible to put a figure on the savings or benefits arising, and intangible benefits, where it is not so easy to assign 'hard' savings.

Tangible benefits

There are many examples in CoreTech of specific intranet applications where it is possible to give a quantifiable figure for savings that have resulted from the use of the intranet. For example, with the CoaT document-management system on the intranet, the cost savings from the initial rollout to 50 000 people have been estimated at £230 million over a four year period. In addition, once the intranet has been implemented fully in CoreTech, as quoted from an internal CoreTech document:

there will be substantial extra quantifiable benefits arising from the cessation of producing, distributing, maintaining, storing and ultimately disposing of paper libraries, very conservatively estimated at £55M p.a.

The document also gives specific examples of where savings have been and will continue to be made:

- Updates to the safety manual incur a distribution cost of approximately £2.50 per person per issue and thus a saving of £300 000 is made each time.
- Internal telephone directory, as mentioned earlier. Of the more than 100 000 searches per day, half are straightforward searches on individuals, the rest are made up of investigations into job titles, hierarchies and other CoreTech organisational information. This is additional functionality, which was unavailable prior to the intranet. The last time the directory was printed, the production cost (excluding distribution) was £750 000.

The 'intangibles'

In addition to the readily quantifiable benefits that arise from the use of the intranet, there are also a number of benefits that arise for which it is difficult to identify the extent of the 'saving' or the benefit to CoreTech that arises from the consequent increase in effectiveness and efficiency of employees. In this context, intangible benefits include the benefit that arises from having access to information that, prior to the intranet, would not have been realistically available. Such benefits can be rather large. As an example, as mentioned earlier, one of the benefits of the intranet in CoreTech is that it facilitates automatic remote distribution of software to desktop PCs. Prior to the intranet, such activities would have required a software engineer/technician to physically visit each PC and to manually install an updated version of the appropriate software. Now with remote software distribution available, this removes the need for technicians to visit each PC and it also saves time from the end-user perspective in that the PC does not have to be taken out of service while the upgrading process is performed.

Another intangible benefit that arises from the use of the intranet is that employees can get information directly from the appropriate intranet web page. The CoreTech intranet manager explained that prior to the intranet, news typically got to people via the 'grapevine' long before any official communications got to them. She added that sometimes before the official internal communication got to employees they would probably have seen it reported a few days earlier on TV or in a newspaper. However, with the intranet in place, employees can access the electronic version of the official communication the moment that it is made available, and be confident that the information is current and up to date. The intranet manager commented that 'this removes a lot of the worry and speculation that people would have had previously'.

A good example of an intangible benefit was the issue of how much time was saved by people being able to access technical support information on an intranet website rather than having to ring a helpdesk. In one particular case, a support engineer, whose group has a home page which is used as a central repository for a fairly reasonable amount of information commented that the intranet has minimised the time he spends on the helpdesk answering the same question 'literally hundreds of times'. He added that people can now access the support information on the intranet and then only ring the helpdesk if they need clarification or further information not contained on the website.

The intranet manager pointed out that the easier flow of information is contributing to a 'better work environment' and that the use of intranet, in addition to allowing the flow of information to bypass the hierarchy also facilitates access to information not previously available. She gave the example of information on her Director's strategy and plans, information which can be accessed openly on the intranet, but which prior to the intranet would not have been made available. She commented that this open approach to information sharing has led to a much more 'open working environment' in the company and that people now expect to have access to all such information.

Reviewing the benefits

Managers in CoreTech are very positive about the benefits that they have extracted from the use of intranet technologies. However, given that CoreTech is now selling intranet technology and solutions to external companies, their estimates of the benefits accruing from intranets need to be viewed objectively. For example, an internal CoreTech document cites that:

> a general increase in effectiveness of 45–50 per cent was recorded from a recent internal CoreTech survey. Given an average employee cost of £28k p.a., this converts to a gain of around £14k p.a. per person. This can be viewed in a positive light as a good reason to put in a business case for new intranet access. It can also be considered as an opportunity cost for every delayed connection.

CoreTech also had intranet benefits reviewed by an external consultancy who reported that implicit in the calculation process is that all effectiveness gains by staff are immediately translated into more work by the same number of staff, or the same amount of work by fewer staff. In practice, it will take time for the increases which employees perceive in their effectiveness to translate into cost savings. For example, if a group of three employees perceive themselves each to be 50 per cent more effective as a result of having access to intranet, it will take some time before their workload builds to take up the capacity of an extra 1.5 staff who would otherwise be recruited. Conversely, if the workload were to remain constant, the translation of the effectiveness gain into cost saving would only occur when one of the three is removed and the space and supervision and support costs are also shed. The external consultants concluded that overall, if all effectiveness gains are being employed in additional productive work, the cost savings will be real, but there exists the possibility of over-statement of productivity-related cost savings in the short term.

Although CoreTech has realised significant tangible and intangible benefits from the deployment and use of an intranet, some senior managers believe that the biggest opportunities of intranets are yet to come. One manager commented that, by and large, the benefits seen at present stem from using the intranet to do the 'obvious things' such as eliminating paper and just sharing information generally. He added that the true benefits will come when everybody in the company begins to exploit the information that is available on the intranet in order to improve not just the work of their teams but also how their teams interact with other teams across the organisation.

5.4.2   Downsides

The rapid growth in the use of the intranet and the opportunities that it brought about for sharing and accessing information led to some problems with meeting people's expectations. The intranet manager commented that:

> what this (intranet) is starting to become is like the nerve centre of the company and now the expectation from people is, although it wasn't built up as a business critical tool, that's what's it is starting to be viewed as. So now we have having problems because we've got to manage it in that way.

She commented that people in CoreTech are developing uses for the intranet that were not initially envisaged and added that the more people use the intranet, the more information goes into the system. Also, more capacity in terms of web-servers and bandwidth must be added; otherwise, as more and more information gets put onto the intranet, the system will slow down. The intranet manager commented that if an employee is dealing with a customer over the telephone and the system slows down while he is trying to access information to give to the customer, then not only is that situation frustrating, it can also be quite embarrassing as the employee strives to talk over the gap while waiting for the information to appear on the screen. She added that such a situation is obviously not acceptable but acknowledged that it is partially due to the success of the intranet.

An example of one of the applications that was not originally envisaged was the use of the intranet as a front-end to existing systems and databases in the company. In the past two years or so, there has been a very rapid development of Internet technology in general to support this, and this has made the task of putting a web-front-end onto databases relatively easy. This has meant that there are relatively few databases in CoreTech that are not now accessible via the intranet and this has led to a sharp increase in the amount of information flowing across the intranet. The intranet manager added that this is not so much a downside, as more of a problem that has been created through the success of the intranet. She commented that it is 'a good problem to have' and that 'it is much better than lots of problems that we could have'.

There were also a number of downsides relating to the changes that have accompanied the implementation of the intranet. There is some resistance to the use of intranet because some people fear the changes that are resulting. The removal of paper from the business has meant that many people feel concerned about how their roles will change. An example of this is some middle managers who feel that elements of their job are disappearing because they no longer control the flow of information.

Another downside and a concern that was noted by a number of senior managers in the company was the worry that the use of the intranet may lead to a tendency to use the machine as a substitute for talking to people, resulting in an imbalance between personal relationships and the machine. A personnel manager commented:

> the technology can help you manage your time better, but it is to give you time to build relationships with your customers and your colleagues – it is not about making those relationships electronic.

5.4.3   Aspects of use

Training

One of the ways of supporting and encouraging people to use the intranet is through the provision of appropriate training. However, many people pointed out that they actually received little or no formal training on how to use the intranet. Any training or instruction that people did receive was typically very informal and often entailed being shown how to use the intranet by a colleague. For example, an engineer commented that when all the PCs in his office were connected to the intranet, the people in the office were given no instruction on how to access it, what information was available, or what it could be used for. He added that fortunately, one of his colleagues was familiar with the use of the Internet and was able to show others how to use the intranet. The intranet manager pointed out that in her experience a lot of training on how to use the intranet comes from people 'learning by doing'. She added that users also have to overcome the hurdle and potential barriers to switching the PC on and learning to find their way around the system. She pointed out that there is also a new 'language' that accompanies the intranet, and users need to learn the meaning of phrases such as browsing, downloading, websites, and electronic publishing.

Use of intranet by senior managers

There appears to be evidence that senior managers value the more direct flow of information that is facilitated by the intranet. The intranet manager commented that most of the senior managers are very keen to use the intranet, particularly since a homepage was set up for the CEO. The CEO encourages people to send comments and feedback via his website.

Another good example of senior managers using the intranet for direct communications is the homepage of the Director of Global Sales. He has an area on his page called 'Ask Bill', where anyone in his directorate, irrespective of grade or position in the hierarchy, can ask a question of him and have it answered. Senior managers perhaps have realised that use of the intranet in this way can be beneficial in that it allows them to get across their messages and to get feedback directly from people at all levels, without it going back up the management chain and perhaps some aspects or details of the feedback being altered.

A manager in the knowledge management unit commented that an interesting aspect to the use of homepages by senior managers is that many appear to be establishing their own website as a result of peer pressure, that is other directors already having one, rather that any strong desire to use the technology to facilitate easier sharing of information. She added that:

> so they're all starting to get them now. It's like a fashion thing, you have to have a website. I suppose the thing is how do you get them not just to have a website – the so called vanity publishing, here's a picture of me and my team – but how do you get them to actually use it for knowledge sharing as opposed to just putting a one way flow of information on there.

Effects on work roles

There is evidence that the use of intranet amongst those employees that have access is now apparently taken for granted. While this may appear to be a rather sweeping comment, it was specifically mentioned by a number of interviewees. Many people commented that they could not go back to a situation where the intranet did not exist, as they would lose most of the information they use daily to perform their job. For some people the intranet 'has gradually taken over' and although their roles have become totally dependent on the intranet, they believe that its use has actually improved the quality of what they do.

For those people who do not yet have access, the potential effect on their roles is rather different. For example, a senior manager pointed that in some cases the use of the intranet will make some jobs redundant and this will obviously be a barrier to encouraging intranet use among those employees who do not yet have access. Typically, the type of job that will no longer exist will be the job where someone takes a piece of paper and keys it into a database or other electronic system. She commented that:

> so I think there is a big issue around how do you encourage people to want the technology when what you are doing on occasions is asking turkeys to vote for Christmas.

Although some types of jobs will no longer exist, it will not necessarily be the case that the people currently doing these jobs will be made redundant. Indeed, it was pointed out that there are retraining programmes available that will support people and enable them to avail the opportunities elsewhere in the company. She commented that in some cases, the need to learn computer skills is a big barrier to some employees, particularly those who are in their late 40s and early 50s. She added that many of these people will decide that they cannot make the transition from the 'old and predictable' ways of doing things to 'a new more flexible, intranet-facilitated, way of working'.

Middle managers

It is interesting to note that in addition to supporting the flow of information across the organisation, the intranet is also facilitating a flow of information which bypasses the hierarchy in CoreTech and leaves a number of middle managers feeling very uncomfortable. A general manager (efficiency) commented that these middle managers 'feel exposed and threatened'. He explained that they feel threatened because people who work for them now have direct access to their managing director (MD) to give feedback or seek further information, the reply from the MD also comes back directly, and the middle managers are no longer in the loop. He added that in the 'old days', even if someone wrote to the MD, the reply would still have come down the management chain to the individual's line manager. He commented that:

> and your immediate line manager would have given you a hell of a bollocking 'why did you write to him, why didn't you tell me?'

The effect of this direct flow of communications means that the success criteria for middle and senior managers has changed. He added that:

> power is no longer 'I have control over people and I have information and that information gives me power' – power is now about what are my personal competences, what are my skill sets and how can I manage information and relationships across boundaries?

The intranet manager in commenting on the changing role of middle managers added that although they see elements of their job disappearing, this will actually give them more time to concentrate on their team's objectives and more time to coach their team towards achieving their objectives. A general manager added that 'if it is appropriate for information to bypass middle mangers, then this should not worry them. If managers are being bypassed then they need to ensure that they are not being bypassed for the wrong reasons'. He commented that if they are being bypassed unreasonably then they need to look at the way their team operates and how they use information.

A final aspect relating to the 'free flow' of information facilitated by the intranet was that highlighted by a project manager who commented that the open access to information on the intranet is helping to reduce people's reliance on their manager for information. He added that in a sense the intranet is 'a force for democratisation and increasing people's autonomy, increasing the number of people who can make informed judgements and who are thus going to be less dependent on their manager or their manager's manager telling them what they can and cannot do'.

5.5   Other issues arising

This section presents data on other issues that arose from the introduction and use of the intranet in the organisation.

5.5.1   Information overload

A number of people commented that the use of the intranet has led to a problem of information overload. A general manager commented that up to a point the volume of information on the intranet overwhelms people, especially when they first begin to use it. He added that after a relatively short period of time, people get used to being able to find what information they want and through using 'bookmarks' they gradually build up their own 'sign-posting' through the system. He commented that:

> there's such a wealth of information on there now, it's difficult to keep up with it all but at least you know it's there. If you're stuck for anything you can find it.

However, other users pointed out that trying to find specific items of information can be difficult 'unless you know where to look'. A typical comment was that there was a need for easier-to-use search engines on the intranet as trying to find specific information using the existing search engine can be very frustrating. A general manager commented that new users in particular, who enter what they feel is a fairly focused search, and then become overwhelmed with 10 000 pieces of information because they do not understand how the search engine works, tend to view this as a barrier to intranet use. He added that what can happen is that some users confine themselves to certain pages on the intranet and this can inhibit them from exploiting the full resource of information actually available. However, he noted that as more and more information comes onto the intranet, it will become increasingly difficult and very time consuming for such users to find the information they want. He commented that:

> and it's only going to be through a search engine or some form of either pushing certain information to you that you will be able to get

that information without taking a long, long time about it, and let's be clear about this, you can find out far more through the intranet or using the Internet to get information than through any of the other traditional methods that we've had in the past.

He commented that there are also 'cultural' barriers to people getting information from the intranet rather than from their 'traditional sources'. He added that people are used to information being 'pushed' to them and they still complain when it is not the right sort of information and it does not come at the right time, or it is not the right amount. However, they are content to sit back and let the information be fed to them, into their in-tray and their e-mail inbox. This 'push' approach to information distribution is now being replaced by a 'pull' approach. A general manager explained that the 'pull' approach basically allows people to choose how much information they want, when to get, and how to get it through the 'new' source, the intranet. However, he noted that it will take time to change people's behaviour and their attitude, and that one way of achieving this is to 'switch off' the alternative sources of information. The other way he mentioned was to make it as easy as possible to use and to give as much encouragement and support as people need to be able to really utilise the investment that has been made in the intranet.

5.5.2   Relationships

The issue of the use of the intranet affecting relationships within CoreTech was identified by several interviewees. For example, the intranet manager commented that she believes that it is helping to break down the 'barriers' between the different grades (i.e. levels in the hierarchy) and the company is becoming much less grade-conscious. Because of the easy access to information on people and their role, employees now tend to use the intranet to be proactive in identifying others in the company who may be able to help them with aspects of their job. The intranet manager added that having located someone in the organisation who looks as though he may be able to help, they would then be contacted directly. She added that in the CoreTech of 'old', this would not have been possible for two reasons. Firstly, it would have been nearly impossible to be able to find out if someone else in the organisation, beyond one's own team was doing similar work. Secondly, any contact with people in other sections or divisions would have had to go via line managers and this was seen as a barrier.

Similarly, other managers pointed out that although the intranet facilitates easier flow of information within and across sections and divisions, there will be, for some considerable time, lots of forces which are militating against cooperation across the organisation and in favour of competition. Examples of such 'forces' include the 'traditional competition' between units in the organisation and also the fact that although employees are encouraged strongly to work as a team, they are rewarded individually. Before full exploitation of the opportunities afforded by the intranet can be achieved, there will need to be a degree of 'unfreezing' of these attitudes. This unfreezing while being precipitated by the use of the intranet, is perhaps more of an issue related to change management rather than a specific intranet issue. However, it is likely that it will take some time and effort to achieve.

However, a business services manager while recognising the improvement in communications facilitated by the use of the intranet, suggested that there may be other reasons why there appears to be an improvement in the degree of collaboration between divisions. He commented that the other major influence on collaboration is the degree to which people are facing ever more demanding targets, ever more demanding customers, but their resources to meet these demands are continually being 'squeezed'. He added that this means that people are a lot more willing to seek and accept help than they would have in the past, and that working together across divisions is actually helped by being very tightly squeezed, as to some extent people do not have any choice but to cooperate.

5.5.3 Controlling access to information

Access to the CoreTech intranet also gives users access to the external Internet and the use of e-mail. CoreTech also has a policy that defines the extent to which employees can make use of the Internet and e-mail. The policy recognises that access to business-related information on the Internet has the potential to be of great benefit to CoreTech and thus the use of the Internet to gather information where there is a 'justifiable business benefit' to the company, is to be encouraged. The policy also points out that it is the responsibility of line management to 'sensibly implement' and monitor the policy. Also defined in the policy is inappropriate use of the Internet, which refers to 'anything which may bring the company or individuals into disrepute'. This includes accessing pornographic material, accessing material that could offend others because of its racist or political nature, conducting personal business transactions via the Internet, and unauthorised contributions to external discussions or newsgroups.

Rather than trusting that employees will adhere to the policy, the document also makes it clear that filters will be employed to deny users access to known Internet sites which encourage improper use as defined above. Indeed, it also highlights the fact that the web servers have the ability to record any Internet access in a log which shows which user the request came from, and that all accesses to the Internet from the intranet may be intercepted, monitored and analysed.

The effect of the policy on intranet use

The policy also points out that 'improper use' of the Internet and e-mail will be dealt with severely and may lead to dismissal. For many users, particularly new users who are unfamiliar with using the technology such warnings can actually inhibit them from experimenting with and making use of the intranet. As noted earlier, lack of training also contributes to these inhibitions. For example, a software engineer commented that most of the people in his office only use the intranet to access the Desktop Directory:

> because they've been frightened by all the dire warnings of retaliatory action by CoreTech for anyone found surfing the Internet.

A relative newcomer to using the intranet pointed out that the problem with the controls and the filters is that if one has not used the intranet before then one cannot actually tell the difference between internal pages on the intranet and external pages on the Internet and thus people may not use the system because of the fear that they might inadvertently access inappropriate external sites.

This point was noted by a number of users and there was general agreement that 'CoreTech's sledgehammer approach leaves a lot to be desired'. An intranet user commented that most CoreTech people are responsible enough not to need this sort of heavy-handed approach and that 'these threats simply breed resentment'.

As noted above, the policy informs users that appropriate filters are used to deny access to Internet sites that encourage improper use of the Internet. When such a site is accessed, either intentionally or unintentionally, the user receives a message 'FORBIDDEN SITE – CONTACT YOUR LINE MANAGER' on their browser indicating that access has been denied and that their improper use has been logged. New users in particular are likely to find such messages rather daunting and this has the effect of discouraging use of the intranet. A business manager, in acknowledging that the policy discourages new users from exploring and learning to gain the benefits of the system, added that:

> when you get that idiot page telling you that access is blocked but you can have access if you can justify that the information is needed for your job, that could only have been devised by someone totally ignorant of how the Internet works, or someone who knows how the Internet works and is determined to deprive CoreTech of its benefits.

Other people commented that the restrictions can usually be got round by anyone who wants to badly enough, so it tends to be the 'ordinary' users who are most affected. In fact, although the restrictions do cause inefficiency, their main 'damage' is apparently done through the 'repressive atmosphere' they engender and thus frighten off new users who would otherwise benefit.

5.5.4 Two intranets

In examining the role of the intranet, it is interesting to note that there are effectively two intranets in use in the company. The main one is referred to as the licensed intranet (where information has to adhere to specific publication guidelines and people must obtain approval to put information onto intranet sites), and the unlicensed intranet – referred to by some as the 'undernet' (primarily focussed at the company's R&D facility where anybody can put information onto web pages without needing to seek permission). While it is recognised by senior managers that the 'undernet' was very useful in the early stages of the intranet as it allowed people to experiment with the intranet and thus assisted with gaining momentum for widespread deployment, as the intranet matured and as the importance to the business grew, it was recognised that a more formal controlled environment was required.

Framework for information management

Initially, people searching on the intranet could search and access information on both sets of pages (i.e. 'licensed' and 'unlicensed'). However, in recognising the growing business criticality of the intranet, a recent initiative aimed at introducing an information management framework on the intranet has meant that the search engine now only searches on licensed pages. Also the fact that the intranet began to be used as a front-end to existing IT systems and for other applications that were not envisaged initially, puts greater pressure on the infrastructure and forced a rethink of how best to manage the information on the intranet. A framework for information management, including publishing guidelines, was thus developed. Internal CoreTech documents describe this as introducing a 'pragmatic framework that ensures that the basic disciplines of information management are adhered to'. The documents point out that this is essential as the system is used by customer-facing people who must be able to trust the information they retrieve from the intranet and be confident that they can use it in a direct interaction with a customer. This is obviously a challenge with such a distributed information system.

Responsibility for implementing the information management standards rests with a *Franchise Holder* in each operating division of CoreTech who 'licenses' the information providers to create and maintain content. Thus, if someone wishes to publish information on the licensed intranet, they must first contact their divisional franchise holder who holds responsibility for authorising new applications for intranet server space and also for the integrity and validity of all information published within their allocated area. The franchise holder also has responsibility for linking in new pages to the existing information structure and thus only licensed information can be linked in.

Intranet applications have been developed which support these principles. A key application is the page management application. Every published page on the licensed part of the CoreTech intranet has a review date and an owner. These are visible from the page. Each night a software routine runs on the server, which reviews all the pages and automatically sends an e-mail to the owner if a page is within ten days of its review date. If the owner fails to update the page by the review date, then it is replaced by a 'sorry' page – 'sorry this information has been temporarily removed and will be replaced once updates are received' – which links to the contact details of the person who is responsible for the page. After a further 5 days the page is removed completely. The review date is set by the information provider dependant on the type of content. For example, documents of record may only need to be reviewed every twelve months, whereas those relating to, say, major customer accounts need to be updated far more frequently. The intranet manager commented that this approach has proved very successful, with very few 'sorry' pages appearing on the system.

Migrating information to the licensed intranet

In early 1999, it was announced by the CRU, responsible for managing the CoreTech intranet, that from April 1999 all new intranet pages would be published on a new intranet server, known as the 'intra.ct' server. They also announced that existing content on the intranet would be migrated to this new server and that in the process, the existing content would have to meet the requirements of the framework for information management. Although the unlicensed pages were still there, in migrating existing content into this framework, hyperlinks to unlicensed pages were removed. Furthermore, the announcement added that from 31 March 2000, all non-licensed intranet servers would be switched off. However, when revisiting the company after this date, it was found that many non-licensed servers are still in operation. It is interesting to note that not all of the information that was on official servers has migrated to the new official intra.ct server. Also of interest is that when users attempt to access information that was previously on official servers, they are directed to a website known as the 'Missing Pages Bureau' which is actually on an unlicensed web server.

The campaign for intranet freedom

The plans to migrate existing content into a managed environment initially met with protests from many people who had developed unlicensed websites and they set up a 'Campaign for Intranet Freedom' page to air their views. They commented that:

> the CoreTech intranet has been built up by the work of thousands of our people. We believe these people deserve to be properly consulted and listened to before radical changes to the system are imposed (such as closing down the sites they have developed). Consultation will help improve the system by identifying flawed ideas and promoting those which are likely to work. Technologies such as e-mail, websites and bulletin boards make consultation easily affordable.
>
> The Campaign for Intranet Freedom recognises the many positive aspects of the new policy and the need for official web pages with guaranteed standards for content. However, we feel that the denial of unofficial web sites on the CoreTech intranet is ultimately misguided and will reduce the benefits to CoreTech of having a company-wide intranet.

They also highlighted their main concern as follows:

> if information provision is bureaucratised, then the free sharing of information will be discouraged. The Campaign for Intranet Freedom

recognises that certain types of information, such as official policy, should be regulated and kept up to date. However there are types of information that do not require such restrictions.

The 'leaders' of the campaign for intranet freedom also had a number of proposals that while recognising the benefits of an information management framework would also allow the licensed and unlicensed web pages to co-exist. They noted that:

> the CRU intranet policy is designed to address problems which we feel could be solved with less draconian measures.

Their proposals for coexistence included the suggestion that official web pages should state clearly that the information provided is official and is guaranteed to be up to date. Also they suggest that links from official to unofficial pages should be marked clearly to show that they are unofficial and that the data supplied may be out of date or inaccurate. Finally, they proposed that the entire intranet, that is both the official and unofficial sites, should be indexed so as to allow the users, when searching the intranet, to choose between official and unofficial servers. This would satisfy those who needed to be sure that the information was current, as well as satisfying those who in addition wanted to know what other information on the particular topic was available.

Perspectives on the migration to a licensed intranet

Not surprisingly, there were a number of different perspectives on the migration to a licensed environment. Providers of unlicensed web pages tended to be rather vociferous with their opinions. For example, a software engineer commented that:

> what will it take to make 'the powers that be' listen to the USERS, not providers of the intranet, and actually give them what they want? It's all very well stating that moving sites to managed servers gives a 'benefits package' (e.g. page management applications), but a moment's thought would make it obvious that the real benefits of intranet sites aren't to the people maintaining them, but to those using the information, and they can't choose whether the information they require is on a 'supported' or 'unofficial' server. By all means plan to migrate pages onto managed servers, but the fact remains that a large proportion of content is currently on unofficial

servers, and wilfully denying users the ability to search these valuable resources is bureaucratic obstructionism at its worst.

A web developer questioned the need for rules on web publishing and added that the idea of making information 'official' is interesting, but was not sure if this was really an issue. He added that:

> most paper reports I read don't have a 'review date' or other 'best before' indicator on them, why should the web have to be any different? Isn't it just that such rules exist simply to give those who like writing rules something to do? They can write them and follow them for all I care, so long as they keep out of the way of those of us trying to use these tools to do our work.

A second web developer in commenting on this pointed out that there is a lot of information on unofficial servers and that this situation is likely to remain, as the task of running a small web server is very easy. He added that:

> hoping that everyone will use official servers is like hoping that everyone would use the typing pool when word processors became available.

However, the perspectives of the intranet manager and franchise holders tend to be quite different. For example, one of the franchise holders commented that the rules are essentially common sense and are there so as to ensure that the information on the intranet is managed in a consistent fashion and so that users can trust that the information they retrieve meets specified criteria in terms of being valid and up to date.

Similarly, the intranet manager added that there are likely to be many unofficial servers around for a very long time. While this is not perceived to be an issue in the short term, in the long term, as CoreTech moves towards 'knowledge management', it is envisaged that the intranet will play a key role in the facilitation of this. The intranet manager commented that the CRU is thus trying to encourage information providers to move from the unofficial to the official servers:

> because that's the only way we're ever going to be able to find out what have they learned of use to the company and share it with the rest of us.

A final perspective on this issue comes from a business services manager who commented that there is a balance between allowing people to be creative with their use of the intranet and having a degree of control in place. He added that while the Internet is quite anarchical, you need 'a different approach in a business situation', especially as the intranet is becoming 'business critical' to CoreTech.

5.5.5   Discussion forums

The intranet facilitates a number of different types of discussion forum. These include a large number of internal newsgroups of a style similar to those that exist on the Internet and a number of different bulletin board type systems based on web pages. At the time of the case study there were approximately 150 internal newsgroups, each 'devoted' to a specific topic or work area. Access to external newsgroups is also possible, but as noted earlier, employees need permission before posting messages to external newsgroups.

Newsgroups

The newsgroups are actually accessible to anybody in the company that has an intranet connection, although until recently a lack of technical knowledge on how to access the groups has meant that the newsgroups have tended to be used mainly by employees with a technical or engineering background. Also, new users in particular are very reluctant to use newsgroups as they are worried about posting (accidentally) to external newsgroups, something which is specifically prohibited by the CoreTech policy on intranet/Internet access.

Many people commented that the most useful newsgroups were formed '*bottom-up*' by people needing the discussion forum and that as a result, most managers in CoreTech are still unaware of the existence of the internal newsgroups.

Web-page based discussion forums

The web-page based discussion forums essentially perform the same function as the newsgroups but have a more user-friendly interface. Examples of such systems are Sorting Information For Tomorrow (SIFT) used by HR people, and the Executive Calling System (ECS) used by executive directors to swap information with the sales force.

Communities of interest

The discussion forums facilitate the setting up and support of communities of interest across the company. For example, the use of the SIFT system is confined to the HR community and the ECS is confined to board members, very senior managers, and sales account directors. Through the use of such forums the communities of interest involved, in addition to building relationships, also build up knowledge. As a project manager explained:

> this is a community of interest building up knowledge. Here you have the added advantage in the sense of it being committed to print, so that you can't in a sense be out of earshot of an interesting nugget. You can go back to it and say 'oh that looks an interesting topic', I can listen in and learn from it. So it's less ephemeral than the chit-chat of a conventional meeting place.

The fact that the discussions on newsgroups and the web-based forums are 'captured' electronically has the advantage that they can be archived and searched at a later date, and this is indeed possible, however, only via an unofficial intranet page. Moreover, the discussions on the newsgroups tend to be initiated when someone is looking for information on a specific topic and very often the replies consist of others imparting their tacit knowledge. Other people who need this knowledge can then search through the archives and retrieve what they require. Thus, many people see the discussion forums potentially performing the role of a basic form of a knowledge repository. For example, a software engineer added that:

> newsgroups are the best way of a quick answer to a simple query once most of the obvious avenues have been tried. For example, my CD-ROM wouldn't play audio CDs – after having upgraded the software, read the manuals, and got confused, someone pointed out the counter intuitive answer in less than an hour.

One noteworthy aspect of the use of the newsgroups is that people seem to either love them or hate them. Those who 'love' them emphasise the benefits of the groups. One of the issues that arose on a number of occasions was the sense of 'community' or 'togetherness' that use of the newsgroups to share information engenders. One particular newsgroup 'ct.misc' displayed this aspect very strongly.

This newsgroup is the most heavily used newsgroup and receives approximately 10 000 'hits' per day from people right across the company. Even though the users of the group acknowledge the fact that a lot of the discussion on the group is non-business related they believe strongly that there are benefits in those discussions. One user commented that the ct.misc newsgroup is the:

> electronic equivalent of standing around having a cup of coffee, but with everybody in the company. Although people may be having a bit of a frivolous chat, there is a sense of togetherness, a sense of shared . . . we're all in this together, lads.

A second user commented that:

> I think ct.misc is a resource CoreTech is very lucky to have. I treat it like a virtual tea bar. It provides a source of 'togetherness' especially for people who are scattered all over CoreTech. The trivial stuff in this newsgroup actually serves a useful purpose even if perhaps over-used a tad. Many opportunities for helping each other out would be lost if we did not have the trivia to keep people interested.

The sense of 'togetherness' that users of ct.misc apparently feel is very strong. For example, a software engineer commented that:

> newsgroups also fulfil the role of tea break banter and so for me change the feel of the company from many people all working on their own, to a single set of people doing things for the same overall purpose. I've actually met in person only two or three regular posters on ct.misc, yet I would no more leave CoreTech without saying goodbye to posters here, than I would not say goodbye to my group. In fact I've probably had more meaningful intelligent communication with some people on ct.misc than I have with people three desks away.

Opposition to the use of newsgroups

However, there are people in the company who disapprove of the news-groups. For example, a manager in the Organisational Development unit in expressing his dislike of internal newsgroups commented that:

> they are dominated by techie discussions or puerile graduate discus-sions such as on ct.misc. Some of that is shocking. I cannot believe that we're allowing people that amount of time. But some of the shit that's on there, I think 'Are we paying these people to sit there and talk a complete load of nonsense?'

In a similar vein, the intranet manager added that the newsgroups are a bit of a sore point with lots of people inside the company. However, she did mention that many people have also commented that the newsgroups provide a very useful function in helping users to share information on an informal basis. With respect to the ct.misc newsgroup, she added that if it was within her remit to do so, she would actually switch this group off because in her opinion it contains too much discussion of non-business related issues. She commented that as a forum for discussion it is more 'abused than used'.

Users of the ct.misc newsgroup vehemently defend their use of the newsgroups and point out that attempting to regulate newsgroups to work topics only, leads to loss of social interaction and loss of work effectiveness. One user added that:

> It also encourages discontent and negative attitudes, initially focused on the 'Internet Gestapo', but later spreading to all the management.

Users of the ct.misc newsgroup themselves recognise that some of the uses of the newsgroup may be inappropriate and they suggest that some of the extreme views of some users need to be 'toned down'.

A manager offered the following 'cultural perspective' on the use of newsgroups:

> I think there's the question of how comfortable people are in sharing their problems and their views with what is actually the whole of the company. And this company comes from a culture where, to a reasonable significant degree, information is power. And I think this newsgroup type idea challenges it because you can publicly expose yourself to 'oh didn't he know that?' and also if you give an answer it becomes public domain and then no one needs to speak to you anymore about that. So what made my phone ring is now gone and because a lot of people feel uncertain about their role in life because they know the sort of changes going on and people like to pull things in. And there's also a built in mind-set that what I've just done 'is not normal'. In fact I felt quite weird that I was writing to somebody and every single word I wrote could be visible to whoever, whether it's the Chairman, my MD or Bill Bloggs in Aberdeen, and that felt quite weird.

5.5.6 Time management issues

An issue related to how people use the intranet is the fear amongst some managers that the use of intranets introduces a new set of problems related to managing people and managing how they spend their time. However, the evidence from the case study is that a lot of the people management issues are the same as ever, that is people pretending to work. As one project manager commented:

> all issues such as security and 'cyberskiving' were with us before the Internet. The use of intranets doesn't create new problems – but may expose some that you've already got.

Some people commented that there is almost an implicit assumption that people using the intranet/Internet are in fact 'cyberskiving', that is leisurely browsing the intranet rather than actually working. For example, a manager in the Knowledge Management unit explained that:

> I tend to maybe have a quick look over lunch time, if I've having a sandwich I'll have a little browse around and see what's happening but again people see you surfing around on the intranet and it's slightly frowned on, it's like well you're not working.

However, a communications manager (Networks) commented that probably everybody 'surfs the Net' for their own amusement. He pointed out that if it involves just a few minutes while waiting for a phone call for example, then it is not really a problem and in fact can help people get used to using the technology. An analogy given was that of employees making personal phone calls, where limited use is tolerated but abuse of the 'privilege' is a disciplinary issue. He commented that these management issues have always been there and added that:

> it's the same as taking a break to have a fag, it's the same as how much time do you spend chatting to your mate next to you. And with all of those things, there are issues to do with whether you are wasting time, but there are also issues to do with, well, it's good to talk with your work colleagues.

If the intranet exposes existing people management problems, it also offers an interesting new method of controlling them. One particular example arose on the ct.misc newsgroup. A communications manager explained that one user, referred to as Peter, was spending a large amount of time on the ct.misc discussion group, and this was obvious from the number of messages he was posting. Someone, unidentified but also a user of the newsgroup, reported Peter to his manager for spending too much time on the group. Peter was then reprimanded and instructed to curtail severely his use of the newsgroups. The communications manager added that this has led to the phrase 'being Peter-ed out' being used on the group.

During the process of gathering data for this case study, the 'Petering-out' of some users actually occurred. The following 'conversation' from ct.misc is a good example of how users feel about this:

Subject: Wes & JP
Date: 18 March 1999 15:06:40
From: Dave Thomas
This is a quick message just to say that Wes and JP will no longer be on ct.misc chatting about life with you on their breaks anymore. It seems that someone informed Wes's boss about him using ct.misc and that he wasn't doing any work and he was severely reprimanded. I can honestly say (as I sit next to him) that Wes was indeed working. He was running tests all day and as the tests were processing he'd do a quick ALT + TAB just to see what you guys were up to. His posts were few but the replies were long and it was for this that he got into trouble. He is no longer allowed to use ct.misc and JP has decided to stop as well.
As for me I'll post occasionally when I really need your advice (like when my car next breaks down as I'm sure it will) but I'll be starting my ct.misc diet today. Hope the informer is happy with themself.
Dave

Subject: RE: Wes & JP
Date: 18 March 1999 15:14:22
From: Paul Richards

Dave Thomas wrote:
>*(snip) the tale of Wes and JP*

I'm really sorry to hear this. The ghost of being 'Peter-ed Out' haunts ct.misc still. OK, Wes was an irritating little shite, but he certainly kicked the ant heap over and provoked discussion! Perhaps someone (Dave?) should have had a quiet word with him before the 'Official Fun Spoilers' became involved.

Paul

As a final note on how people management issues are being affected by the use of intranet, a software engineer commented that:

> the intranet and access to the Internet has improved the way my manager regards me – reading a paper manual was considered time-wasting when I should be developing code, but reading the same information from the intranet is considered working.

5.5.7   Towards knowledge management

The benefits of using an intranet for improving the efficiency of existing processes have been well received by managers. However, people are now beginning to explore the use of the intranet to facilitate processes that previously were not possible. A key element of these 'new' processes is that they all involve aspects of how best to exploit the information sharing capability of the intranet and are exploring how to use the intranet as a platform to facilitate a company-wide knowledge management system.

A senior manager in the Organisational Development unit, in commenting on the role of the intranet in facilitating and supporting knowledge management in CoreTech, added that 'because the intranet allows for all pervasive connectivity it actually has a crucial role'. However, he pointed out that 'a downside to the intranet is that you get people who become more and more addicted to sitting in front of a screen, whereas for knowledge management to be effective you need to get people to go and talk to each other'. He pointed out that the intranet can facilitate this as it can help people to identify who they need to talk to about particular issues (see earlier description of use of the Desktop Directory application).

While some of the people interviewed feel that the intranet is just a facilitator for knowledge management in CoreTech, others believe that it is actually a 'knowledge management system', or at the very least a repository of CoreTech knowledge. For example, in discussing the role of the intranet in facilitating a move towards knowledge management in CoreTech, a general manager commented that:

> the intranet is the knowledge bank for CoreTech, and it allows completely open access for people in the company to get information on anything that's going on in an easy fashion because rather than having to work out who do I speak to about that, the search functions and the cataloguing gives you really easy open access to find anything on any topic anywhere in CoreTech.

The role of newsgroups

A number of people also mentioned the role of newsgroups in CoreTech in facilitating knowledge sharing across the organisation. For example, a user of the ct.misc newsgroup commented that this newsgroup is a place where one can ask questions of, and get answers from, 'a company-wide knowledge base'. He added that this is a very effective way of finding answers to issues that fall outside the field of knowledge of one's own team or workgroup. Users of the newsgroups also appear to be quite keen to share their knowledge in helping to answer questions posed by other users. For example, one user added that:

> I can find answers to technical queries from the wide readership of internal newsgroups, and also contribute answers to technical queries posted on newsgroups, saving the questioner from re-inventing a wheel.

Bearing in mind that many managers do not use, or are not even aware of the existence of newsgroups, it is unlikely that this altruistic behaviour to helping others resolve problems receives any acknowledgement, except from other users of the newsgroup. The obvious question then is why do these people spend time helping other people whom they do not know and are very unlikely ever to meet?

Intranet as an enabler

Many managers in CoreTech have recognised that as competition continues to increase, they will need to find new ways to create value in their products and services. It was pointed out by a senior manager that the only way they can achieve this is by getting better intelligence collectively in the organisation. A project manager in HR pointed out that while a key part of knowledge management involves capturing and sharing knowledge and information, a more important issue is how to actually use this knowledge for business advantage. While the use of an intranet can certainly facilitate the capturing and sharing of knowledge, it can have but little influence on how such knowledge is actually used. The HR project manager explained that when looked at from this perspective, the intranet is not an end in itself, but 'it is merely an enabler that allows people to do things such as knowledge management'.

A manager in the knowledge management unit also commented that there is more to knowledge management than simply having an intranet. He added that just having a 'wonderful' intranet does not necessarily mean that everyone will use it. He pointed out that while the use of the intranet can encourage people to access information, there is also a need to encourage people to share information and to publish it on the intranet.

Despite problems of information overload, many people have exploited the intranet to broaden their network of contacts and so are in a sense beginning to build up their personal knowledge management system. For example, as one manager commented, 'knowledge management is not just about putting people in contact with information, it is much more to do with putting people in contact with people'. He added that this is where the real value comes from.

5.5.8   Perspectives on the role of the intranet

As the intranet has rolled out across the company, its importance has apparently grown. Senior managers talk of it as being the 'central nervous system' of the organisation, and the use of the intranet facilities is now considered to be business critical. For example, a general manager pointed out that the intranet is now 'the most important IT system in the company'. Other managers commented that intranet access is no longer just something nice to have, it has become an essential part of the way that many people work.

In summing up the role of the intranet, it is believed by many people in CoreTech that its importance will continue to grow, especially as the company is now exploring the use of the intranet to cross organisational boundaries out to customers and suppliers. Also many people commented that because the use of the intranet is now taken for granted, its actual use is underestimated. For example, a senior manager commented that:

> I think first of all it's underestimated. It's not until you have a conversation like this that you really begin to realise how much change the intranet has brought about. But I still see it as tip of the iceberg. I believe we've done some of the obvious things. So, tip of the iceberg and my gut feel still is that we use it far more than we ever realise.

Although there is a great deal of interest and widespread use of the intranet in CoreTech and while the intranet manager views it as a business critical system, the opinions of others differ. For example, a communications manager (Networks) commented that 'although it is an extremely useful tool, it is not going to solve all of CoreTech's problems by any means'.

5.6 Summary

This case study investigated the issues that arose when an intranet was used both to improve efficiency of ways of sharing information and the facilitation of new ways of sharing information within the organisation. Having presented an overview of the problems of information flow being experienced in the company, and presented data on the origin and implementation of the intranet, examples of how its use has affected the flow of information were presented. Of particular interest is the extent to which the use of the intranet has facilitated a change not only in the way that people receive information but also in their attitude to the type of information to which they have access. However, some people, for example some middle managers, feel rather threatened by the free-flow of information, over which they no longer have control.

In contrast, many senior managers are very positive about the intranet even if some of them appear to be using it currently as a mechanism for self-projection rather than facilitating a two-way flow of information with employees.

It is interesting to note that while the CoreTech policy on the use of the intranet and access to the Internet seems to encourage the use of such systems as a way of obtaining business-related information, the policy actually discourages users from obtaining fully the benefits of using these systems. The use of heavy censorship of the Internet in most parts of the company, threats of disciplinary action, and a general attitude which apparently frowns upon browsing the intranet, engenders a fear among users that they may inadvertently access improper material. The fact that many employees received little or no training in how to use the intranet, and what training they did receive was very informal, did not help matters. The net effect is that many users, particularly new users, curtail severely their use of the system and stick to the use of 'safe' applications such as the Desktop Directory. This has a secondary effect in that not only are such users not availing of the benefits of the intranet, but CoreTech as an 'organisation' is also being deprived of the full benefits of the system.

The use of internal newsgroups as facilitated by the intranet also raises a number of interesting issues. First, while some managers would prefer to see such forums shut down, users see benefits in these on-line communities and defend strongly the sense of community and togetherness that these forums engender. Second, the ability to search and retrieve information from earlier posts in the newsgroups means that the groups may be viewed as a useful repository of knowledge.

It is rather interesting that those managers who see the intranet facilitating knowledge management across the company are also the ones who 'condemn' the newsgroups. Perhaps the real issue is who has control of the information and knowledge. There is very little control over the newsgroups, other than that imposed by the users, who already operate a self-policing mechanism ('Petering-out').

Finally, in terms of assessing the overall role of the intranet, it is apparent that its importance to the company is high and will continue to grow. Its rapid ascent to the status of perhaps being the most important IT system in the company is rather impressive, but bearing in mind that its use to date has been confined to rather obvious tasks such as replacing paper and electronic publishing, its status would appear to be safe. However, there are still a number of associated organisational issues that need to be addressed. Such issues include the effect on the structure of the organisation, the continued impact of policies restricting access to the Internet and the effect of this on intranet use, and encouraging people to contribute information and knowledge to the system despite the controls imposed by the 'Framework for Information Management'. Perhaps if these issues can be addressed then the belief among senior managers that the intranet has become the central nervous system of the company can be justified.

Having presented above the data from the study of an intranet, Chapters 6 and 7 present the data from the two case studies that investigated the use of extranets.

6
Case Study – Research and Technology Organisation

This chapter presents the second of the three case studies. This particular case study focuses on the use of an extranet and investigates the issues that arose as a result of using Internet technologies to facilitate new ways of sharing information with other organisations. Table 6.1 illustrates how this case study sits in relation to the other two case studies. As mentioned in Chapter 4 when discussing the research methodology, the purpose of the table is just to show the initial objective for deployment of the intranet/extranet in each of the three case studies. As will be seen, a wide range of issues arose during the case study and the limitations of this table will be discussed later in Chapter 9. Nevertheless, the table serves as a useful starting point.

The data in this chapter are presented under a number of headings. The first section presents background information on the company and the business context in which the use of Internet technologies is seen as providing a solution. Before describing the origin and implementation of the system, data are presented on the situation that was extant prior to the implementation. This helps to provide an understanding of the context in which the system was introduced and also provides a basis with which to identify changes that occurred subsequently. The post-implementation outcomes and issues are categorised under the headings of benefits, downsides, aspects of use of the system and effects on people's role. Other issues that arose include how internal and external relationships were being affected. Finally, in an attempt to ascertain the level of importance associated with the use of Internet technologies in this case, both now and in the future, some perspectives of the role of the system discussed are presented.

Table 6.1   The ATI case study in relation to the other two cases

	Internal use – intranet	External use – extranet
Improving efficiency	Improving efficiency of current ways of sharing information within an organisation	Improving efficiency of existing links with other organisations Neotany UK (HQ in London)
Facilitating new ways of sharing information	Facilitating new ways of sharing information within an organisation Core Technologies (CoreTech) (HQ in London)	*Facilitating new ways of sharing information with other organisations* *ATI* *(based in Birmingham)*

6.1   Background

This case study is centred on a research and technology organisation (RTO) and its use of Internet technology (via an application called RTOnet) to facilitate new ways of sharing information with other organisations. The company in question, ATI (formerly The Advanced Technologies Institute), was established over 50 years ago and is a world authority on all specialist materials technologies. It is one of Europe's largest independent contract research and technology organisations and employs around 430 people who, with a blend of technical backgrounds, international experience and language skills, work with industry worldwide to apply specialist materials technology. ATI also operates a professional engineering institution and has an international training and certification unit. The majority of the company's employees are based at a large site near Birmingham, England. Over 2500 companies in over 50 countries use ATI services. More than 60 per cent of the member companies are based outside the United Kingdom. The company's annual turnover is in the region of £22 million.

The company is unusual in the sense that it is limited by guarantee and is in effect owned by its 2500 industrial members who include all major global industrial corporations and scientific organisations. These members pay an annual subscription, the size of which is dependent on the size of their organisation, and this gives the members certain privileges. These privileges include copies of regular research reports produced by ATI, access to information services, and direct access to numerous experts in all fields of materials technologies.

ATI adheres to the 'membership principle' regarding what companies it will work for in that until a company has paid a membership fee to be an industrial member then ATI will not work for that company. Because of the nature of the research that ATI conducts, the overheads in terms of capital investment and maintenance tend to be high and as a result the membership fees are also quite high. For example, the membership fee for a large company may be approximately £50 000 per annum. While a fee of this size may not be much to a large multinational, such high fees tend to exclude small and medium size enterprises (SMEs).

ATI lists its core business activities as: information provision and core research, contract R&D services, consultancy and project support, training, qualifications and personal membership and technology transfer services. The company's projects include many kinds of specialist technology developments, and range from the design of a wing for a new generation jumbo jet, to the sealing of nuclear waste-containing cylinders to joining the various parts of disposable nappies. The majority of these projects assist manufacturers in designing new products and testing new technologies. This means that ATI enjoy a very close working relationship with senior strategists and technologists in their member organisations, work on products in their earliest stages of the design cycle, and assist in not just developing the new technologies needed, but also provide consultancy support in implementing them. For example, the type of information that a welding engineer may require from ATI would be information on using specialist materials that he/she probably has not used before but which have been used in the design of a new product, or information on automating part or all of an existing development process.

6.1.1 The business context

ATI do not have any direct competitors for their complete range of services; indeed in the United Kingdom they are unique in terms of the breadth and depth of information and expertise that they can offer to members. There is a view among senior managers in ATI that the market for ATI services both with member and non-member companies is not being addressed adequately. For example in the United Kingdom, ATI has 790 small companies in membership but there are 140 000 small manufacturing companies that could potentially use ATI's services. Also when one looks in detail at any one of their membership relationships with a big company, that relationship is also not being exploited fully and there is considerable scope for increasing the amount of interaction between ATI and the individual member companies.

A typical example cited by a senior manager in ATI was the relationship with a major multinational car manufacturer. ATI deals with about 30–35 engineers in this particular manufacturer. However, on a global basis the manufacturer has around 79 000 engineers, of which approximately 2000 are concerned with riveting, which is just one of the ATI's technologies. Thus, there is a view among senior managers in ATI that not only are ATI not delivering their capability to the mass market, they are not delivering their capability to their key clients. Also, a senior manager pointed out that if the full complement of such engineers from just one member tried to access ATI expertise using ATI's current methods of transferring information and knowledge (via paper and direct personal interaction with ATI experts) ATI would simply not be able to cope.

Despite the fact that ATI's business revenues continue to grow and that the company enjoys little competition and operates in largely unsaturated markets, recent changes within the marketplace have led to ATI reviewing its own operating methods. Over the past few years large corporates, including many ATI members, have passed their core R&D activities down into their supply chains and, as a result, created the need for organisations such as ATI to interface with a larger number of often smaller companies operating in fragmented technology areas.

ATI's store of information and experience, accumulated over the past 50 years, is disseminated through written reports, 'word of mouth', training courses and other information channels. Demand for ATI information and consultancy services continues to increase. The limit on how much business that ATI can do currently is determined largely by the number of staff employed. The view of a number of people in the organisation is that while there is a desire to increase the level of business activity, they do not entertain the idea that this should be achieved by simply employing more staff. The consensus view within ATI is that there must be another way.

6.1.2   Internal structure of the organisation

The organisation is led by a CEO. He has three executive directors reporting to him and they are responsible for actually running the business. The CEO answers directly to the Research Board which consists of selected members from the member companies. The function of the Research Board is to oversee the performance of the company. A view of the organisational structure is shown in Figure 6.1.

One of the three executive directors (Director of Financial Affairs) is in charge of corporate finance and administration. The responsibilities for the rest of the company's activities are split between the business development director (BDD) and the director of research and technology (DRT). The organisation operates in a matrix fashion. The DRT is responsible for the 'vertical' part of the business, that is the physical assets such as engineers and the capital plant. These are organised into departments, such as 'Advanced Materials Processing' and 'Arcs and Lasers', which operate on a cost centre basis, and which comprise individually around 40 people. Departments are then sub-divided into technology groups comprising project managers, technology experts, engineers and technicians. The 'horizontal' part of the business is the responsibility of the business development director whose role incorporates responsibility for the services side of the business. This includes the actual delivery of services and products to the member organisations. He is thus responsible for membership services, which account for approximately 25 per cent of ATI's turnover.

Included in the services side of the business is the technology transfer department (TTD) which is where the idea originated of using Internet technology to facilitate knowledge and information trading with member companies. The TTD (the structure of which is illustrated in Figure 6.2 below) is very different from 'traditional' departments in ATI in many respects.

From a 'structural' point of view, as explained by an IT manager in the TTD:

> here in this office we have six managers, whereas if you look in the research department you tend to have a manager, four engineers under them, and then 10 technicians under them, they are very triangular.

In the TTD, in addition to the Head of Department there is also the role of product manager. The product manager, who is responsible for managing the extranet initiative described later (and known as RTOnet), is at the same 'hierarchical level' as a Head of Department.

6.1.3 Identification of roles

It is useful at this stage to identify the roles of various people who appear in the case study. The majority of roles in the case are of people employed in ATI. The key roles are shown in Table 6.2:

In addition to the above roles there are a number of people external to ATI whose roles are relevant to this case study (Table 6.3).

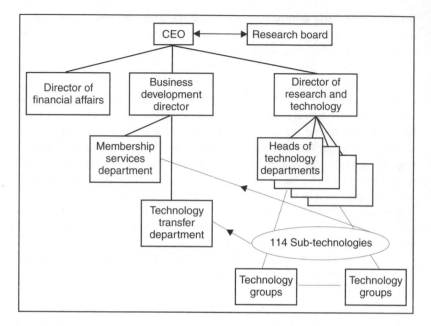

Figure 6.1   ATI organizational structure.

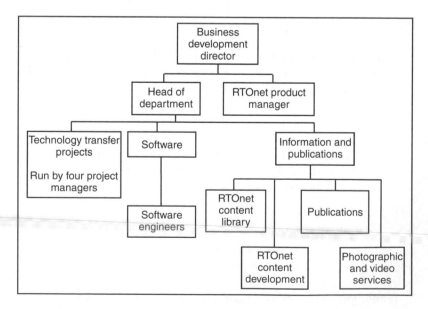

Figure 6.2   Structure of the technology transfer department.

Table 6.2 Main roles of ATI personnel in the case study

Business Development Director	The BDD has responsibility for the services provided by ATI to its members. Below the level of director there are a number of *heads of department* whose role is to manage their respective departments
Associate Director for Professional Affairs	This role is concerned with the part of ATI that deals with the engineering profession links. There are about 6000 professional society members and this role carries responsibility for the services and benefits offered to professional members
Product Manager	This role carries responsibility for the development and implementation of the RTOnet system
Project Managers	Typically, a project manager will have management responsibilities for a number of engineers who in turn will have responsibilities for a number of technicians. However, the role of a project manager in the TTD department is quite different. In the TTD a project manager may often have project responsibilities but no staff management responsibilities
Technical Experts	The role of technical expert involves some project management responsibilities but also involves technical consultancy tasks

Table 6.3 Main roles of non-ATI personnel in the case study

Manufacturing Engineering Manager (MEM)	This role, at a major car manufacturer (one of ATI's members), carries responsibility for manufacturing process technology
New Technologies Manager (NTM)	This role, at another car manufacturer, carries responsibility for investigating new and developing technologies

6.2 The situation prior to RTOnet – up to 1996

This section presents an overview of the situation that existed prior to the development and implementation of RTOnet. It includes data on how enquiries for information or assistance were handled, and presents an overview of the main flows of information from ATI to members and non-members.

6.2.1   A progenitor to RTOnet

Prior to the development of RTOnet, what is now the TTD was initially set up to run a technology transfer programme (called the RTO Technology Transfer Programme), funded by the Department of Trade and Industry, UK (DTI), and was based around the supply of services to SMEs who were not members of RTOnet. The programme, launched in 1994, was designed at the time to use 'traditional' methods (telephones, faxes, visits, feasibility studies, process reviews) to disseminate information. However, one of the key conclusions of the programme was that the 'traditional' methods did not work very well with SMEs. Bearing in mind that under the RTO technology transfer programme, ATI were offering their services free of charge, the take-up among SMEs was very low.

One result of the RTO technology transfer programme was that ATI found there was a huge demand for materials technologies information amongst SMEs. During the programme, around 10 000 enquiries per year were received, of which around 2000 per year were actually significant enquiries. The other 8000 were often fairly low-level sourcing enquiries, information about standards designations and the sort of information that, in the opinion of senior managers in ATI, a good IT-based system ought to be able to service very easily without human intervention.

6.2.2   Processing enquiries

It is useful to look at how enquiries were handled prior to RTOnet, as enquiries from members and non-members came in via the same route, typically via a telephone call. However, the enquiries were processed differently depending on the source of the enquiry.

Enquiries from members

Prior to RTOnet, there were a number of ways in which enquiries from customers could be handled. The majority of enquiries are from members and each member company is issued with a guide to ATI expertise. This guide, called 'Who Knows?' is essentially a directory of technical experts in ATI. The guide is now also available to members through RTOnet.

In the case of an enquiry from a member who knew what information was required, the process was fairly straightforward. He/she would look up the appropriate expert in the 'Who Knows?' directory and telephone him and being able to contact the expert directly is one of the privileges of membership. The expert would then discuss the problem with the enquirer and then forward information in the form of reports or articles if appropriate.

In the case of an enquiry from a member who did not know who in ATI to talk to, then the first call would be to a technical enquiry officer at ATI who would talk the problem through with the enquirer. If the technical enquiry officer was not able to resolve the problem, the appropriate expert could then be identified and put in contact with the enquirer.

A technical expert interviewed pointed out that while some enquiries could be dealt with in about five minutes, others can get more complex and may require some contract research in order to address the enquiry. Typically, if dealing with the enquiry takes more than an hour, then the possibility of conducting some contract research to resolve the query is discussed. A project manager added that most of the enquiries that come in from members tend to be relatively easy to answer. Often the member just wants reassurance of something that they are already doing or clarification of something they are about to do.

Non-member enquiries

In dealing with an enquiry from a non-member, the initial enquiry would be routed through to a technical enquiry officer. This officer would then give as much time as he saw fit in dealing with the enquiry, depending on the complexity of the problem, whether he needed to get some more information, or whether he thought it was a membership prospect. Also in dealing with non-member enquiries there are often other factors to consider such as whether the company is working for a member, or whether the enquirer is a partner in a collaborative project in which case ATI have the opportunity to get further referrals for information.

The approach to non-member enquiries, adopted by a former technical enquiry officer, was to ideally answer all such enquiries over the phone and to avoid replying by letter or fax unless it was absolutely essential. However, while part of the reason for this may have been a natural reluctance not to give too much free information to non-members, a project manager added that it was preferred to handle non-member enquiries by phone only:

> because otherwise that generated paper and work and we don't have any way of satisfactorily capturing or retaining or doing anything with the knowledge in response that we got. So, for example, we had no way of knowing how many times that man rings up and asks for information.

A technical expert added that ATI cannot afford to be subsidising non-member enquiries. He pointed out non-members have a tendency not to want to pay for information from ATI. He added that the difficulty is, as soon as non-members are informed that they will have to pay for the information they require, the response typically is that they are no longer interested and they will get the information elsewhere. He added that:

> it's a real hurdle that people do not perceive that information is worth money.

The project manager responsible for RTOnet content commented that people will pay for photocopies but as that is a legal requirement due to copyright issues, most people will accept that some payment is expected. For members, the photocopy charge would be taken from what is referred to as the 'free advice' part of their membership fee. For people or companies who have membership of ATI's professional institution, there is a specified rate for photocopies. Non-members pay double this rate. However, she explained that while some will pay 'under protest' others simply refuse to pay and say that they will get the information somewhere else. In the majority of such cases the information is not actually available anywhere else, or if it is, it will not be free.

6.2.3   Flow of information prior to RTOnet

Prior to RTOnet the main flow of information from ATI to members was typically in the form of research reports, regular journals such as *Connect*, and magazine articles. All of these were delivered in paper form. Other forms of dissemination included training courses and telephone discussions with ATI experts. Similarly, professional members also received information via these routes. In the case of non-members, typically information either came from the technical enquiry officer or from the technical library, assuming that they were prepared to pay whatever fee was requested by the library staff.

The primary source of the information disseminated by ATI is the researchers and engineers in the various technology departments. In addition to the information on all aspects of materials technologies that ATI has built up over the years, ATI conducts a wide variety of research and development activities that contribute to its pool of knowledge. A secondary, albeit minor, source of information is third parties, which include manufacturers of welding consumables, manufacturers of sheet metals, and component manufacturers. Such information tends to

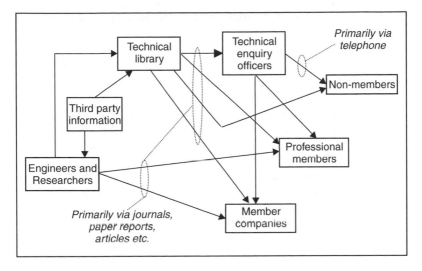

Figure 6.3 Main flow of information prior to RTOnet.

centre on the physical characteristics and specification of materials and thus is of interest both to ATI researchers and member companies.

Figure 6.3 summarises the main flows of information from ATI to members and non-members.

6.3 Origin and implementation of the RTOnet application

This section presents data on the background and development of RTOnet.

6.3.1 The RTOnet system

RTOnet is a multi-user system based on an Internet client–server model, offering access to on-line content. Users contact the RTOnet application in the same manner that any other Internet site is accessed, by selecting or entering its Internet address (URL). Users are identified using a password, which determines access privileges and charging method, set according to the contract with ATI. Typically, contracts would specify pre-paid, subscription-based, or post-paid invoicing methods. Users can also access information on a pay per view basis by credit card payment or micro payment. Furthermore, a default content-set is available for guests (no contract) to browse and purchase information if required.

There are three levels of RTOnet service with varying degrees of inter-activity:

1. Call off information including data sheets, best practice guides, sector-relevant news, directories of suppliers, standards information, hyper-text links to accredited service suppliers.
2. Interactive software: a series of materials technology toolkits, ori-ginal equipment manufacturer (OEM) bid specification and supplier response sets. In most cases the software packages that users access via RTOnet are packages that were developed by experts in ATI and thus are essentially interactive expert systems. The software pack-ages accessible via RTOnet are in fact the same packages that ATI experts use when resolving enquiries.
3. Technical discussion groups and expert 'surgeries'.

The system allows the majority of enquiries for information to be satisfied directly, on-line, with automatic charging for the information received. This frees ATI's people to concentrate on tasks with greater value-added content, such as consultancy and research and development projects, providing the basis for further information for members and customers. Another outcome of the use of the system is that it frees ATI experts from the routine of answering the same question or dealing with the same enquiry time after time.

The ATI Business Development Director added that he sees RTOnet as:

> a step change in the business, so strategically it sits in one of the business areas that's designed to revolutionise the business. It is a major strategic outlet for knowledge in that it's expanding our pene-tration of the market place.

While RTOnet has the perceived advantage of providing a new income stream for ATI, there is a problem in that managers in ATI do not know the potential size of this income stream. They believe that it is going to be substantial and could even grow larger than the income generated by the current business activities.

Although it is difficult to substantiate just how many people are likely to use RTOnet, ATI take heart from the number of people who access ATI's Internet home page, and in particular the high proportion of people who return to the site at a later stage. At the time of the case study the number of 'hits' on the ATI home page was averaging around 130 000 per month, of which 70–80 per cent were repeated visitors, that is people who had visited the site on at least one earlier occasion.

The RTOnet system offers benefits, to both knowledge providers and users, as a range of services that aid the transfer of knowledge on a pay-as-you-go basis from an authoritative source to an enquirer. An ATI project manager added that the biggest value is in the original content being provided rather than the Internet technology itself.

6.3.2 The history of RTOnet

The concept of RTOnet originated in ATI in late 1995. In one sense the concept was a follow on from the recognition, gained from the RTO technology transfer programme (outlined in Section 6.2.1), that if ATI wanted to grow its business without dramatically increasing staff numbers, then the 'traditional' ways of information dissemination and knowledge transfer were not adequate. In another sense the concept of RTOnet arose from the recognition by a senior manager (who became the RTOnet product manager) that the growing interest in the use of Internet technologies could be viewed from ATI's perspective as a terrific opportunity for new ways of disseminating information or a major threat to ATI's business.

Although ATI had a large volume of information that could be potentially transferred via the use of Internet technologies, the RTOnet product manager realised that one of the major requirements in terms of developing such an information system was a strong competence in telecommunications, which ATI did not possess. Thus, an approach was made to British Telecommunications plc (BT) to ascertain their interest in participating in the development of the application. The approach to BT proved positive and the first demonstrator of the RTOnet concept was displayed in late 1996 and was viewed as being very successful in showing how knowledge could be traded over the Internet. This demonstrator was developed jointly by BT and ATI, who were responsible for providing the information and knowledge content. During the period April–August 1997 an increasing number of ATI customers were exposed to RTOnet. These customers included most of the world's major car manufacturers, aerospace companies and a number of RTOs similar to ATI.

The RTOnet demonstrator generated widespread interest from the member companies and it was planned to launch the system, on a trial basis, in January 1998. However, some technical problems meant that the start of the trial was delayed by about four months. For the purposes of the trial the billing process, whereby users are charged for obtaining information from RTOnet, is based on a decrementing credit basis.

Members who wish to become registered users of RTOnet pay an initial charge of £2000, which is decremented as they purchase information from the system. As this credit decrements to zero the members are offered the option to renew their credit. In addition to being able to test the market for RTOnet and test the actual application, an important aspect of the trial from ATI's perspective is to gather data on how people actually use the system. It is envisaged that this will help ATI to determine where the bulk of the content provision activities should be focused.

The initial target market for the trial, and indeed the full launch of RTOnet, is the automotive sector of the manufacturing industry. All of the companies involved in the trial were industrial members of ATI and are automotive OEMs and companies who supply both the members and their supply chains with manufacturing systems and consumables. The reason for the trial focusing on the automotive sector was because the original thrust of RTOnet, as funded by the DTI, was related to the automotive sectors and the aluminium market. Each of the companies involved in the trial has between two and ten registered users.

It was anticipated that the trial phase would last for about six months before the system was launched commercially. At the time of concluding the data collection for this case, the trial was still in operation. Subsequently, the commercial launch took place in 1999.

6.3.3   Sources of information for RTOnet

The TTD is responsible for collecting and putting the content onto RTOnet. The primary source of information for RTOnet is the large volume of information that ATI has accumulated during its many years of research. This information is in many forms such as magazine articles, technical papers, and various types of reports and publications. ATI also maintains one of the largest materials technologies libraries in the world.

A second major source of information is the material that was produced, with DTI funding, under the RTO technology transfer programme mentioned earlier. This material includes a series of 'Best Practice Guides' and software used for 'techno-economic analysis' of materials technologies processes.

In addition to the above software packages ATI also has quite a number of other software packages which they have developed and which they plan to make available through RTOnet. These packages are designed to help materials technology engineers perform specific technology calculations. However, ATI has not been able to sell many of the packages, as the price has tended to be a barrier. Rather than use this type of software package everyday, an engineer may only need to use it occasionally and thus may feel that a price of around £500 is too expensive and difficult to justify its purchase. However, through the use of RTOnet, ATI will be able to offer the opportunity of a once-off use of the software for a much smaller fee, a figure of around £20 was suggested. The exact fee for these and other services to be delivered through RTOnet will be determined following the trial of the system.

Third party information

In addition to the information accumulated by ATI, the RTOnet application will also contain complementary information from third parties. These third party content providers see RTOnet as a way of increasing interest in their products. From ATI's perspective the inclusion of third party information enhances the credibility of the RTOnet site and makes it more attractive to users as it means the site has the potential to become a 'one-stop-shop' for all information on materials technologies and associated areas. Furthermore, although the third party information is being added free of charge for the initial phase of RTOnet, a project manager added that, in due course, ATI might well charge for the provision of third party information via RTOnet. This could provide ATI with an additional source of revenue in the future.

Keeping the content up to date

As just seen there will be a wealth of information and resources available via the RTOnet application. However, a number of people commented that the issues of how to maintain the information up to date, and also how to fund the activities associated with updating the content, have not been given full consideration.

The project manager in charge of content development for RTOnet explained that a review process will need to be introduced so that the material on the system can be reviewed to ensure that it is still up to date. Because of the fact that each department in ATI operates on an individual cost centre basis, there will be a need for some cost transfer mechanism or funding that can be released to experts to allow them to recover their costs associated with keeping the RTOnet content up to date.

Different levels of access to RTOnet

When the commercial version of RTOnet is launched there will be different levels of access to information. There will be a public access area which will be free to access and contains general information on areas such as the RTOnet application, ATI and its business services, training courses, and qualifications in materials technologies. There will also be an issue of *Connect*, which is ATI's general magazine. This is the limit of what can be obtained, without charge, from the system. To access further information the user will be required to go through a registration process. This process results in a profile being set up for the user so that their membership status or other association with ATI can be identified. This will allow information access to be tailored so that, for example, some categories of information could be restricted to industrial members only, or some material may be restricted to members of certain companies. This also gives ATI the facility to charge different rates for the same item of information depending on whether the user is an industrial member, a professional member, or some other preferred status.

The registration process also allows the user to identify preferences for the type of information they would probably be accessing so this should make it easier for them to find the information they require when they access the system.

Evolution of RTOnet content management

The view of the project manager responsible for RTOnet content is that the processing of the content and getting it into a form suitable for direct publishing on RTOnet will become more automated in the near future. The content management team is the driving force behind both the structure and the actual content of the system. The content manager sees this evolving to a situation where the people generating the information, for example the expert welders, will be more involved in guiding the structure and content. However, it will still be the case that the content management team will be deciding what information is appropriate for dissemination via RTOnet.

6.3.4   Potential customers for RTOnet

Senior managers in ATI believe that the customers for RTOnet will come initially from their existing membership base, but they also hope to attract a significant number of non-member companies, especially from the SME sector. The RTOnet product manager has identified four types of customers for RTOnet, as follows:

1.   The first type of customer, referred to as the 'technically literate', includes large blue chip multinational manufacturers who have a good understanding of where technology is going. These customers are also in discussions with ATI about a direct interface between their intranets and RTOnet.

2. The second type of customers are companies who have a well-developed idea of what they want to do with their business, but do not really have a technical strategy for how to do it. Typically these companies sell welding and joining materials and consumables. For these customers, the use of RTOnet is seen as offering them a commercially neutral marketing tool that will raise their technical profile and their respectability by virtue of the fact that information on their products and services can appear on the RTOnet system. This is essentially a form of affinity marketing.

3. The third category of customers is probably the majority and they are having problems with their structure and their markets. They are probably about two to three years behind in terms of understanding how Internet technologies could affect their business.

4. The last category of customers is the 'unknown'. These are companies that ATI neither know nor contact at the moment, and include many SMEs. ATI estimate that there are around 140 000 SMEs in the United Kingdom, of which only 790 are currently members of ATI.

6.4 Post-implementation outcomes

This section presents data on the changes and outcomes that resulted from the deployment and use of the RTOnet system. However, as mentioned earlier, for technical reasons the full commercial deployment and launch of the system did not occur until after the data collection phase of this case study had finished. Thus this section contains opinions, perspectives and outcomes of the trial of the system rather than the full commercial launch.

6.4.1 Flow of information following the advent of RTOnet

With the advent of RTOnet, the main change in terms of the flow of information is that RTOnet now plays a key role in the transfer of information and knowledge, as illustrated in Figure 6.4.

The primary sources of material for RTOnet are still ATI's engineers and researchers. The Technical Library is also shown as a source of information in that this represents the wealth of existing information that ATI has built up over the years. Responsibility for the library now rests with the RTOnet Content Management Team and a major part of their activity currently is migrating existing content onto RTOnet.

As noted above, there will also be information on RTOnet from third parties such as manufacturers of welding consumables and raw materials

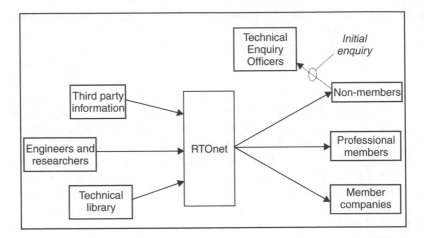

Figure 6.4   Main flow of information following the implementation of RTOnet.

such as aluminium and steel. This information is a significant addition to the information that ATI would have disseminated normally. This should serve to enhance the attractiveness of RTOnet as a source of information relating to all aspects of materials technologies.

From a member's perspective, rather than receiving copious quantities of reports in paper form the same information can now be accessed electronically. In the case of non-members, rather than spending time and effort dealing with enquiries as before, the Technical Enquiry Officer can now simply direct the enquirer to RTOnet.

Following the implementation of RTOnet and the changes that resulted in the flows of information, it is possible to identify a number of consequent benefits and downsides. The key ones are identified below.

6.4.2   Benefits

There are a number of benefits that accrue from the use of RTOnet, both from an ATI perspective and the perspective of people who use ATI information. The most obvious one is the benefit that arises from not having to use paper as a key method of information and knowledge transfer.

Removing paper

One benefit cited by the Associate Director for Professional affairs was that the use of RTOnet could eliminate the mass mailing of bulky printed material to the 6000 professional members. He added that 'there are probably a lot of people who are tired of receiving articles and reports which are of no particular interest to them but because they are members, they receive them automatically'. Now RTOnet is available, ATI can send brief summaries of reports to members, with the full reports available on RTOnet. Large cost savings are anticipated with this approach. Additional cost savings are also anticipated if a similar approach was taken with the industrial members of ATI.

People at the member companies participating in the trial also commented on the benefits of having the information on-line rather than on paper. The Manufacturing Engineering Manager at one company explained that 'it is much easier and quicker for me to find information electronically than to store all the bits of paper that I receive and then trying to remember where I have left the paper when I need to find out some information'. He added that with a large company like his, there is always a great difficulty in keeping everybody's knowledge at the same level, and although they have a large library with lots of information, he is never sure how much his engineers make use of that information. He commented that:

RTOnet will bring information to their desktop so that it's so easy to access it that they couldn't possibly do the job without looking at the background information and that's good for our business. So I think it's good, great potential as an information source.

Just as RTOnet will make it easier for members to access information, it will also make it easier for ATI to deliver information. For example, a Head of Department pointed out that:

at the moment it's a nightmare to impart information, it's tucked away all over the place, and it would be a great efficiency if we could just find it on the system and direct it to them electronically.

Access to more information

Although members receive various journals and reports as part of their membership, there are often additional reports that ATI produce and for which members have to pay an additional fee. Typically these reports may be produced as an output of some specific contractual research for which members would have contributed additional funds. As it would be unfair to then make the results of such research freely available to members who have not contributed to the research, an additional fee is payable. Unfortunately, such reports may prove to be rather expensive, especially if a member is only interested in a small section of the report. A New Technologies Manager at a member company gave an example of a project that ATI was conducting, where to participate in the project would have cost around £10 000, or to buy the report produced by the project would have cost several hundred pounds. He explained that he could not justify spending these amounts of money to either join the project or to purchase the report, as he was only interested in one particular aspect of the work. However, with RTOnet, he sees advantages in being able to specify what parts of the report he would like to view and to pay a small fee, such as a few pounds, just to get that information. Thus, he will be able to get access to specific, almost customised information, which previously would have been prohibitively expensive. Thus, from the member's perspective he can get a specific item of information at a reasonable cost whereas prior to RTOnet he would not have been prepared to pay for the full report and would have been denied access to that information. From ATI's perspective, the member is providing extra revenue.

Increasing the amount of business

As far as RTOnet is concerned, one of the big opportunities for ATI is that it will allow them to increase the number of members that they assist. For example, prior to RTOnet an expert could often have six one-hour conversations a day, dealing with the same query, where in each of the conversations he has got to start at the beginning and take the enquirer right through the particular process or problem solving routine. Whereas with RTOnet, the same expert could have say, 20 ten-minute conversations, because the enquirer will already have gone through a large part of the process on RTOnet, qualified his knowledge to a large extent, and thus only need some reassurance and final piece of advice that he is doing the right thing. A project manager commented that:

> at the end he can just ring up ATI and say 'okay I know what the solution is, I know this is the process I need, all I need to know is just am I doing the right thing in ordering five million of these rivets?' And that's the end of the conversation as opposed to an hour and a half.

While this will obviously save the expert a lot of time, it has a commercial benefit for ATI in that while the enquirer is trawling through RTOnet qualifying his knowledge and answering his own questions, he is actually spending money via usage charges.

Just as RTOnet can provide a first port of call for members trying to obtain assistance, it can also act as a first port of call for non-members. One of the things senior managers are trying to change at ATI is the number of non-member enquiries that they get and which can tie up the enquiry service. Prior to RTOnet, the expert was often in a slightly difficult position of informing non-members that ATI cannot answer their enquiries or give them any information until they become members. This was particularly troublesome in the case of an enquiry concerning health and safety issues.

However, as RTOnet comes on stream, ATI now have a real alternative in that they can direct non-member enquiries to RTOnet. The system will allow the non-member to view the appropriate information on a pay-per-view basis or even to avail themselves of one of the other types of subscription options available.

Problem solving

The easier access to information facilitated by RTOnet offers benefits to member companies in that it can reduce the time it will take them to solve problems and resolve queries. The new technologies manager (NTM) at one member company gave the following example of how RTOnet will facilitate faster resolution of problems. First, prior to RTOnet he would have contacted the appropriate expert in ATI and asked the questions or discussed the issues to be resolved. Typically, this would have involved the expert in retrieving the relevant information and sending it to the enquirer, a time consuming process. However, sometimes the process could get rather complicated and take even longer. The NTM gave the example of where he was having a problem with a new design and the ATI expert needed to actually see the drawings before attempting to resolve the issue. Unfortunately, the drawings were on a proprietary CAD system and thus needed to be rescaled and printed so that they could be sent to ATI. In this example it actually took three days before the drawings were in a suitable format to be sent. Having received the drawings, the expert at ATI then searches for the information needed to solve the problem, and this information is then sent back to the member. The NTM added that in this particular case it took around a week to get the answer they were looking for. However, he explained that as he already knew what the problem was, if he had been able to use RTOnet and interrogate the databases he could have picked up the appropriate information in half a day.

Similarly, the MEM at another member company added that even when the ATI expert sends information in response to an enquiry, it often raises other issues and the whole process could take several days. However, he explained that with RTOnet he does not have to wait for the information to be received in the post. He can read the information on-line and then process any follow-up enquiries on-line as well. He added that:

> it's got a lot of potential to make the information gathering a lot slicker and also because it's a database system, it won't forget things whereas the expert that I might be talking to might have forgotten that they did this or maybe it was his mate that did it, so it no longer requires people to have brilliant memories and I have a lot of sympathy with that because I have an absolutely crap memory. So I think that will be a good aspect of RTOnet as well.

6.4.3   Downsides

A number of downsides related to the use of RTOnet were identified and these are highlighted below.

Timescales

While many people in ATI recognise that RTOnet can offer the company significant opportunities and indeed may be the way ATI will do business in the future, there are some concerns about how ATI should make the transition from its current way of delivering services to members. There is also an additional concern that ATI, and the TTD in particular, may be moving too far ahead technologically, and too fast, compared to the rest of industry.

For example, the project manager responsible for membership services pointed out that the time period that the rest of industry needs in order to get up to speed with RTOnet and what the TTD are proposing should not be underestimated. He added that while he believes that the use of Internet technologies is definitely the way of the future, ATI need to maintain their existing business and 'ways of doing things' until the rest of industry catches up. He added that unfortunately the problem is that no one knows how long this will take.

He gave the following example of what the differences in opinion, as regards to the appropriate timescales, can mean in practice. He had been away on business for six weeks, when on his first day back in the office, John Williams, the manager responsible for membership communications came to see him. He came with the news that the first fully electronic version of the magazine *Connect* was going to be made available in November 1998. This was possible because the contributors were now generating the information in the right format for electronic publishing. John then added that there would probably be an overlap period of three to six months. When asked what was meant by an overlap period, John added that obviously there will be a need to produce a paper version for about three months before the magazine will be published in electronic format only. The membership services manager continued with the example:

> So I said 'just a minute John. Are you telling me that all 3000 of our members are going to be geared up to receiving, about 12 000 copies, and all those 12 000 people are going to be happy that in three months time they are going to be told that this is now available only in electronic format?' I said 'sorry, you are way ahead of the game. There's no way you can think about abolishing the paper version in that time frame'. He said 'well I've got to cut down budgets and if there's budget going on this then I can't do this and so on'. And I said 'sorry if that's the way you think then you're way out because industry is not ready for this yet'.

He added that while some people in ATI may believe that industry at large may only need six months or so to 'catch up', others believe that it may take up to five years, if not more. Indeed, the Manufacturing Engineering Manager at one of the member companies commented that he believes it is going to take some time to educate industry that retrieving information via systems such as RTOnet is a useful step forward. He pointed out that the technology is actually capable of moving much faster than the time it will take to change people's attitudes and that this will be 'a massive job'. He added that:

> it will take several years to get to the stage that ATI goes round and tells people about now. This is a not a six month project. It might be a six year project.

A project manager in membership services commented that RTOnet should be viewed as just another medium and cautioned that there is 'a danger that ATI will rush into things and say that RTOnet is the only way forward'. He added that while RTOnet is a new and exciting medium, 'it is only one of a number of media used for disseminating information and that managers in ATI would do well to keep this issue in context'. He expressed concern that if ATI give out the message that this is the way they are going to do business from now on and that there will be no more paper, then 'this approach is dangerous and could ruin ATI's existing business'.

Impact on membership fees

A final downside of the use of RTOnet relates to the impact on membership fees of users having to pay to access information on RTOnet. For example, a project manager responsible for membership services commented that expecting members to pay to access information on RTOnet, in addition to their membership fees, is a big risk. He explained that some companies are already paying £50 000 a year for existing services. This membership fee entitles them to services such as telephone support, and copies of all the reports and journals produced by ATI. The membership services project manager commented that if ATI then tell such companies that they will have to pay extra to access the information via RTOnet, then the company may well question the need to pay such a high membership fee. He pointed out that the risk in charging members additionally to access information on RTOnet is that ATI could 'alienate the 4.2 million membership'. He added that:

> we're justifying it because we're saying it's more efficient, but they're saying 'well hang on we were getting it on paper anyway and we'll stick with that thank you very much', and if we say, 'well it's not going to be available any more that way, you've got to pay for it', well that's one of the things that is a big risk.

The idea that attempting to use RTOnet as a way of extracting additional fees from members carries a degree of risk is borne out by what members say about this issue. For example, the Manufacturing Engineering Manager at one member company commented that if it comes to paying additional money to access information via RTOnet, then:

> providing it's a reasonable amount of money then I think that's okay. I mean it does give us a bit of a problem as a company because with our population of engineers if they all use ATI and other systems and pull down bits of information that cost money, we've got a slightly unpredictable bill and no accountant likes unpredictable bills. So somehow we need to find a way around that.

The people in the member companies interviewed during this research commented that they expected ATI's charging structure to change so that it can recognise the difference between a member company and a non-member. One member commented that if ATI come up with a fair and reasonable charging structure then he does not foresee a problem. Another member commented that over a period of time he expects his company's annual subscription to ATI to reduce but that this will be broadly balanced by the cost of the information that they retrieve from RTOnet. His expectation is that some proportion of the membership fee will be replaced by revenue gained from members using RTOnet.

6.4.4   Dealing with enquiries

After RTOnet

With the advent of RTOnet, member companies will have the option of obtaining information from the RTOnet platform in addition to being able to contact individuals at ATI. It is expected that the volume of 'low-level' enquiries, that is relatively simple enquiries, in particular will be affected, but opinions differ as to whether the volume of such enquiries will increase or decrease. For example, the content library project manager commented that one of the things that ATI is hoping to be able to do is take more of the low-level enquiries and requests for basic information, via RTOnet. He added that this will leave ATI engineers and researchers with more time to devote to their contract work as it will reduce the number of interruptions they receive in order to resolve low-level enquiries. A technical expert commented that he would save a minimum of four hours a week as a result of not having to deal with very low-level enquiries.

However, a Head of Department commented that in her view the volume of low-level enquiries will increase purely because more people will be aware of the kind of expertise that ATI possesses. She added that increasing the volume of low-level enquiries may not be a bad thing as long as ATI can find a way of turning an enquiry into an opportunity for future work or even membership.

An additional advantage that will come from answering queries via RTOnet is that the answered can be 'standardised'. The content library project manager explained that prior to RTOnet each of the technical enquiry officers or even experts, when answering an enquiry, may have given slightly different answers. This is because each has their own individual experience and preferences and thus may give different, albeit all correct, answers. With RTOnet, the answers can be standardised, so that the answer to a specific query will always be exactly the same.

Problems with a simple question–answer approach

However, a technical expert expressed some caution about the use of standard answers. He explained that sometimes it is difficult to know how to answer enquiries because some of the questions they receive are 'verging on the dangerous'. He added that:

> people will ask a question and the simple answer is 'you do this'. And you ask a little bit more and you find that the fellow has absolutely no idea of what he's doing and ultimately the construction is going to fall to bits and maybe kill somebody. So you have to say 'well the answer to the question you asked was this but you'd better be aware that this, this and this might happen and you'd better go back to the design engineer and' . . . well, the answer is not yours to give it's his decision to make the lid of out this that or the other, but it's just unbelievable. I find some of the design engineer people just frightening, terrifying.

A project manager added that how to actually build this 'capability' into an electronic system is a difficult issue. This capability essentially would mean that the system in addition to answering the question that has been asked would also be able to answer the questions that the enquirer has not asked. One suggestion was that the system needs to be able to recognise when enough contradictory questions have been asked and to recommend to the enquirer that he should contact ATI for more advice.

6.4.5   Aspects of use and effects on roles

Availability of Internet access

When considering aspects relating to how RTOnet will be used it is worth remembering that users will require Internet access in order to be able to connect to RTOnet. Indeed, one of the key underlying assumptions about RTOnet is that potential users have Internet access. However, not everybody is happy with this assumption. For example, a project manager commented that he feels that very few member companies are actually geared up to be able to use RTOnet. He added that the RTO technology transfer programme demonstrated to ATI that it is very difficult to get SMEs, for example, interested in new technology unless everything is free. His view is that this is likely to be repeated with Internet technologies, and while there may be a small number of innovative SMEs who are keen to exploit such technology, the majority will not have the time or resources to do so. He added that large organisations are more likely to have some people dedicated to working with Internet technology and thus it may be possible to get such companies interested in using RTOnet.

In commenting on this, the project manager responsible for the RTOnet trial pointed out that the companies selected for the trial already had established Internet capability and that there was no need to convince them of the benefits of the system as they already were, to some extent, 'converted'.

However, from the perspective of two of the participants in the trial the situation was rather different. For example, at one of the companies trialling RTOnet, the NTM pointed out that in theory all the engineers in his company have Internet access. However, in practice, there is only one terminal, which they all share and which needs to be booked in advance. It is also located one floor below where the engineers work. He pointed out that this means that access to RTOnet is not instantly available when an engineer realises he needs to obtain some information. He added that:

> You can't think 'oh I want to know the answer to that I'll just log into RTOnet', well firstly it's a trip downstairs and secondly chances are it's being used and you have to come back in the afternoon or something by which time the urgency is gone or your desire to know is gone or you've got the answer from somewhere else.

When questioned as to why there was only one terminal providing Internet access but potentially hundreds of users, the NTM commented that 'it's to restrict the use, apparently'.

He pointed out that although there are potentially hundreds of users of the terminal, the number who actually use it is far less. He suggested that if one went and looked in the book at the names of people who had been using the Internet terminal then there will probably only be about 20 or so names, and that they will be people who have recently graduated from university and who are used to using the Internet. He added that some of the older engineers are still struggling with getting to grips with e-mail.

Although this particular company has six registered users for the trial, as far as the NTM is aware, he is the only one who has actually used RTOnet. One of the registered users at the company who has not yet used RTOnet commented that he has not even logged onto RTOnet to see what information is available. He added that it is something that he needs to set aside some time to do. He also added that the fact that the terminal he would need to use to access RTOnet is downstairs and needs to be booked in advance, is a big barrier to using the system. If the system is not available when he wants to use it then he will either get the information elsewhere or he will go and perform some other task instead.

The NTM commented that ATI is probably different from a lot of companies in that ATI see Internet access as an on-going cost to their business, and they are trying to convince senior managers in member companies that getting information is a part of their businesses. However, he expressed the view that a lot of senior managers do not actually see it this way. They see it as a 'fact' that if an engineer, for example, is spending time obtaining information then he is not doing the work that he is supposed to be doing, despite the fact that he needs the information in order to actually do the work.

The problem of members not having easy access to the Internet was echoed by the Manufacturing Engineering Manager at another member company involved in the RTOnet trial. He commented that the biggest single problem he had in getting the 12 people that he wanted on the RTOnet trial was actually getting them Internet access. He explained that he believes the reason for this is that Internet access is not something that people get automatically because his company has not yet realised the benefits of giving engineers access to the Internet generally, not specifically RTOnet. The view is that senior managers are probably still concerned about the potential downsides of engineers spending time surfing the net rather than doing what they are supposed to be doing which is delivering solutions to particular technical problems.

Internet access in ATI

As mentioned above, one of the key underlying assumptions concerning the potential use of RTOnet is that engineers (and other potential users) of RTOnet will have easy access to the Internet and thence to RTOnet. However, it is interesting to compare the situation inside ATI and reflect on the level of Internet access that is permitted to ATI staff. While a lot of ATI staff have access to the Internet, private use is not allowed and the general guideline is that it should not be used unless it is essential. If this is the guideline that operates in ATI, where the belief is that they are very much switched on to using the technology, then if similar guidelines operate in other companies, and the indications from the member companies are that this is indeed the case, then the assumption that engineers in the member companies will have easy access to RTOnet appears difficult to substantiate. There is an apparent contradiction in ATI's attitude to the use of the Internet in that, while the objective of RTOnet is to make the Internet a primary mechanism for service provision, the realisation of this objective requires that member companies permit their staff to have easy access to the Internet in order to be able to access RTOnet. A second requirement is the recognition of the Internet as a legitimate source of information for engineers. It also requires that engineers are actually encouraged to use electronically provided services such as RTOnet, rather than being frowned upon for seemingly wasting time.

However, in ATI only around 100 people actually have Internet access. A project manager in ATI commented that:

> what we should be saying to our staff is that 'the Internet is wonderful, go out and use it, go and get more information to help you in your role'.

It is useful to note that although managers in ATI place great importance on using Internet technologies to trade knowledge and information with members, their use of the same technologies to share information internally is not very advanced. The intranet in ATI is rather basic and largely comprises a staff guide where the users can see pictures of individuals, their phone numbers and their e-mail addresses. Some minutes of internal meetings are also published on the intranet. Finally there is some information on key customers and the type of projects that ATI has conducted for them. However, this information is little more than a list of company names and projects. Even with ATI's intranet, not everybody in the company actually has access. ATI started a policy that meant that everybody who had a PC would also have access to the intranet but this has been a low priority. A project manager commented that:

> we've looked outwardly more than we've looked inwardly with the Net technologies and concentrated most effort on the Internet really.

Work roles

One particular issue that was mentioned by a number of people concerned how people's roles were changing and are likely to continue changing. Traditionally, people entered ATI as technicians and their progression through the organisation was very stable and predictable in the sense that right from the beginning their career path was predetermined to a large extent. Also, the technology departments, which they typically join, tend to be very hierarchical and the ways of working tend to be very bureaucratic.

In terms of changing the way people work, the RTOnet product manager explained that among the staff in the TTD are people who have made the change from, for example, the very predictable world of preparing and contributing to publications. He pointed out that they have changed roles because those jobs and other similar jobs will no longer exist. These people are now involved in processing electronic content and customising information for dissemination via RTOnet. In the process they have been turned from being an overhead to actually earning money for the organisation. Their role is likely to continue to change as the contribution of RTOnet to ATI's business increases. The RTOnet product manager added that the real change is getting to a structure and culture that understands there is no stable future state, a far cry from the ATI of old.

One way of characterising the changes is to look at how some of the roles within ATI are being affected. For example, a project manager in the TTD gave the example of people who are 'traditionally' used to producing 'something in a paper format' and who are used to meeting, face to face, the person they are doing the work for, and formally presenting the work to their organisation. Now, they are being told that they are never actually going to meet their customer. They will do the work for somebody who could be the other side of the world, or they may be just down the road. They will exchange a few e-mails, work on a word document for the project together and share it electronically, but they are not going to meet the customer face to face. He added:

> that's a very different way for a lot of people out there and in fairness to them the more senior they are I think the more abhorrent that idea is to them. They don't like that at all but that's something else we're working on.

Another issue that is causing some concern is encouraging people, particularly technical experts, to share more of their knowledge so that it can be disseminated via RTOnet. There are two problems associated with this. The first is that some engineers are unwilling to share their knowledge. The second is that at present there is no funding available to pay for the time that the expert needs to spend in 'sharing' his knowledge in this way. The Business Development Director pointed out that there are not too many experts who are reluctant to 'divulge' their knowledge and that 'for every one who behaves that way there are a whole bunch of people that are quite open and quite happy'. He added that the way to overcome these problems is to find funding for experts to convert and share their knowledge and then to isolate the ones who will not do it, and then to decide what to do with such people as and when their knowledge becomes critical.

6.4.6   Changes in ATI

It is interesting to look at the changes in ATI that have accompanied the advent of the RTOnet initiative. The RTOnet product manager commented that there is an awareness creeping in that there is an alternative way of running ATI than just running it as a collection of deep wells of technical expertise, and that advanced communications give ATI a way of linking those wells of expertise in new ways.

The Business Development Director added that some resistance to the changes have surfaced, for example the expert not wanting to 'leak his knowledge', and some departmental resistance in the sense of 'what's in it for me?' However, he seemed rather pleased that nobody has really opposed the idea, and that the only objections seem to centre around how it is actually being done.

In terms of changes in the organisational structure, perhaps the most significant has been the refocusing of the Technology Transfer Department (originally set up as part of the RTO technology transfer programme and now numbering around 45 people) so that its focus is on how ATI deliver technology to customers. The RTOnet product manager commented that in the early part of 1998 when ATI was given substantial funding for RTOnet from DTI, that things started happening fast. The department was reorganised and the jobs of around 40 people were reprofiled and the people retrained. The RTOnet product manager commented that people did not really like the changes at first, but the vast majority quickly accepted the changes. He added that:

> I think there are still one or two who are sort of, unsure, and they think it's all going to go away like a big black cloud, the sun will come out again and they can have coffee in the morning from 10:30 till 11:00 and isn't it all lovely.

6.5   Other issues arising

This section presents data on other issues that arose as a result of the use of RTOnet and the consequent changes. The main issues concern relationships, information ownership and the perceived role of RTOnet.

6.5.1   Relationships

The issue of how the use of RTOnet may impact on the relationship between ATI and its members was identified by a number of people. Also, the impact of the changes in ATI resulting from the advent of RTOnet was identified as having an impact on internal relationships in ATI itself. Perspectives on these issues are presented below.

Internal relationships in ATI

The presence of tension between the TTD and the other departments is an issue that was mentioned by a number of people. For example, a Head of Department commented that there is very much a 'them and us' situation between the TTD and the rest of the organisation. Part of the reason for this is that the TTD have moved so far ahead in terms of use of technology that some departments have not yet got access to basic tools and technologies that the TTD now consider to be out of date. She added that people in the TTD have mobile phones, they are getting home computers, and they have mobile systems for presentations. Also, the RTOnet team have an accepted 'philosophy' for home working. She commented that none of this is the same for the rest of the Institute, and as a result there is a big barrier because 'basically the TTD have absolutely no concept of the whole organisation'. She cautioned that:

> you can't continue with a total lack of realism for too long. I think you've got to bring them in and make them more aware of what ATI's business as a whole is, and the realism and the constraints that we have to work under that they don't have.

The perspective of the RTOnet product manager was, not surprisingly, somewhat different. He pointed out that a certain amount of the tension comes into the field of 'understandable jealously' in that people outside the TTD see the RTOnet team getting home computers, mobile phones, and ISDN lines in their homes, but they do not understand the reasons for this. The RTOnet team needs to be able to understand how electronic working changes their business and the way they work as individuals, and thus in a sense they are experimenting on themselves. He added that if they cannot do this then how are they expected to 'plot a way forward for the rest of the organisation?'

While people in ATI acknowledge the presence of this tension, there are signs that it is affecting the internal relationships in ATI. For example, the RTOnet product manager commented that there are people who come into conflict with the TTD because their business processes and their view of ATI's future are very different. Part of the conflict is also due to the level of communication that the TTD is able to sustain with the other departments. The RTOnet product manager pointed out that it is a balance between the speed with which his department is moving and the amount of resource he can devote to keeping the other departments up to date. He added that:

> I'm fast getting to the point of saying 'well actually chaps you ought to do your homework here because if you think you're a technologist and you don't know much about these technologies then there's a deficiency in your development'. But it's not necessarily very productive to actually point that out. It's getting close.

A readily identifiable source of tension is the conflict between the desire of the TTD to move as fast as possible towards RTOnet as the way that ATI should do business, and the desire of the membership department to ensure that the existing ways of doing business are maintained until such time that members have made the transition to the 'RTOnet way of working'. It is interesting to note that the RTOnet product manager and the person in charge of membership services both have the same line manager, the BDD. It is essentially his responsibility to manage the tensions and ensure that the relationships are maintained. The RTOnet product manager explained the position of the BDD as follows:

> he's got a pretty unenviable task because at the corporate level the risk stops at his desk. I think he's doing a reasonable job of it, which means that basically we're all moderately dissatisfied with him. He's not moving fast enough for me and other people reckon he's a dangerous revolutionary.

The fact that a major source of content for RTOnet is actually the other departments in ATI means that good working relationships need to be maintained. The project manager responsible for RTOnet content development commented that the content management area and all the things associated with it are probably the areas most fraught with potential difficulty in terms of people problems. The RTOnet content management team cannot work in isolation as they need to work closely with the other departments. He suggested that there may be a need for a content advisory board consisting of people from different departments who could provide advice on the types of content and make the content team aware of information and activities that they may not necessarily be aware of. He added that the relationship building needs to go both ways and that in addition to the TTD ensuring that they are aware of new developments (and potential content) in the research departments, there is also a need to ensure that the rest of ATI is made fully aware of what the TTD is trying to do.

Maintaining the relationship with members – the advantages of paper

Although an aim of RTOnet is to encourage people to access information electronically, there are still advantages associated with members receiving information from ATI in paper form. People in the membership department in ATI stressed the importance of regular communications on paper in maintaining the relationships with members. They commented that having RTOnet as the sole way in which ATI delivers information to members will actually result in a reduction in the number of members. The head of membership services gave the following example to illustrate how this could happen. One of the things that ATI stopped doing a few years ago was sending out copies of all research reports to all members. Instead they send members a briefing letting them know what reports are available and then members can request a copy of the full report. Even now ATI get members saying that they have not had any research reports from ATI for two years, and enquiring if ATI is still doing research. The head of membership services added:

> that's with paper where we've actually sent a letter. Can you imagine if we sent an email out to him that says 'from now on all research reports will be available on the Internet and we're not going to send them out'. Some people will read it, some people might but the vast majority of people will ignore it. And then six months down the line people will have forgotten us and will say 'what happened to ATI, does it still exist?'

Similarly, a project manager pointed out that sending a journal or even a piece of paper to a member is actually interaction and the members can physically see that ATI is supplying them with something. He added that although there are disadvantages with sending paper, for example the cost of sending journals to thousands of members in nearly 60 countries, it is a physical manifestation of how ATI are in touch with their members. It is physically and consciously reminding member companies about ATI and the benefits that they receive from being a member, and thus it helps to maintain the relationship.

The manager responsible for membership services pointed out that the impact of ceasing to send information in paper form to members, and instead relying on members to access the information via RTOnet, is actually unknown. It is difficult to ascertain what the impact is on ATI's business, of a paper journal or report arriving on a member's desk. On one level it is a physical reminder that ATI is still around. On a second level, as a project manager explained, further contract work for ATI might come from the fact that a member has seen a specific article in a journal while he was browsing the contents.

A project manager in membership services commented that there is definitely a need to encourage members to access ATI information via RTOnet rather than relying on paper. He pointed out that 'there is a need to encourage members to set aside time to access RTOnet. Engineers in the member companies tend to be rather busy and so it can be difficult for them to even find the time to read the paper journals produced by ATI.' However, he added that at least when the paper journal arrives the engineers can quickly scan the contents and decide what is of interest. If the information is on RTOnet the problem that ATI faces is how to get the engineers to actually access RTOnet and browse the journal contents there. The membership services project manager commented that the obvious way would be to 'starve them of everything else' and tell them that the only place where they can get the information is on RTOnet. However, he added:

> that's dangerous because if you say you can only get it that way then you've lost contact. And with our members, they would pay various sums of money for their annual fee but it could be up to £50 000, now if you're not actually in regular contact in terms of sending them information then you lose the whole relationship.

It is interesting to note that people in the member companies also acknowledge the value of information, in paper form, arriving from ATI. For example, the Manufacturing Engineering Manager at one member company commented that there is a value in *Connect* coming in paper form as it acts as a 'catalyst' to remind him that some new information is available. He added that at this stage he is probably not disciplined enough to regularly access RTOnet to see what new information is available and thus there is a value in the paper journal in that it triggers him to take a look at the RTOnet. However, he acknowledged that the 'trigger' does not necessarily have to be paper and that an e-mail would be acceptable.

However, the New Technologies Manager at another member company commented that if ATI stopped producing the paper journals and only made them available via RTOnet then this would cause him difficulties. He added that he still suffers with the 'problem' that although information may be available in electronic form he would prefer to read it in paper form.

Relationship maintenance

A number of people in ATI, while acknowledging the potential of RTOnet as a way of delivering information to members, commented that 'personal interaction' is still needed in order to maintain the relationship with members. A project manager in membership services added that ATI's business revolves around knowing the customer and having an interaction that is based on personal communication and trust.

The RTOnet product manager highlighted the importance of ATI maintaining good relationships with members. He commented that ATI is actually a 'relationship business' and added that:

> If you think about the fundamental of our business, it works because our members are in the position of shareholders essentially and we charge them large amounts of money just to talk to us. In other words before you get to talk to us you have to pay us lots of money. You have to understand how to manipulate, control relationships. And it's developed over the years and we know how to do it actually. However, those relationships can change fundamentally. They are going to be impacted by this new medium that's coming along. We have got to understand where our members are going and how to control the development of the relationship with them – that's crucial.

Despite the above reservations that the use of RTOnet may impair relationships with members, others view RTOnet as a way of actually strengthening these relationships. For example, the Business Development Director pointed out that RTOnet, in allowing ATI to increase its penetration amongst engineers in member companies, would actually result in a stronger relationship with members.

6.5.2   Ownership of information

Bypassing experts

In discussing the problems of generating and managing content for RTOnet, the project manager commented that some of the technical experts in ATI are somewhat concerned about RTOnet. He added that they believe it will diminish the opportunity for them to gain contract work because if members can access information via RTOnet then it will reduce the need for them to contact an expert directly.

He pointed out that there have been instances where experts quite like the fact that people are constantly trying to ring them. He added that:

> it makes them feel important. There are people like that here, inevitably and who you would have great difficulty with because they don't like sharing anything because to them knowledge is power.

However, other experts actually see advantages in having RTOnet 'handle' enquiries. For example, a welding expert commented that he was quite happy about the fact that members will be able to use RTOnet to answer their own questions. He added that:

> I used to work for a large steel company and there used to be a thing about welding engineering being a black art. And a lot of welding engineers used to retain their knowledge in order to ... they used to like confusing people basically. They used to like that black art image because then it gave them power because they had the knowledge and everyone else didn't. But I'm all for disseminating it, I really am.

He commented that he always has plenty of contract work that keeps him very busy and so the more information that can be disseminated via RTOnet then the more time he will have available to devote to his contract work.

6.5.3 Perspectives on the role of RTOnet

In commenting on the role of RTOnet, people pointed out that it should be viewed initially as a delivery mechanism that enables ATI to transfer information and knowledge in an electronic format. Many people also noted that they see RTOnet becoming more important in that it will become ATI's primary mechanism for transferring information.

However, others were more cautious regarding the role of RTOnet and in particular the timescales related to its projected widespread uptake. For example, a technical expert commented that:

> at the moment, I don't think it's terribly important. We're all managing quite well without it and we'll continue to do so. I think it's

important in the long term. But at the moment I don't think it's going to make any difference really, but medium to long term yes I think it will.

In summing up the role of RTOnet, a technical expert stressed that it needs to be viewed in the context of what ATI is good at. He added that:

it would be nice if we could believe in that particular area, but at the end of the day our core competence is providing information on specialist materials technologies, it's not about being a world leader in the fanciest Internet page and the advanced communications area.

6.6   Summary

This case study investigated the issues that arose when the objective of the use of Internet technology was to facilitate new ways of sharing information with other organisations.

Having presented the context in which the RTOnet system was implemented some examples of how its use has affected the flow of information were presented. Also, while many people acknowledge the benefits of not sending information in paper format, others believe that information sent to members on paper is a key part of maintaining contact with the membership. They would prefer a delay in moving towards using RTOnet as the sole means of information and knowledge transfer, until such time as they are fully confident that member companies are capable of accessing information electronically.

The primary source of information for RTOnet is the expertise and experience of ATI's engineers and researchers. Although a degree of their knowledge is already available on RTOnet in the form of expert-systems type software packages and various types of research reports, the engineers will also provide the basis for new information and knowledge.

It is interesting to note that ATI makes assumptions about how other companies access and use the Internet. A key factor in the success of RTOnet will be that engineers and others who wish to use RTOnet will have ready access to the Internet. However, this was not the case in the member companies visited. Also similar restrictions on Internet use in ATI appear to be in place, even though one would not have expected this to be the case.

In terms of changes to people's roles, RTOnet will allow the majority of routine enquiries to be satisfied on-line and while this is advantageous in that it frees ATI engineers from having to deal with routine enquiries, it also reduces the amount of contact that they have with prospective clients for contract work. Moreover, many researchers, while performing the same type of tasks, may no longer have face to face communication with members. Some people interviewed believe that face to face communication is a very important part of maintaining the relationship with members and thus feel that relationships may suffer. However, others feel that because RTOnet will increase the penetration of ATI within member companies it will actually strengthen rather than weaken the relationship with members.

The speed with which the TTD is moving forward in terms of developing RTOnet as a key part of ATI's business is leading to some tensions between the TTD and other departments. There needs to be a balance between the speed of migration to the new way of doing business and the need to maintain the existing ways of doing business until such time as the new approach is seen to be successful. If the speed of advance is too fast there is a danger that many members will be alienated because they are not sufficiently capable of accessing information electronically. Such capability includes the technical capability as well as the capability to recognise the Internet as a valuable source of information for engineers. If the speed of advance is too slow, then the initiative may be lost and ATI may be perceived by some members as being incapable of satisfying their needs, and their suppliers' needs, for information.

Having presented in Chapter 5 the data from the study of an intranet, and in this chapter one aspect of the use of an extranet, Chapter 7 presents the data from the case study that investigated the use of the technology to improve the efficiency of existing links with other organisations.

7
Case Study – Automotive Sales and Service

This chapter presents the last of the three case studies. This case study focuses on the use of an extranet to improve the efficiency of existing links between organisations.

As a reminder, Table 7.1 illustrates how this case study sits in relation to the case studies presented in Chapters 5 and 6. As mentioned in Chapter 4, when discussing the research methodology, the purpose of the table is to show the initial objective for deployment of the respective system in each of the three cases. As will be seen, a wide range of issues arose during the case study and the limitations of this table will be discussed in Chapter 9. As in the previous two case studies, the table thus serves as a useful starting point.

The data are presented under a number of headings. To begin with, background information on the organisations involved and the roles of participants in the case study are presented. Before describing the origin and implementation of the extranet, data are presented on the situation that was extant prior to the implementation. This helps to provide an understanding of the context in which the extranet was introduced and also provides a basis with which to identify changes that occurred subsequently. The post-implementation outcomes are categorised under the headings of benefits, downsides, aspects of extranet use and effects on the roles of people in the case study.

There were also a number of other issues that arose as a result of the implementation and use of the extranet. Such issues included information overload, ownership of information, and effects on internal and external relationships. Finally, in an attempt to ascertain the level of importance associated with the extranet, both now and in the future, some perspectives are presented of future applications and the role of the extranet.

Table 7.1   The Neotany case study in relation to the other two cases

	Internal use – intranet	**External use – extranet**
Improving efficiency	Improving efficiency of current ways of sharing information within an organisation	*Improving efficiency of existing links with other organisations* *Neotany UK (HQ in London)*
Facilitating new ways of sharing information	Facilitating new ways of sharing information within an organisation Core Technologies (CoreTech) (HQ in London)	Facilitating new ways of sharing information with other organisations ATI (based in Birmingham)

7.1   Background

This case study is centred around the use of an extranet to link the UK headquarters of a car manufacturer (referred to in the case study as Neotany) and its retail dealerships. The UK headquarters are located in London and the European headquarters of the company are in Amsterdam. The technical section responsible for after-sales support in Europe is based in Düsseldorf.

The dealerships number approximately 300 and are located across Britain and Ireland. The vast majority of dealerships are independent companies who operate under a franchise arrangement with Neotany for the retail and after-sales support of the vehicles. As part of this arrangement, dealerships have to maintain a minimum standard of operation which involves procedures for maintaining documentation and general rules and procedures for the day-to-day running of the dealership. Although Neotany has recently set up a small number of wholly owned dealerships, the majority of dealerships are either PLCs, parts of large groups, small family-owned companies, or somewhere in between.

7.1.1   Roles of people involved in the case study

This section presents background information on the roles of people involved in the case study. Firstly, in addition to the roles of salespeople and receptionists, the main roles at a typical dealership are as indicated in Table 7.2. Secondly, for the purposes of this case study, the main roles in Neotany are as illustrated in Table 7.3.

The next section presents an overview of how some of the above roles were performed prior to the implementation of the extranet.

Table 7.2   Main roles at a Neotany dealership

Dealer Principal (DP)	This is essentially the person who runs the dealership. He would typically own the franchise
General Manager	This, as the name implies, is someone who actually runs the dealerships on a daily basis, on behalf of the DP
Service Manager	This is the person who runs the service department in the dealership and who has overall responsibility for all aspects concerning the servicing, repair and maintenance of vehicles. Part of their role is to take control of the technical bulletins that Neotany issue to the dealers, and to make sure they are read and circulated around the dealership
HITEQ	This is the name given to the 'hi-tech' or senior technician in the service department. His role is to actually carry out all the necessary work on the vehicles. This involves referring to the appropriate service manuals and technical bulletins in order to get the information needed to repair the vehicles
Parts Manager	This role involves managing the purchase, and return if appropriate, of all vehicle parts and accessories required by the dealership

7.2   Prior to the extranet

Typical interactions between Neotany and the dealerships involve the exchange of information on sales and marketing, pricing, ordering, and maintenance of vehicles, spare parts and accessories. Prior to the implementation of the extranet, the majority of information sent from Neotany to the dealerships was in paper form. Typically such information included service manuals, technical bulletins, service bulletins, price lists, paint manuals, sales and marketing information, and bromides for use in advertising.

Prior to the extranet, information referring to the repair and servicing of vehicles which dealerships needed to be made aware of, was faxed in summary form, then sent by post, and then followed up by a phone call to make sure that everything had arrived. However, rather than having people in Neotany print and mail the material to the dealerships, information that Neotany required to be sent to dealerships was initially sent to external agencies who printed out the information on Neotany headed paper, collated it and then mailed this to individual dealerships. As an example of the costs involved, Neotany had been spending around £100 000 a year just printing and distributing the

Table 7.3 Main roles of Neotany employees in the case study

Head of IT	This is the person who runs the IT department at Neotany and who is responsible overall for the extranet
Extranet Manager	This is the person who is responsible for the technical development of the extranet including the development of new applications
Product Support Administrator (PSA)	This role involves providing technical backup to the dealerships. They deal with the technicians and service managers. As well as providing the technical bulletins they also make sure that the dealerships have all the service manuals that they require. There are around 20 PSAs located at Neotany HQ
Dealer Operations Manager (DOM)	This role is essentially that of a mobile sales force that looks after the dealerships. A key part of the role is to ensure that the dealership is meeting the standards required of the franchise agreement. There are around 30 DOMs operating from Neotany HQ
Brand Controller	This is essentially a strategic marketing role and the responsibility addresses product specification, pricing, and communications nationally on a strategic level rather than on a tactical level
Technical Field Engineer	This role involves going out and helping dealerships when they have a 'difficult to fix' technical problem of if there is a customer relations issue that cannot be resolved at the dealership. There are four field engineers operating out of Neotany HQ

monthly price lists to the dealerships. The master pricing set was actually a 40-page document and with every single car (and model variants) and every single price on it, it was quite complex. It included the customer price list, that is the prices that the end customer sees, as well as the wholesale prices, that is the price at which the dealership can buy the car. The cost of £100 000 related to the price list alone, the printing and distribution of marketing brochures, technical bulletins and any other information incurred additional costs.

It is also worth noting that the pricing information, marketing brochures, and technical bulletin information originated in different departments in Neotany HQ and that the distribution of the information to the dealerships was not coordinated within Neotany. If the external agency was aware that information from different departments was due to be sent to dealerships, then the agency would coordinate the mailings where possible in order to reduce mailing costs. However, this was not always possible, so it was not unusual for a dealership to receive multiple mailings from Neotany on a daily basis.

7.2.1   Technical and service bulletins – prior to the extranet

A large part of the information sent from Neotany HQ to dealerships is in the form of technical and service bulletins and prior to the extranet these were all sent out in paper form. Typically a technical bulletin would contain tips on how to fix a vehicle, and although averaging five double sided A4 pages, could often be as much as eight or nine double sided A4 pages. All bulletins were stored in their own binders which related to different vehicle models. The bulletins were also filed in a set of dividers that relate to the sections of the service manual, for example, clutch, maintenance, brakes. There are different types of bulletins: service action bulletins which mean that the next time the vehicle comes into the dealership they should carry out the work detailed in the bulletin; technical information, which is the most common one; and a service manual amendment. When an amendment to a service manual is issued, the service manager or HITEQ is supposed to replace the appropriate pages in his copy of the manual. However, a product support administrator (PSA) acknowledged that not all dealerships actually do this even though they are required to do so under the terms of their franchise agreement. The service manager and the technicians were required to read all technical and service bulletins and then to sign their name at the bottom of the bulletin to indicate that they had read it. The bulletins were then stored in special binders for future reference. This is what was supposed to happen. The reality in some cases was rather different.

A PSA explained that when technical and service bulletins were sent to a dealership, invariably they end up in the service manager's in-tray because it is part of his role to read the bulletins before passing them on to the technicians and the parts manager. However, not every service manager actually passed the bulletins on as required and in some cases, the trigger to pass the bulletins on was the fact that the service manager's in-tray was full. The result of this would be that the HITEQ would typically receive up to three month's worth of bulletins in the same afternoon, all in one go.

7.2.2   The dealer communications system (DCS)

Prior to the implementation of the extranet, there was already a DCS in use. This system, accessed at the dealer end via PCs leased from Neotany, was a low-speed (2.4 kbits per second) dial-up link to the Neotany mainframe computer. This link, accessed via a dumb 3270 terminal adapter client on the PC, only allowed dealers to connect to the

Neotany mainframe to check availability and place orders for vehicles, parts and accessories. With the DCS, dealers were only allowed to run Neotany applications on the PCs. Also, the system only facilitated basic communications between dealers and Neotany. It was not possible for dealers to communicate with each other via the system.

7.2.3   Dealer operation managers (DOMs)

The DOMs provide the main contact between Neotany and the dealerships. Each DOM is responsible for an average of nine dealerships. This role involves liaising between the dealers and the Neotany head office in terms of sales targets, general running of the dealership in terms of abiding by the franchise agreement, and sorting out any issues that may be affecting how well the dealership is performing. Any information that was sent to the dealers was also sent firstly to the DOM so that he was fully aware of what information the dealers are receiving and would be in a position to be able to anticipate any issues that may arise.

7.2.4   Flow of information prior to the extranet

Figure 7.1 illustrates the main flows of information between the dealerships and Neotany prior to the extranet. As shown in the figure, information to be sent to the dealerships originated in a number of departments in Neotany head office. This information was then sent to an external agency for printing and onward distribution to the dealerships. At the same time as sending the information to the external agency, the information was also copied to the DOMs so that they had prior awareness of what the dealerships would be receiving.

In the case of technical and service bulletins, and any information concerning the parts, accessories, repair and maintenance of vehicles, the recipient would typically be the service manager. The service manager would then decide what information should be passed on to the parts manager and to the HITEQ and other technicians. Even in the case where Neotany send information directly to the HITEQ and where the envelope is specifically addressed to the HITEQ, in the majority of cases this information would be 'intercepted' by the receptionist (or person who deals with incoming post) in the dealership and passed to the service manager, who again would decide whether or not to pass on the information.

Information from Neotany concerning sales and marketing would be directed to the sales manager, although in small dealerships the roles of sales manager and service manager may actually be performed by the

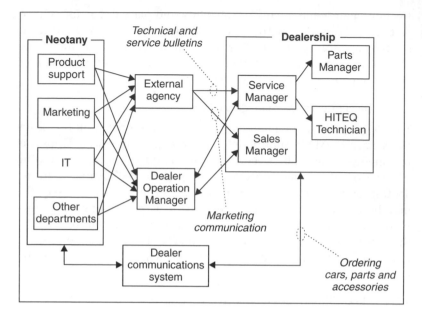

Figure 7.1   Illustration of main flows of information prior to the extranet.

same person. Other more detailed sales and marketing information such as sales reports and sales targets would come into the dealerships via the DOM and this would often involve a two-way flow of information between the DOM and the dealership. Similarly, the DOM would also convey information to the service manager and the sales manager concerning changes to the standards of operation that the dealerships were required to adhere to under the terms of the franchise agreement.

Information would also come into the dealerships via the DCS. This information was confined to details of availability and ordering information for vehicles, spare parts, and accessories. Similarly, information in terms of the actual orders flowed via the DCS back to Neotany.

7.3   Origin and implementation of the extranet

In February 1997, old hardware used for supporting the DCS was due to be written off and this provided the IT department at Neotany with the opportunity for a substantial review of how they communicated with dealers. The new hardware to support the DCS involved PCs running Windows NT and Windows95 operating systems. The PCs at the dealerships were also replaced with machines with up-to-date specifications. The new DCS also benefited from an upgrade in the speed of the dial-up communications to ISDN standard which, using data compression techniques, allowed a data throughput of 256 kbits per second to dealerships.

However, in the early stages of upgrading the hardware supporting the DCS, the use of extranet was not a part of the plan. The Head of IT commented that it was only about half-way through the upgrade process when he spotted the potential of web technologies. With the new DCS providing an appropriate infrastructure for deployment of web technologies, he decided at the time to investigate what could be done with the technology. The person who subsequently became the extranet manager, the Head of IT, and a contractor spent a couple of months experimenting with the technology and putting some ideas together for how it could be potentially used. The extranet manager commented that 'at the time we just played about at first really'. The outcome of these experiments with the technology formed the basis for 'selling' the deployment of an extranet to the IT Director.

The business case for deploying the extranet was justified essentially on the basis of anticipated cost savings. Although issues such as ease of use of the technology and the fact that it appeared to offer a better method of disseminating information to dealers were important, the fact that electronic publishing showed substantial cost savings when compared to the then current methods of disseminating information to dealerships meant that the business case was easy to justify.

When it came to deploying the extranet, the Head of IT decided to have a small team within the IT department which although driving and managing the technical infrastructure would only provide a limited amount of support to the other departments in Neotany who would use the extranet for disseminating information to dealers. He explained his reasoning for this as follows:

> we would encourage the different departments to do their own thing, which was whatever they wanted to disseminate it was entirely up to them, we would help them but we would expect the individual department to do the coding, generating the pages, putting in whatever structures they wanted, which we did deliberately so that it wasn't seen as IT attempting to control the information flow because we didn't want to, we never have done and we didn't see why if we did electronic publishing we ought to start doing that now.

Following a trial involving ten dealerships in the latter half of 1997, the Head of IT with backing from the IT Director decided to roll out an extranet across the entire dealership population, the newly upgraded DCS providing the necessary hardware infrastructure. With the necessary hardware already in place, the actual roll out process simply involved the installation of a web browser on each PC at the dealerships and the installation of a web server at Neotany HQ. The web browser that was installed was Microsoft Explorer, which was free to install and use.

Neotany actually own the terminals that the dealers use to access the extranet and the mainframe. The dealers pay rental of £180 per month on each PC plus they also pay for calls which they initiate to access the extranet. The leasing fee also covers all maintenance and installation of any updates or upgrades, and there is also a helpline that dealers can ring if they encounter any problems with the system. Dealers can stay permanently logged on to the extranet, but to save on phone bills the line is automatically disconnected when not in use.

With the deployment of the new DCS equipment, the actual hardware that the dealers needed to run the extranet was already there and they were already paying the leasing fees for this. Thus, as far as the dealerships were concerned, the deployment of the extranet simply entailed installing the browser, and hence they essentially got the extranet 'for free'. At Neotany head office, additional PCs were installed to act as servers for the extranet and a web browser was installed on all other PCs. The new DCS thus 'evolved' into the extranet.

Managers in Neotany were so pleased with the extranet that from the beginning of 1999 it was decided to use it for all communications with dealers. At the time of conducting the case study the extranet was used primarily as a flexible publishing tool. A wide variety of information was available including newsletters, service bulletins, technical data, price lists, support manuals and bromides for use in car advertising. The PCs in the dealerships still allowed access to the Neotany mainframe for the purposes of ordering vehicles, parts and accessories but it was planned to migrate this capability to an extranet application within a year or so.

7.3.1   Information flow – following the advent of the extranet

Figure 7.2 illustrates the main flows of information between the dealerships and Neotany following the advent of the extranet. An important change to be noted is that *all* information sent by Neotany to the dealerships goes via the extranet. Also, the extranet facilitates easy communications from the dealerships back to Neotany, either via extranet e-mail or via forms-based extranet pages.

As shown in Figure 7.2, information to be sent to the dealerships still originates in a number of departments in Neotany head office, but in contrast to the situation that was extant prior to the extranet, the DOMs now get access to information at the same time and in the same way as people in the dealerships. Previously, they were 'forewarned' of what information was about to be sent to the dealerships.

At the time of conducting the case study, the DOMs still exchanged dealership-specific sales and marketing information with the sales managers, and also passed on information concerning changes to the dealership operating principles. However, based on the growing relevance and importance of the extranet as the means of communications between Neotany and the dealerships, it is likely that before very long this information too will also go via the extranet. Indeed, even at the time of conducting the case study, there was no technical reason or impediment preventing the communication of such information via the extranet.

In terms of receiving information via the extranet from Neotany, providing there are no restrictions on access to or use of the extranet, every

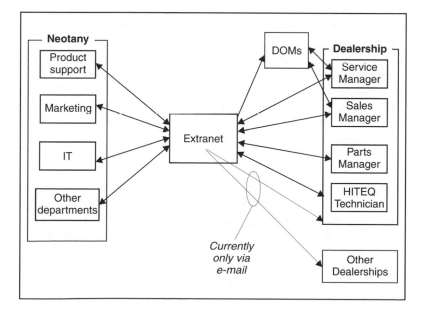

Figure 7.2 Illustration of main flows of information after the advent of the extranet.

member of staff in a dealership has equal and total access to all information published by Neotany on the extranet. This is in contrast to the situation prior to the extranet when, for example, the service manager played a pivotal role in deciding what information was passed onto the parts manager and the technicians.

Finally, it is also interesting to note that the e-mail application which runs over the extranet facilitates easy communications between dealerships. Prior to the extranet, the only way that dealers could communicate on a day-to-day basis was via the telephone.

7.3.2   What the dealer sees

A key issue relating to the development of the extranet was making it easy for people in the dealerships to use. Unlike the previous DCS access to the Neotany mainframe which was rather complicated, accessing information on the extranet is simply a matter of 'point and click'. The front screen of the extranet that the dealer sees is a graphical image depicting a dealer showroom showing the different areas that the dealer can use. So for example, if the dealer required information relating to the servicing and maintenance of vehicles he would simply click on the icon depicting the entrance door into the service department. For sales information he would click on the icon on the desk in the 'virtual showroom' and this would give access to this information.

It is interesting to note that following the decision to deploy an extranet, the initial reaction from people in the dealerships to the presentations of the extranet was a sense of foreboding. A PSA explained that in 1997 when the first presentation was made to HITEQs, a lot of the technicians seemed initially to fear having to use a PC. However, she added that once they had a chance to 'play with the extranet', they seemed to be very happy with the use of the technology.

7.3.3   Sources of material for the extranet

To begin with, the information that was initially published on the extranet came from simply taking existing paper information and digitising it. The material that is published on the extranet originates from a number of sources. Some of it is simply a case of passing on information from Neotany Europe or the factory in the United Kingdom. Some of the material such as the paint manual originates in the United States of America. However, some of the material comes from the experience of field engineers who record and pass on tips and techniques for fixing vehicles. Some of the key sources from different perspectives are outlined below.

Brand Management department

In terms of the material published by the Brand Management department, most of it relates to new car marketing rather than accessory marketing or used car marketing. A brand controller commented that the information sent out by his department is a mixture of information that originates in the European head office (relating to major changes to vehicle models and/or specifications) and information originating in his department in the United Kingdom (relating mainly to the specification of the vehicles that will be sold into the UK market).

Technical and service bulletins

The information that goes into the technical and service bulletins also originates from a number of sources, including Neotany HQ in Japan, Neotany Europe and Neotany UK. One of the problems that the PSAs encounter with compiling information for publication on the extranet is how best to deal with high resolution images. A PSA commented that they experience a lot of problems with scanned images because the type of images they have to scan, for example wiring diagrams, tend to be very complex. Complex diagrams need to be scanned with very high resolution, but the higher the resolution the longer it takes for the images to download when a dealer wishes to read the bulletin. These diagrams, and other images that the PSA needs to scan, actually come from Neotany Europe and they are sent to Neotany UK in hard copy format only. The PSA commented that although they have tried to get the images in electronic format this has not, as yet, been possible. The Head of IT added that Neotany as a European company is looking at publishing the technical bulletins from scratch and that this will render the activities associated with scanning images obsolete. He pointed out that although the information will come straight from Neotany Europe, either as html or Microsoft Word or PDF files, the people at Neotany UK will still have to modify the bulletins to reflect the local content for the UK market.

Following the introduction of the extranet, bulletins were published initially on the extranet in addition to being mailed in the usual way. However, after a period of three months during which bulletins were both published on the extranet and posted to dealerships as usual, it was decided by managers in Neotany that the bulletins would no longer be posted to dealers but would only be published on the extranet.

7.3.4 Examples of extranet applications

An example of an application facilitated by the extranet includes the ability to install software upgrades remotely rather than having to visit each dealer in turn and install upgrades on an individual basis. Also, using the extranet, Neotany's help desk can take remote control of a dealer's PC to diagnose and fix faults.

A second example of an extranet application concerns computer based training (CBT) for dealers. Previously, this used to go to a third party who sent floppy discs, with the questions on, to each dealership. The answers were saved back onto the floppy discs and then sent back to the outside company who processed them and sent the results back to the training department in Neotany. With the deployment of the extranet this process changed. The first stage now is to make the training material available on the extranet. When the trainee completes the assessment part on-line, the results get sent back automatically to the databases at Neotany HQ and the people in charge of training can access the results almost instantaneously and give immediate feedback.

At the time of conducting the case study, the engineers were also trialling some more advanced applications on the extranet. One example given was the use of a video link, over the extranet, to dealers. The idea being that rather than engineers having to physically travel to the dealers to resolve a problem on a vehicle, they will be able to investigate the problem remotely via a live video link over the extranet. However, the engineers acknowledged that it will take a year or so before that application could be rolled out to all dealerships.

7.4   Post-implementation outcomes

Following the implementation of the extranet and the changes that resulted in the flows of information, it is possible to identify a number of consequent benefits and downsides. The key ones are identified below.

7.4.1   Benefits

As mentioned in Section 7.2, the sending of information from Neotany to the dealerships was typically a three-stage process of faxing, posting, and telephoning. With the advent of the extranet this has been replaced by a two-stage process of publishing the information on the extranet and then e-mailing dealers to let them know that new information has been published. This also has an advantage in that it allows the product support personnel to point a technician towards the relevant information on the extranet, when he telephones the Product Support Department looking for assistance in fixing a problem on a vehicle. A field engineer commenting on what happens when a dealer rings to say he has got a problem with a vehicle that he cannot fix, added that:

> Before I go to a dealer I will actually check the extranet and usually this is how it should be done, we should always be the last thing to go out. But it does happen and I'll get this problem and I think we've issued a bulletin on this, and I'll ask the dealer 'why haven't you done this?' and he'll reply 'I haven't got the bulletin'. Well now I simply tell him 'yes you have it's on the extranet'.

The change in the way the pricing information is disseminated provides an illustrative example of the use of the extranet. Rather than printing and distributing hundreds of copies of the 40-page price list as before, using the extranet allows dealers to print off selected prices, for example, just the prices of a particular model which can then be handed to a prospective customer. The sole means of distributing the price list now is via the extranet and as the Head of IT commented:

> it means that when it gets to the other end the first thing they do is sit down and print it out, but that's okay because it cuts down our central costs significantly and it means they can print as many copies as they like.

At the time of conducting the case study, dealers still had to dial into the Neotany mainframe (using the same terminal with which they access the extranet) to place orders and check availability of vehicles. It is planned to move this facility to the extranet in the near future.

Thus, with the introduction of the extranet, Neotany can publish the information on the extranet and then e-mail dealers to let them know that the information is available. Also, by examining the extranet access logs, Neotany can tell which dealer has actually accessed the appropriate pages on the extranet.

Saving time

Additional benefits of distributing the information via the extranet is that the information gets to dealerships more quickly and having the information on-line can save users a lot of time in terms of being able to find information when required. This benefit was cited both by people in the dealerships as well as by Neotany field engineers. The speed of communication and the time saved in having the information on-line was also noted by a Neotany brand controller. Moreover, he added that the extranet allows him to distribute much more information than previously was possible when information was sent out in hard copy. Similarly, Neotany PSAs are also putting a lot more information on the extranet than was previously distributed to dealers on paper.

Advantages of having a standard platform

The benefit of having the extranet at the dealerships was cited by the Head of IT as being a great advantage to Neotany as it gives them a standard platform on which to develop further applications. The Head of IT commented that his department is now moving beyond simply publishing information and is actually deploying software applications that will run on the extranet. He gave the example of a finance company, recently launched by Neotany, for which the entire point of sale is an extranet application. He pointed out that this application in particular has shown that the IT department can move beyond just publishing information, which mostly was there already, albeit in a different format, to actually integrating this information with applications as well. He stressed that using the extranet as a platform for application deployment has allowed him to develop and use applications that would have not been possible without the extranet, or which could only have been done with a significantly greater expenditure.

The use of the extranet as a standard platform for applications also offers advantages in that it can provide a more 'user-friendly' interface to existing applications resident on the Neotany mainframe. As explained by the Head of IT, a lot of the Neotany core business systems are still mainframe based and there are still a lot of costs associated with mainframe development. However, he noted that with the extranet, information that originates on the mainframe can be presented in a more user-friendly fashion and incorporated into a web application.

Who benefits most?

One issue that is useful to address in this case study is the attribution of benefits to the dealerships and to Neotany. While dealers do acknowledge that the use of the extranet can save them time, their main role is to run a successful and profitable dealership and one of them commented that he does not believe that the use of the extranet actually contributes much to running the dealership. Indeed, the perception of the dealers interviewed was that the benefits of the system are loaded towards Neotany and that the use of the extranet has shifted costs from Neotany onto the dealerships. This is clearly the case when one considers that the use of the extranet for electronic publishing has allowed Neotany to cut significantly their costs but at the expense of the dealers who as one said 'print off no end of stuff now'.

The majority of the costs related to the printing of bulletins, price lists and other information from the system. Dealerships were also concerned about the call charges incurred when they were on-line downloading information from the extranet. A parts manager gave the following illustrative example:

> in the past Neotany would produce an accessory catalogue, they would have printed 27 pages, with glossy pictures, and post that out to every dealer. Now you've got to go onto the system, you've got to stay on-line, which is expensive, you have then got to print every page off on an expensive colour printer, and it takes time to download 27 glossy pages to the printer, and the cost of the ink alone on a colour printer to print 27 pages must be phenomenal. But you see it's not Neotany that's paying that. They've suddenly lost the cost of 300 copies of those 27 pages and they have just sent it out to the dealers. That's just saved them money. Now that isn't progress, that's called passing the buck.

There was clearly some confusion in the dealerships about what information they actually need to print off. For example, in the dealerships visited, technical and service bulletins were usually printed off and filed away in the relevant binders as was the case prior to the extranet. Yet when talking to people in Neotany, they pointed out that this was not really necessary and if a dealer can demonstrate that he uses the extranet sufficiently often so that he is always up to date with the bulletins being published on the extranet, then Neotany are quite happy for the dealer to use the extranet as the primary source of the bulletins and thus obviating the need to print out the bulletins. This has obviously not been made clear to people in the dealerships.

As a final comment on who benefits most from the extranet, it is worth pointing out that Neotany have invested around £2 million in the extranet but most of this will be recouped in leasing fees, and Neotany estimate cost savings of at least £250 000 a year.

7.4.2 Downsides

One of the negative issues arising from the deployment of the extranet was the concern that the dealers were not necessarily accessing and reading the information available on the extranet. A brand controller commented that when his department was sending out information in paper format, although there was no guarantee that the paper was actually read, at least the dealer was aware that information was arriving. With the extranet approach to publishing information, if the dealer is not actually making use of the extranet then not only is he not reading information but he is also unaware that new information has been published.

A PSA, however, was more concerned about the implications of dealers not accessing the system and potentially missing important bulletins. She explained that the worst thing that could happen if they published a technical bulletin and it is not seen by the appropriate people at the dealership, is that a car arrives at the dealership with the problem addressed in the bulletin and the technician is unable to fix it. When he then rings the help desk at Neotany for advice, he is told that he should have read the bulletin and is directed to the location of the bulletin on the extranet.

However, problems caused by dealers not being aware of information on the extranet could potentially be very serious. For example, should a bulletin be issued detailing a safety recall of vehicles, dealers who had not been using the extranet would be unaware of the recall and a lot of unsafe vehicles may remain on the road.

7.4.3   Aspects of extranet use and effects on people's roles

It is useful to examine how the different players in the case study actually make use of the extranet. To begin with, some of the people in Neotany who were previously compiling and preparing information for publication in bulletins were initially reluctant to publish information on the extranet. The extranet development manager explained that there were two main reasons for this. Firstly, they were unsure as to whether the people in the dealerships would actually read the information when it was on the extranet. Secondly, she commented that some people seemed to be 'a bit scared' of the technology because they believe that it is unlike anything that they have had to use before.

Product support administrators

The perspective of a PSA adds more detail. One PSA added that having to use the extranet has actually made her role more difficult. Using the extranet for publishing documents rather than publishing them the 'old way' on paper can mean it takes longer for them to actually produce a bulletin. The PSA explained that problems and delays arise because of the need to scan fairly complex figures, such as wiring diagrams, for inclusion in the bulletin. These diagrams need to be scanned with a high resolution so as to ensure that the details in the diagram can still be read when the figure is incorporated into a bulletin. However, the higher the resolution of the image, the longer it will take for the bulletin to be downloaded by a dealer, thereby increasing the dealer's on-line call charges and potentially causing disillusionment with the system because of an apparent slowness of response.

It is interesting to note that when the PSAs receive the bulletins on the extranet (just as the dealers do) they print them off and file them just in the same way they used to prior to the extranet. However, the reason for this is that they simply prefer to have the information on paper. One of the PSAs commented:

> isn't that awful? We're as bad as the dealers. It's ease of use. So we prefer to have a paper copy, it's easier for us to use. I mean really we should practice what we preach. We should get rid of them but everybody's much happier with a paper copy and I know that's not ideal but it's what happens.

She went on to note that when the information is on paper she personally believes it is easier to find specific items of information that one is searching for. However, she did comment that because the extranet is fairly new to her, she is experiencing a rather steep learning curve at the moment. She added that she felt sure that in a year or two her views of the system would be very different.

Despite the fact that the PSA felt that use of the extranet to distribute information was causing some initial difficulties, she did comment that it does actually make it easier and far quicker for her to give the dealers up-to-date information.

Brand controllers

Prior to the extranet, information from brand controllers and others in the brand management department, covering things such as a change in specification or a change in pricing, would have been sent out by letter to each dealer principal (DP) and sales manager and they would then communicate this within the dealership. With the advent of the extranet, there was a period where the information continued to go out on hard copy as well as appear on the extranet. Following a decision to stop this duplication and only publish the information electronically on the extranet, there was some concern that dealers were not actually reading the material, and it was felt that the brand management department needed to do more to encourage the dealers to use the system.

The approach taken to try and achieve this was to make the information on the extranet interactive and easy for the user to direct the flow of information rather than forcing the user to read the document on screen similar to the way he would have read the information on paper.

Prior to the extranet, dealers would often ring the Brand Management Department and ask for details of specifications, for example, saying that they never received the appropriate bulletin in the post and asking for a copy to be faxed to them. However, now when they call, the response is that they are instructed to go to the extranet to retrieve the information. The brand controller pointed out that there has not been much 'resistance' from the dealer network to using the extranet, but cautioned that this does not mean that the dealers are fully convinced of the benefits of the extranet and are fully using it.

He used the example of what are referred to as 'dealer bromides' to illustrate the type of response they have had from dealers. Bromides are images, typically background images, that dealers use for local advertising, for example, in local newspapers. Typically, the dealer would put together an advert based on his logo and address but using images supplied by Neotany of the various models.

Prior to the extranet, all the bromides were sent out on paper but now they are only available on the extranet. However, the brand controller commented that when the bromides were on paper, the dealers were saying:

> 'well this is silly because all printers nowadays use electronic media, so please can we have it on disc?' The funny thing is now we're all basically fully electronic, there's some dealers now ring up and say 'well, can we still not have it on paper?' So you can't win really.

However, he did add that there have been some problems with the images and with the electronic files containing the images. Just as the PSAs experience problems with scanning complex diagrams, the marketing people experience problems with scanning high quality images. There is a balance between getting images of high enough quality and the time it takes to download the file from the extranet. The higher the quality, the longer it takes to download the file. The brand controller expressed hope that this balance had now been achieved but acknowledged that without feedback from the dealers it was difficult to ascertain if this was actually the case.

However, in discussing this issue with a sales manager, it was apparent that the issue had not been resolved. The manager in question showed an example of a bromide that he recently retrieved from the extranet. The images showed three car models with some typed information alongside each one, but the images were slightly blurred and the text was scarcely legible. The sales manager compiled the advert and sent it off to the local newspaper. Someone from the newspaper subsequently rang and told him that the text was unusable and so the dealer had to type out the information and send it on. While acknowledging that images downloaded from the extranet should not have this problem, he did not feel it worthwhile feeding this back to Neotany. He added that while he could telephone someone at Neotany and get the hard copies of the images if need be, he preferred to download them from the extranet because it meant that he could get images more quickly and at very short notice.

Field engineers

Because a main part of the field engineer's role is to visit dealers to resolve various issues, they need to refer to manuals and technical bulletins before they travel to the dealer's premises and typically the engineers would travel directly from home rather than from Neotany head office. Prior to the extranet, field engineers would have maintained a small set of manuals at home. Sometimes they may have had to travel to Neotany HQ to retrieve information before visiting the dealer or more often they would have to phone Neotany HQ requesting that certain material be faxed to them. As the engineer would be attempting to find information to help him solve the problem, this would often entail multiple faxes and would be very time consuming both for the engineer and his colleague at head office who would be retrieving the information and faxing it to the engineer.

Following the deployment of the extranet, the engineers can now dial-in to the extranet, search for the appropriate information and either print it out at home or copy the information to their laptop which accompanies them when they visit the dealerships. The engineers interviewed reported that prior to visiting a dealership they now always check the extranet for relevant information. Indeed, prior to leaving to visit the dealership, the engineers actually ring the dealer to ensure that the dealer has used all the information he has available to attempt to solve the problem. One engineer commented:

> before I go I'll ring and ask 'have you checked a, b, c, d?' If they say 'well no I haven't got anything on it', I'll say 'well you have because I've got it here, it's on extranet'. And they'll say 'what does it say?'

And I won't tell them, but 'you go and find it, I'll wait on the phone'. And if it's the same then we're not going to go out. The dealer will then get a bollocking for that.

Views from the dealerships

The efforts put in by Neotany to make the extranet easy to use appear to have been successful. One dealer commented:

> it's easy to use, it just takes a bit of time to get used to it really, but it is easy enough to use ... We use it for a number of things, it's really good. It's a help towards the business really, if you know how to use it.

This dealer had been noted by Neotany as a dealer who uses the extranet a lot and it was clear he had a good understanding of the system and how to use it. He pointed out that the extranet is used every day, not just by him, but others in the dealership as well. When the system was introduced, his initial impression was 'oh no, what have they done here?' but he added that the only aspect that worries him is having people remember to go onto the system and retrieve the relevant information. He pointed out that there is a need to make time for using the extranet and that one needs to be disciplined to regularly access the system so as to ensure that new bulletins or other information are not being missed.

In terms of the type of information that his dealership retrieves from the extranet, he added:

> there is an awful lot on it ... you can go into 'Service Department' and get all the new service bulletins out of it, which you've got to because they're not coming through any other way. So you've got to use it for that. 'Parts', you get all the updates and parts prices. For sales, you get all the advertising bromides and then with all the updated information all the time, you can print it off. So you can get all the good stuff with that. And 'Marketing' again, it gives you Neotany's ideas of how they want to market it.

In contrast to the above dealer, the views from a dealership that did not use the extranet very much were rather different. The main issue in this dealership seemed to be the time taken to physically retrieve information from the extranet. As the parts manager explained:

> we have our tried and tested ways of doing things and we don't have time to sit and play around with space invaders I think is the best

way of describing it, the extranet is not the be all and end all that they are trying to make it out to be.

It is interesting to note that people in this dealership believed that they were still required to print off all bulletins and maintain the complete set in hard copy, as was the case prior to the extranet. This was not an uncommon situation. As mentioned earlier if a dealership is using the extranet to access all the bulletins then it is not necessary for them to actually print out the bulletins as well. Thus, not surprisingly, most of the comments from the above dealership related to how much time they have to spend printing the bulletins off and maintaining the paper-work. Yet at the same time they seemed to recognise the benefits of just accessing the information on-line when required. For example, the parts manager commented:

> bulletins, now then, there are all the various bulletins for different things. It is mandatory that all of these are all filed away in the various places, but they're there if you want them. What is the point in printing them all out? For example, here is a bulletin. It's all nice on there, and somebody spent a lot of time on it, and click here to view the attached documents. So that's it, that's your page. Fair enough, no problem. That's all the information I need, but it's there if I want it, why do I need to print it? It's all there.

Service managers

In some dealerships the ability of the HITEQ to access information on the extranet, and much more than he previously would have had access to, is a cause of concern with the service managers. A PSA pointed out that the HITEQs are bypassing the service managers in that they can now retrieve information themselves directly from the extranet rather than waiting on the service manager to go through his in-tray and decide whether he wanted to pass on to the technicians the information received in the post from Neotany.

She observed that some of the service managers are not too happy about this because:

> it sort of undermines their role. It takes away the importance of 'I'm in charge of the service department, I will decide what you see and what you don't see', but now the service manager doesn't really have that.

She added that having met some of the service managers and spoken to the HITEQs about what goes on in the dealerships, it was clear that the service managers do not like the fact that the technicians can bypass them and retrieve information directly from the extranet.

From a PSA's perspective, there is a concern that the HITEQ technicians are not reading the information, not because they do not want to but rather they are not being permitted to access the extranet at the dealership. Part of the reason for this stems from the lack of recognition of the HITEQ's role in the dealership. As one administrator explained:

> quite often I'll ring a dealer and I'll say to the receptionist can I speak to your HITEQ technician please? And they'll say 'pardon, what's a hi-tech technician, what's one of those?' Especially if you get through to sales, their view of the HITEQs is that they are the 'greasy little oiks the other side of the wall'.

However, with the advent of the extranet, the HITEQs now have the facility to go and get the bulletins and other information directly from the system as soon as it is published. Furthermore, she commented that this may be another reason why some of the HITEQs struggle with access to a screen because usually the PC in a dealership is in the service manager's office and 'he doesn't want some greasy oik in his overalls with his mucky fingerprints all over the keyboard'. The contrast of attitudes in dealerships relating to the HITEQ having access to the extranet is quite marked. In the words of a PSA:

> some dealers are absolutely terrific and allow HITEQs time to come in and print bulletins off, he's allowed access whenever he needs to and that's ideal. But then we hear some real horror stories. One dealer's HITEQ told us that they have surveillance cameras, in the showroom and the only terminals are in the showroom and he's not allowed to walk through the showroom in his overalls and even if there is nobody about and he does, he gets seen on camera and he gets told off and he can get a warning for going into the showroom in his overalls, even though he is going in to get the information that he needs in order to fix a customer's vehicle. I mean how can you work? So we've got like very, very different stories and we need to try and make everybody understand the importance of it, and get terminals in the workshop.

A field engineer commenting on this issue added that with some of the newer dealerships, which may have cost up to £2 million to build, they might only have two or three PCs that give access to the extranet, these typically being located in the offices or maybe in the showroom and the general rule being that the technicians cannot go into these areas to access the information but there will be someone who can retrieve the information and print it off.

If the HITEQs are not getting access to the extranet then they are not getting the information they need to actually perform their role of servicing and repairing vehicles. If the HITEQs are not getting access to the extranet to retrieve bulletins, then they have to contact Neotany head office to request the information. As noted by a PSA this wastes both the technician's time and the time of the product support personnel.

However, resolving the access problem for HITEQs is not easy. A field engineer added that if the product support people get a complaint from a HITEQ that he cannot get access, then a PSA will contact the DP. He added:

> it's a case of phoning the DP and saying well it's not yours, it's ours if you like, we own the system, you've got to let him in. The dealer can refuse because the dealer doesn't work for us at the end of the day, he works for his shareholders and whatever. So he can turn around and say no.

A PSA commented that service managers need to be made more aware of how important the system is and that if the HITEQ is not getting the information from the extranet, either directly or indirectly, then he cannot do his job properly. She stressed the need to get a terminal in the workshop, which would enable the technicians to get access, and suggested that one idea is for Neotany to pay for the workshop terminal initially and then introduce it as a part of the dealer operating standards.

A dealer's perspective

However, the perspective from a dealership gives a deeper understanding of the issue of allowing a technician access to the extranet. A parts manager at one of the dealerships commented that when the information was sent through on paper they knew that it needed to be filed away and the physical presence of the paper they received made them aware that new information was available. However, he pointed out that with the extranet there is so much information available that it would take someone a great deal of time to access the extranet and to retrieve the information.

When questioned if he thought that the retrieval of the bulletins from the extranet should actually be part of the HITEQ's job, he gave the following reply:

> no, the reason being that he's earning in the region of £30 an hour, and if he spent an hour a day, that's costing the dealership £30 a day, which is £150 a week, which is £600 a month, just to pull the bulletins out. Multiply that by 12 and it's £7200 per year, for him to spend one hour. It's a silly example but it's practical. So basically what will happen is, the cheapest most junior person available will be given the job to do it because you're not just talking about an hour, you're talking about hours, several hours.

In order to help people at the dealerships identify what has recently been added to the extranet there is a 'what's new' page on the extranet that contains a list of, and links to, information that has recently been added. This is sorted according to the date when it was added. Thus, a regular user can go onto the system, see what has been added and retrieve the information if required. However, confusion about how the system works can lead to misunderstandings of how to use even this relatively simple 'what's new' page. For example, a general manager commented that:

> okay so there's a listing of what's just been added, but how does it know you've actually pulled off what was new last time? They're only assuming that if they send it today, you'll get it tomorrow. And what comes out the next day is new. How do they know that you've got them, they don't.

The DOMs

As noted earlier, the role of the dealer operations managers (DOMs) is to be the dealerships' main point of contact with Neotany and all information from Neotany to the dealerships are supposed to go via the DOMs, or the DOM is supposed to get a copy of the information before the dealerships. With the advent of the extranet, where dealers can retrieve information directly from Neotany, it is plausible to assume that the DOMs may feel that their role is under threat. A brand controller commented that when they put information on the extranet they send an e-mail to DOMs and other internal staff who need to know ahead of the dealers. However, he pointed out that with the extranet, when information is published then it is accessible immediately to all users.

Thus the DOM gets such information, not before the dealers as was previously the case, but at the same time. Also, all DOMs now have a laptop PC and they can dial into the extranet and retrieve bulletins remotely as well as their reports on sales figures and sales targets.

It is feasible to assume that as more information continues to go to dealers via the extranet, the role of the DOM may be undermined and a reduction in the number of DOMs should be possible. A general manager at one of the dealerships commented that since the extranet became the main route by which he receives information, he hardly ever sees his DOM.

However, as noted by the Head of IT at Neotany:

> there was some initial, very deep initial reluctance from the DOMs because there they are saying 'we've been set up as the single point of contact between Neotany and the dealer and now you're publishing all this information electronically over which we don't have any control'. And there was some big fears expressed very early on. It's no longer an issue. They've seen how it works, they are happy with it. We're publishing, as well as the reports, there's also a dealer management plan application which they use to organize their lives with dealers, which pulls in information on what the dealers are up to, what his sales are like, and again that's entirely web based. So, I think the DOMs have come round to it, it was certainly seen as a threat initially.

Despite repeated requests, it was not possible to actually arrange an interview with a DOM in order to ascertain their perspective on this issue. The reason given was that the DOMs were 'far too busy'.

7.5   Other issues arising

7.5.1   Information overload

In terms of the volume of information on the extranet, the dominant view from the dealerships is different to that from the Neotany HQ. For example, the above dealer assumes that everything that appears on the extranet needs to be printed off and filed away as before and thus he feels overwhelmed with a deluge of information. A parts manager commented that there is just too much information on the extranet and that because of lack of time or personnel to regularly check for new information, should a particularly important piece be published then he is likely to miss it.

The view of the field engineers and the Head of IT was there is a lot more information being made available to dealerships via the extranet than previously was the case, but that it is not expected that anyone would actually read all the information. There is bound to be information on the extranet that no one in the dealerships will ever read but a field engineer pointed out that if someone is likely to access a piece of information just once, then that is sufficient justification for having the information on the extranet.

Overloaded with e-mail

The need to set aside some time to regularly check the extranet also applies to the e-mail application that is part of the extranet. As noted above when a bulletin has been added to the extranet an e-mail is sent to remind dealers that the information is there. However, also as mentioned earlier, the extranet system now actually permits dealers to contact each other and many dealers have been taking advantage of this opportunity to sell or exchange spare parts and accessories among themselves. Dealers recognise that this can have certain advantages. However, he added that some dealers use the system to advertise large lists of spare parts and that these e-mails clog up and slow down the system and waste everybody's time. The presence of such 'trivial' messages can mean that a dealer may become disillusioned with the e-mail application and actually miss important messages that he should be reading. For example, prior to the extranet, dealers used to have a fax from TNT couriers who would advise the dealer when they would be collecting parts for return to the Neotany parts warehouse, whereas nowadays rather than fax, an e-mail is sent to the dealership, but unless the e-mail is checked regularly these messages may be missed.

7.5.2   Ownership of information – losing the personal touch

One dealer commented that one of the downsides of the system is that when information appears on the extranet and he has a query he often does not know who to contact. When the information used to come in on paper it was always accompanied by a letter which was signed by the person responsible for publishing the bulletin. However, this practice has not been carried through to the on-line bulletins which just 'appear' on the system. A general manager pointed out that if it is a technical bulletin then they can ring the product support people and be reasonably confident that the query on the bulletin could be resolved. However, with other types of information, for example, promotion material, it is not so easy to find out who to contact. The general manager added that he can get the name of the correct person eventually but that it can take a lot of time to do so. He felt that this lack of ownership of information on the extranet is leading to a decay in the 'personal touch' between the information providers and the information users.

7.5.3 Relationships

One issue that arose during the case study was how the relationships between Neotany and the dealerships were being affected by the use of the extranet. This was a point that was mentioned by the majority of people interviewed, but the views of how relationships were being affected differed. Perspectives on this are presented below. Also presented is a perspective on how dealer–dealer relationships are being affected.

Neotany–dealer relationships – perspectives from Neotany

People interviewed at Neotany commented that they believe the extranet allows them to forge a closer relationship with dealers. For example, a PSA pointed out that:

> I've got to know the dealers an awful lot better since we've been doing this because I now go out to dealers and I actually see what goes on in a dealer so I'm now probably more sympathetic to their problems and to the way they work now than I was a year ago. So I think it has actually brought us closer together.

Similarly a field engineer added that even though the overall impact of the extranet may be that the Neotany product support people get fewer phone calls (as dealerships can access information on-line), he felt that the easier flow of information facilitated by the extranet was having a positive effect on communications between dealerships and Neotany and thus was helping to forge closer relationships.

A second field engineer commented that the use of the extranet is definitely bringing the dealerships and Neotany together, in particular as it instils a lot more confidence in the HITEQ technician. He added:

> In the past the HITEQ would have phoned us up and you could hear the trepidation in his voice, 'I've got this problem' and we know he's lost his index and he's lost everything else, and I say 'yeah it's on the bulletin board', and they're really embarrassed. So the next time he'll think 'I'm not going to phone'. Now there might be something that we don't know about so it stops him phoning the next time and he

gets worried and he thinks he's going to get it wrong. But now he looks at the extranet and if it's not there he's then got the confidence to phone up and say 'I've looked at extranet and there's nothing been issued with this so I'm not wrong, so now can you help me?' And we say 'yes, we can help you now', as long as he's done everything else. As long as he's looked at it, he will then phone us up. So the relationship then becomes a lot closer because it's not stand-offish. Where previously he would have thought I'm going to get this wrong if this is issued information and I haven't read it, 'cause you can hear them on the phone going 'Oh God I should have read this'. There's no excuse for it now.

It is interesting to note that although people from the various departments in Neotany have commented that the use of the extranet is forging a closer relationship between their individual departments and the dealerships, they did not feel that it was facilitating a closer relationship between the individual departments themselves. The one exception was with the IT department with whom people felt they had actually got closer due to the need to learn more about how to use the extranet and how to publish information on the system.

Neotany–dealer relationships – perspectives from the dealerships

The dealerships' views of how relationships may be affected by the use of the extranet are rather different to those of the people at Neotany. One dealer commented that he felt it was actually making him more distant from Neotany. He acknowledged that even though people from the Product Support Department in Neotany had come and helped to set up the extranet at the dealership, he had not seen them since.

The fact that so much information is available on the extranet also has the effect that it reduces significantly the number of occasions on which someone in the dealerships may need to telephone someone at Neotany. A general manager commented that:

> the personal touch is disappearing really, instead of picking up the phone and saying 'Jack I need to do this, this, and this'. It's all becoming a bit impersonal. I don't see how they can say they're getting closer to the dealers.

A parts manager in another dealership voiced rather stronger opinions. He commented that:

Neotany head office, they're not in the real world down there. The people up there think they know what's happening but they've probably never left their office in the last three years, and somebody who's on 30 grand a year comes up with some silly idea that everybody thinks is brilliant and every dealer in the country laughs at it, and just gets on with the job that everybody gets paid to do.

Dealer–dealer relationships

One of the things that extranet technology facilitates is the use of newsgroups or discussion groups which are only accessible by users connected to the extranet. It was interesting to note that this facility is not actually supported on the extranet in this case study. When asked about this the Head of IT commented that discussion groups was a facility that he had demonstrated early on in the development of the extranet but that the groups were never deployed. He explained the reason for this as follows:

> there is a feeling in the business that they'd rather dealers didn't talk to each other, which does make it tricky if we ease that communication, because in the past all you've ever had is complaints. There are regular seminars and forums where dealers do get together and yes it's always bad news, it's never good news. So we've demonstrated it very easily that we could host newsgroups, but no one has yet come up with a non controversial use of one.

He added that the reason for not wanting dealers to talk to each other is because there is a perception in Neotany that the dealers would 'gang up together' against Neotany. However, he did acknowledge that dealers can now e-mail each other quite easily and they do. He added that because all e-mail traffic on the systems goes via a central e-mail server based at Neotany HQ he can monitor the amount of dealer-to-dealer e-mail. He commented that the amount of dealer-to-dealer e-mail traffic is growing significantly.

7.5.4 Looking to the future

Having presented various perspectives on the current use of the extranet it is also useful to examine the perspectives of the different players in terms of how they see the extranet and its use in developing.

Field engineers' reports

As discussed earlier a key part of the role of field engineers is to resolve issues and fix problems when all other avenues, such as the technical bulletins and service manuals, have been exhausted. In order to do this they rely heavily on their experience and knowledge. Also as the solutions to these problems tend to be undocumented it is important that the engineer completes a report explaining how the problem was resolved. An engineer explained that when such a job is cleared they will write an engineer's report, identifying the problem and the solution or outcome, and then file the report in a special set of binders at Neotany HQ in London. He added that these reports are currently being entered onto a database accessible via the extranet. Previously, if an engineer needed to consult one of these reports he would have to phone a colleague in the Product Support Department and ask him/her to go through the reports and then fax him the appropriate one. With the reports going on-line the engineer added:

> we can go into the extranet and then pull out that particular report and read it, from anywhere. That was totally impossible before the extranet. The real difference now is that it's going to be shared, everyone else has also got access to the 800 reports.

However, he later explained that 'everyone' in this sense refers only to people in the Product Support Department and maybe a few people in the Customer Relations Department. He pointed out that the reason for this is that some of the information in the engineer's report may be very sensitive and it may 'condemn' a dealer or a customer. He gave the following example:

> we might actually write in there something like 'this dealer is a prat', we've actually done that. You know, he's a prat and he shouldn't have done this and he was to blame, and we write it because that's what the problem was. If we need to give a customer a copy what we do is we take out the relevant information, put it in a letter format. If the customer says well I want a report to back it up, well you can't get this report because it might say the customer is a complete tosser, he wants his money back because he bought the car and now he can't afford it, so he needs to get out of it, so he needs to find a technical reason to give back the car. So we'll actually say this in the report, so we've got to be really careful.

Service manuals on CDROM – HITEQs need access

One development that will have a major impact is the decision by managers in Neotany to have the service manuals for all vehicles in electronic format and these will be distributed initially on CDROM. The reason they will be initially distributed on CDROM rather than on the extranet is because currently dealerships have to actually pay for the service manuals and the extranet in use has no mechanism for charging users to access specific types or categories of information. Also, introducing charges to access specific categories of information on the extranet is likely to discourage people in the dealerships from using the extranet.

A PSA expressed concern about the migration of service manuals onto CDROM. She pointed out that one of the biggest problems the Product Support Department is experiencing is that HITEQs generally do not have an easy access to the extranet. There is a struggle to make dealers understand the need for and benefits of a terminal in the service department. She added that although she is happy with the theory of service manuals on CDROM, the practice of it is that Neotany have got to ensure that every service department has their own dedicated extranet terminal, otherwise the HITEQ simply will not be able to fix the vehicles.

So in a sense putting the service manuals into CDROM will force the dealers to give access to the HITEQs and while people in the Product Support Department see this as a very positive move, it does create a problem in that the Head of IT did not seem very happy about having to purchase an extra 300 terminals. However, as noted earlier, the capital cost of these machines will be offset to a certain extent by the leasing fees that the dealerships will have to pay.

Extranet as a customer-facing tool – the end of showrooms?

A brand controller commented that he sees the role of the extranet evolving so that it becomes a customer-facing tool, where customers visiting the dealership can look interactively at the various options they can select when choosing to buy a new car. However, the dealers' perspective was rather more ominous. One dealer gave the following perspective:

> the only bit that does worry me slightly is that in the years to come there is no need for us, somebody, a customer can come in on the system and put his bits and pieces on the machine and he'll be able to buy a car. Click a button and it will be delivered to him tomorrow. That does worry me a bit. It's changing the whole concept of dealerships. It will come. Gone are the days of having showrooms, there'll just be service centres.

He commented that he sees technology developing to allow people to order directly from Neotany and thus push dealerships out of the loop. He added that the extranet could well be the first step towards this.

7.5.5   Perspectives on the role of the extranet

Despite the divergence of perspectives on the use of the extranet as noted above, there was an apparent convergence of views on the role of the extranet. For example, a PSA commented that she believes that it is a very good system but that she needs to sit down and try to fully understand how to exploit it properly. She added:

> I think it's made quite an impact. I think it's good. Although we have got a few teething problems, I think long term it's the way we should be moving. It's having a big impact in the dealers and it's going to have an even bigger one whether they like it or not. So I'm all for it. We've got to make much more of an effort to make it work but it's good.

The dealerships' perspective was very similar and one commented that:

> I think it's becoming more and more of an important role to the dealership, for information. It's going to become very important.

However, he added that although the extranet is important it has not yet reached the critical stage where the dealership could not cope without it. However, he did acknowledge that it's only a matter of time before this stage is reached and when the extranet will become a core part of how he runs his business.

However, the view from a field engineer adds a noteworthy perspective on the role of the extranet. He adds that:

> I'm not really worried by the fact that nobody says anything negative about the system, not really. I do expect a bit more feedback because I know for a fact that it can't be that good, it can't be that good. Whether they just don't want to say things in case they are wrong, but let's be perfectly honest, nothing's that good.

7.6   Summary

This case study investigated the issues that arose when the initial motivation for the extranet was to improve the efficiency of existing links between organisations. Having presented the context in which the extranet was implemented, some examples of how its use has affected the flow of information was presented. Of particular interest was the effect on people's roles of the use of the extranet as the primary means of communicating information. For some people such as product support administrators and brand controllers, the effect was arguably minimal in that they used the extranet to send similar types of information (albeit a lot more), as was the case when information was sent on paper. For others, in particular the service managers and the DOMs, the effect is more significant in that where previously they had some degree of control and influence over information flows, the use of the extranet effectively removes this control and influence. While it is clear that service managers do not like the fact that they are being bypassed it was not possible to determine exactly how the DOMs felt about this. However, based on the data presented, it is fair to say that the DOM's role is most under threat.

Using the extranet as the sole means of communicating information to dealerships and taking advantage of the capability to publish more information than was previously the case led to problems of information overload from the perspective of people in the dealerships. Perhaps this view may change over time once dealers realise that providing they can demonstrate they use the extranet sufficiently so as to be aware of what new information is published, then they will not be required to print off copies of all such information.

The problem of information overload was also noted in terms of how dealerships are making use of the e-mail application, where perhaps the novelty of being able to easily contact other dealers has yet to fade, and the dealer-to-dealer communications are yet to move beyond what was referred to as the level of 'trivia'.

Extranet use and the easier flow of information that it facilitates also has an effect on relationships. However, from the Neotany point of view the effect is positive in that it is viewed as enabling a closer relationship with the people in the dealerships, whereas from the dealership perspective the effect is negative in that they see their relationship becoming more remote. The issue of ownership of information and who to contact in the event of a query with an 'unsigned' on-line bulletin was used to illustrate this.

Of interest also is the fact that managers in Neotany have deliberately not implemented the newsgroups facility offered by extranet technology. This was in an attempt to prevent dealers from 'ganging-up' on Neotany, although people in the Product Support Department failed to see this as an issue and actually saw benefits in permitting this type of dealer-to-dealer discussion.

Finally, it is clear from the data that the role and importance of the extranet is set to grow. As more applications are developed for the extranet and as more information such as engineers' reports on problem solving and on-line service manuals are made available, it is likely that its use will become indispensable. Indeed for people such as the HITEQs, lack of access to the extranet will mean that they will be unable to perform their role. Some changes will be necessary in order to ensure that HITEQs actually have access and it was suggested that the most likely change would be for Neotany to supply terminals for use in the service workshop and then to amend the dealerships' principles of operation so that such terminals became compulsory. While this may prevent the service managers or others in the dealership from removing or preventing the installation of these terminals, it will not overcome the problem of service managers being 'upset' about the fact that they can no longer control what information the HITEQs or parts managers can access. But then again, given the potential of the extranet to become a customer-facing tool and to perhaps contribute to the demise of showrooms, perhaps that is a relatively minor issue to be overcome.

Having presented the data from the three case studies, Chapter 8 presents the analysis and discussion of the data from the three cases.

8
Analysis and Discussion

This section discusses findings from the three case studies and situates the findings in the literature. In the first section the discussion focuses on issues relating to the use of IT as reviewed in Chapter 2. In the second section the discussion focuses on issues relating to the knowledge management literature as reviewed in Chapter 3. Finally, a summary of the key points of this chapter is presented.

8.1 Evaluating the findings in the context of the IT literature

Having made use of the literature to guide the research (see Table 4.2) it is now useful to return and discuss the findings in the context of the IT literature. The main themes from the literature review in Chapter 2 which were used to help guide the data collection are now used to structure this discussion. Thus, issues such as integration into corporate strategy, planning and implementation, evaluation, Groupware related issues, and the role and effect of intranets/extranets are discussed below.

8.1.1 Integration into corporate strategy

Integration into corporate strategy covers two key issues; the motives for deploying the IT system and the degree of linkage between business objectives and the objectives of the IT system (Reich and Benbasat 1996). These issues are discussed below.

It is evident from the case study that for CoreTech, its intranet performs a major role in the way information flows within the organisation. The use of an intranet has not only helped to improve the efficiency of current processes but is facilitating new processes that previously were either prohibitively expensive or were just not possible. An example of this is the use of an intranet to support the development of a company-wide knowledge management system. Yet, less than three years ago the intranet was perceived as little more than an office automation tool that would allow easy access to information. Indeed the implementation of the intranet was actually done as an add-on to the more strategic document-management system. The intranet was not viewed as a strategic IT system and therefore a lot of the formal top-down planning procedures such as detailed implementation plans, formal change programmes and fully specified cost/benefit analysis, normally associated with planning and implementing a strategic IT/IS system simply did not apply.

With respect to ATI, the RTOnet system was viewed as being of strategic importance right from the beginning. There are two key indications of this. Firstly, there was the recognition that the existing ways of disseminating knowledge and information were not compatible with the desire to increase the level of business activity without a dramatic increase in staff numbers. Secondly, the recognition of the growing interest in the use of Internet technologies presented to ATI both a good opportunity and a potential major threat to their business. Although the opportunities offered by using RTOnet as the key mechanism for knowledge transfer are recognised, the 'newness' of the use of Internet technologies together with the continued rapid evolution has meant that the strategy was very much an emergent approach. It is interesting to note that the key proponent for change (the RTOnet Product Manager) and the key proponent for maintaining the *status quo* (the head of Membership Services) both report directly to the Business Development Director. He thus has the task of ensuring that the speed with which ATI moves forward is tempered with the need to maintain the existing income and relationships with members. Also, the uncertainty regarding the take-up of knowledge trading among member companies, and the reliance, currently, on external sources of funding for RTOnet, mean that an emergent approach is actually very appropriate.

In the Neotany case, there is very little evidence to suggest that the extranet is important strategically. The original vision associated with the extranet was that it would facilitate more efficient ways of sharing information with the dealerships, and from the perspective of managers in Neotany this has indeed been the case. The use of the extranet was confined to a specific purpose and while it apparently achieved its aim, at least from a Neotany perspective, of making the process of information and knowledge transfer more efficient, its use has not expanded beyond that intended originally.

Thus, of the three cases, only the RTOnet system was viewed initially as being important strategically and indeed may be viewed as an example of what King (1996), when discussing the strategic issues in Groupware, refers to as 'an enterprise-redefining application'. In comparison, whereas the CoreTech intranet became significant strategically, the Neotany extranet remained very much a 'stand-alone' application. Perhaps this is due to the fact that the Neotany extranet was a very focused application whereas the CoreTech intranet was enterprise-wide. Also of significance is the fact that in the CoreTech case, there were, at least initially, few if any restrictions on how users could share information whereas in the Neotany case, facilities for sharing information openly, were denied to users. These issues are discussed later. The Neotany case provides an example of a relatively simple use of an IOS (interorganisational information system) similar to those defined by Bakos (1991b) and Konsynski and McFarlan (1990). It also supports the findings reported by Johnston and Vitale (1988), Bakos (1991a) and Clemons and Row (1992) who explore the use of IT to reduce transaction and coordination costs between firms.

Integration with existing systems

The degree to which new IT systems are integrated into existing IT systems is noted by Benjamin and Scott-Morton (1988) as providing the basis for deriving strategic advantage. With respect to the CoreTech case, the intranet actually provided a platform which facilitated easy access to information stored on existing systems and thus in a sense provided users with a window into existing systems. This capability was perhaps the main factor for the rise in prominence and importance of the intranet in CoreTech.

However, in the case of the Neotany system, there was no integration of the extranet into the existing systems. For example, at the time of the data collection the PC that facilitated access to the extranet was also used by dealers to access the Neotany mainframe to order cars and spare parts. Access to the mainframe was a non-extranet application and while it would have been relatively easy to add a web-front-end so as to allow dealers to access the mainframe from the extranet, this was not implemented. Perhaps if this simple integration had been performed it would have speeded up the acceptance within dealerships of the utility and benefits of the extranet, as it would have increased significantly their use and familiarity with the extranet.

There is no evidence to suggest that in the ATI case any integration with existing IT systems took place either in ATI itself or indeed in the member companies. Furthermore, in terms of transferring knowledge to members prior to RTOnet, this simply did not involve the use of IT systems. Indeed, the use of RTOnet to replace existing methods of transferring knowledge to members is a key source of the internal tensions being experienced in ATI.

8.1.2   Planning and implementation

As noted by Galliers (1994) and Lederer and Salmela (1996) amongst others, planning and implementing IT/IS remains to be one of the key IS management issues. Table 8.1 below indicates the related issues that are discussed below in the context of the three case studies.

As mentioned in Chapter 5, the CoreTech intranet was implemented as part of the CoaT office automation programme, which had already gone through all the various formal planning stages in CoreTech required for such a company-wide programme. The actual implementation of the intranet, at least in the early stages was a relatively straightforward process of installing a web browser on the PCs or workstations of those who were to be given intranet access and the installation of web server software as appropriate. The early implementation of the intranet thus neatly bypassed the normal formal planning processes. Furthermore, although formal planning processes can have benefits in that they are thorough and systematic, these benefits are at the expense of considerable time (Gogan and Cash 1992). It is likely that had such processes been applied to the intranet then the first issue of the 'Plans and Implementation Processes for intranet' would still be in the drafting stage! It is interesting that benefits had already been realised in the time it would normally have taken to conduct a formal strategic plan for such a system. In the latter stages, as the importance of the role of the intranet began to be recognised, senior managers began the formal planning process of how best to manage the information content of the intranet. It is interesting to note that the reaction of certain users (cf. the Campaign for Intranet Freedom) was that such formal planning

Table 8.1   Issues related to IT/IS planning and implementation

Theme	Issues
Planning and Implementation	Amount of time spent in the formal planning process
	Time lag between planning and implementation
	Facilitators and inhibitors to implementation
	The involvement of external expertise in planning
	The involvement of external expertise in implementation

and control of the content of the intranet would stifle its further development. Given that the CoreTech intranet essentially grew from the bottom-up, and a key element of this was that in the early stages users had the freedom to essentially publish whatever information they chose to publish, the fact that formal planning processes were absent in the early stages was thus a key facilitator in its development.

With respect to the Neotany extranet, the planning and implementation process followed a similar path to that of the intranet in CoreTech. The decision to upgrade the existing hardware to support the dealer communication system had already been made when it was decided to introduce the extranet's capabilities as part of the process. Again, the implementation process was fairly straightforward and involved the installation of a web browser on PCs at the dealerships and the installation of a web server at Neotany HQ. A key difference between the Neotany extranet and the CoreTech intranet was that in the content development phase of the implementation the material to be published on the CoreTech intranet was essentially 'free-form' as noted above, whereas in the Neotany case the material needed to fit within an existing structure of bulletins and brochures. The result of this was that the process of sending information to dealerships was simply automated. There was little, if any, scope for innovation in terms of the types of information or the way it was structured before being distributed. This is discussed below.

Whereas the CoreTech and Neotany systems were developed and implemented 'in-house', the situation with ATI and the RTOnet system was rather different. As mentioned in the case, the initial prototype of RTOnet was developed in conjunction with BT. In addition, while RTOnet relies on customers using the Internet to access the system, the actual application itself is very much proprietary. This is in contrast to the CoreTech and Neotany systems which, at least until the latter stages, were implemented using open standard Internet applications. The net effect of this was that ATI faced inhibitors in the planning and implementation processes that the other two companies did not. For example, the lack of dedicated resources up-front to develop the system was perhaps the key factor which impeded progress. ATI's unique financial structure in terms of being owned by its members was a major contributor to this. In both the CoreTech and Neotany systems a key enabler was the fact that the systems were relatively inexpensive to develop, being based on open standards technology.

In addition, the internal 'resistance' in ATI to the changes resulting from the use of RTOnet as a key mechanism for transferring knowledge to members could be seen as an inhibitor in that it has slowed down the rate at which changes in ATI's organisational structure and business operations would otherwise have been made. However, this may actually have benefits in that it gave more time for the members to ramp up their Internet capability, both technically and organisationally in terms of recognising on-line systems as a legitimate source of information for their engineers.

Thus, overall, both the CoreTech and Neotany systems 'escaped' the full formal planning processes and the approach to implementation was relatively informal, at least in the early stages. This was a key enabler in terms of the speed of development, as was the fact that both systems were based on open standards technology. In contrast, the ATI system was more traditional in the sense that RTOnet progressed through formal planning stages, gaining approval from senior managers (a 'generic' facilitator as noted by Ginzberg (1981) and Ives and Olson (1984)), but not the necessary internal funding (a typical inhibitor as noted by King and Grover (1991)). To its credit the fact that ATI has been able to secure external funding has meant that this has not turned out to be the ultimate inhibitor.

8.1.3   Evaluation

As discussed by Wen *et al.* (1998), a typical problem that occurs when evaluating IT systems is that most benefits tend to be qualitative, indirect, and diffuse. Also, as noted by Jurison (1996) and Brynjolfsson (1993) there tends to be a time lag between the implementation of the system and the appearance of benefits. The literature review presented in Chapter 2 identified 'benefits', 'downsides' and 'time before benefits accrue' as categories of measures that can be used in the evaluation of IT systems. These are discussed below.

Benefits and the time to accrue

In the three case studies presented there were elements of the benefits which were qualitative, indirect and diffuse. However, there were also elements of the benefits which were very much quantitative and direct.

With respect to the CoreTech intranet, the fact that the company realised benefits from using an intranet in a remarkably short period of time means that assessing when the benefits accrue is an easier task than is normally the case with IT systems. A 'traditional' problem in researching the organisational role and effect of IT systems is that typically it can take a number of years before their impact is felt at the organisational level and thus longitudinal studies are rare as noted by Jurison (1996). Also as pointed out by Brynjolfsson (1993), time lags between the implementation of IT and the delivery of benefits also make it very difficult to assess the success or effectiveness of IT implementation and use. However, this is not the case with the CoreTech intranet, where tangible benefits such as cost savings were realised within weeks and intangible benefits such as improved flows of information, leading to a more open working environment were in evidence within months rather than years. Intangible benefits were derived from increased efficiencies in processes that previously were paper-based or reliant on people to supply information directly and which are now intranet-based. Examples include the distribution of company briefings, general news and information on the company and its activities, remote distribution of software, and the use of the Desktop Directory to find contact details and other information on colleagues and their work activities.

Similarly with the Neotany extranet, once the initial overlap period had ceased where information was distributed both on paper and electronically on the extranet, then direct cost savings began to accrue to Neotany. Unfortunately, from the perspective of the dealerships this meant that their direct costs began to rise as they were required, at least initially, to print bulletins and other information and process the paper as was the case prior to the extranet. These direct costs can be avoided though if a dealership can demonstrate to Neotany that they are making effective use of the extranet and that bulletins and other information are being accessed as necessary, as there would no longer be a requirement to print the information. Until the issue is resolved of HITEQs and other technicians being allowed easy access to the extranet, these direct costs will still be incurred. When consideration is taken into account of the time and costs involved of printing bulletins and other information at approximately 300 dealerships, then it is fair to say that the overall cost savings that Neotany have obtained are over-shadowed by the increase in costs incurred by the dealerships. Perhaps as time progresses and the people in the dealerships become accustomed to using the extranet, these increased costs will start to reduce and eventually disappear.

In the case of RTOnet, it is clear that it is rather early to evaluate the tangible benefits of the system. However, the likely benefits of the use of the system are potentially large. Firstly, it is expected to provide ATI with a substantial new revenue stream from companies which previously would not have been aware of ATI's expertise or which would not have been capable or willing to pay the necessary membership fees. Secondly, it will increase ATI's penetration amongst the member companies and thus help to preserve the existing revenue stream from membership fees. In terms of intangible benefits the increased penetration amongst member companies will also serve to strengthen ATI's relationship with its members and thus will increase the barriers to the entry of potential competitors to ATI.

Downsides

It is also informative to examine the downsides or disadvantages of the respective systems. With respect to the CoreTech intranet the downsides identified were more related to general issues of change management rather than intranet-specific issues. For example, the use of the intranet is leading to job changes, where roles which previously revolved around processing paper or transferring information from paper to an IT system are disappearing. Perhaps the only intranet-specific downside to the use of the intranet in CoreTech is the fear among senior managers that the use of the intranet will lead to the information exchanges that underpin relationships in the company and with customers becoming less face-to-face and more 'electronic'. However, if by virtue of such relationships becoming 'electronic' leads to an improved relationship then this should actually be viewed as being an additional benefit rather than as a downside.

The nature of the downsides with respect to the Neotany extranet is rather different. Perhaps the most important issue is the concern that information being published on the extranet is not actually being accessed in the dealerships. This downside is of sufficient importance as to outweigh any cost savings or benefits accrued by Neotany. If important information is published electronically on the extranet but is not actually being used or even being accessed in the dealerships then the use of an extranet has achieved little in real terms. Perhaps this will change with time as the use of the extranet within the dealerships increases.

Similarly in the case of RTOnet, if member companies are not willing or even capable of accessing RTOnet via the Internet, then the value of the overall system must be questioned. However, it could be argued that the deployment of RTOnet is actually pump-priming the membership into a position where they can enjoy the benefits of accessing and retrieving information on-line via the Internet, not only from RTOnet but also from the other information providers. A similar argument could be applied to the Neotany extranet.

There are also intangible downsides that have occurred in each of the three cases. For example, in ATI the implementation of RTOnet has led to tensions in the organisation between the 'pro-RTOnet' camp and the 'traditionalists'. In the CoreTech case, similar tensions arose as evidenced

Table 8.2   Benefits and downsides of the respective systems

Measures	CoreTech	ATI	Neotany
Main benefits	Cost savings, easier and more open access to information	Potential cost savings, additional revenue	Little overall benefit, but potentially easier access to information
Main downside	Less 'face-to-face' interactions	Members may not have capability to access the system	Not being used sufficiently

by the 'Campaign for Intranet Freedom'. Finally, in the Neotany case, tensions have arisen concerning the 'attribution' of savings/costs. These issues are concerned with the political aspects of the implementation and use of each respective system and are discussed later.

Overall in terms of evaluating the three systems it is clear that there are many benefits possible but there are also downsides which may outweigh the benefits, especially in the Neotany case. However, it is also prudent to point out that the evaluation of the systems in question took place relatively soon after the implementation and the fact that any tangible benefits were visible after such a short period of time is noteworthy and serves to highlight a characteristic of intranet/extranet and the time before benefits accrue.

Table 8.2 summarises the above discussion of the benefits and downsides. Having discussed the 'traditional' IT issues of integration into corporate strategy, planning and implementation, and overall evaluation, the following section discusses the findings from the case studies in the context of the key themes relating to Groupware.

8.1.4   Intranets/extranets and Groupware

It is interesting to compare the findings from the cases with what has been reported in the literature about Groupware. As noted in Chapter 2 there are similarities between Groupware and intranets, with intranets often viewed as being a 'flavour' of Groupware as noted by Cameron *et al.* (1995). Key themes in the Groupware literature are the 'interaction' between the technology and the people in the organisation who have to use it and the difficulties associated with integrating the technology into work practices (Orlikowski 1996). These issues are akin to the notion of appropriation as discussed by Ciborra (1996), that is the higher the degree of integration then the higher the degree of appropriation. These issues are addressed below.

Integration and appropriation

The degree of integration and appropriation into use in each of the three cases differed, although the exact nature of the problems differed between the cases.

CoreTech

In the CoreTech case, where the intranet grew from the 'bottom-up', integration of the technology was less of an issue initially, as users were very keen to experiment with the capabilities of the technology. These early adopters also tended to have a technical background and were thus more at ease with new technology. However, as the intranet became more widespread it began to include users who did not have a technical background and who were more reluctant to use the technology. Lack of formal training and a policy that threatened disciplinary action for inappropriate use did not exactly help the situation. In fact it meant that new users in particular tended to restrict their use of the intranet to 'safe' applications such as the Desktop Directory. The net effects of this were that the users did not avail themselves of the facilities and benefits offered by the use of the intranet, or that they took longer to gain familiarity with the systems and its capabilities, thus delaying further the benefits to CoreTech as a whole.

Another interesting aspect to the use of the intranet in CoreTech is the reaction that ensued when it was announced that a framework for information management was to be introduced. The emergence of the 'Campaign for Intranet Freedom' showed that a certain body of users who had fully integrated the technology into their roles were reluctant to 'backtrack' on their use of the technology and saw the framework and its implementation as a form of censorship. The fact that they were able to use the technology as a medium with which to voice their opinions is illustrative of the strength of the technology in facilitating and encouraging discussion and feedback amongst users. This also provides an example of what managers in Neotany may have been trying to prevent when they did not permit the setting up of forums such as newsgroups for fear that dealers would 'gang up' on Neotany.

Neotany

With respect to the Neotany extranet, the situation was somewhat different. Here, the end users (at the dealerships) received formal training on how to use the system and how to download information. Unfortunately, in some cases the HITEQs and other technicians to whom a lot of the information in the system was targeted, were not actually permitted to access the information. Also, the sheer volume of information being published on the extranet and the time taken to download and print it at the dealerships did not encourage service managers and others in the dealerships to take full advantage of the system. It is ironic that had the dealerships been able to demonstrate familiarity with the use of the system and to demonstrate that they were accessing the information as appropriate then they would not have needed to continue to print out the information and process the paper as was the case prior to the extranet. Even at Neotany HQ, the 'fit' between the technology and the people was not ideal and there was little integration of the extranet into work practices. For example, the people responsible for producing the bulletins themselves preferred to deal with the information on paper. Perhaps this will change as familiarity with the system grows.

It is clear that in the Neotany case the mismatch between the technology as implemented and the people, in terms of work practices, meant that the system merely automated existing practices rather than facilitating new processes or new methods of collaboration. This helps to explain the lack of overall benefits accrued from the use of the extranet and it stems from the fact that there was little consideration of the Neotany extranet from a strategic perspective (as discussed earlier). As noted by King (1996) a strategic issue in Groupware is the 'fit' between the Groupware solution and the corporate 'culture' and a mismatch between the two may merely automate poor relationships and practices. This is essentially what occurred in the Neotany case. This finding is also corroborated, in the wider context of IT in general, by Short and Venkatraman (1992) who note that using IT to automate existing processes rather than to redesign them often yields disappointing results.

In the Neotany case, key reasons for the mismatch and lack of integration include the fact that the system only permitted a one-way flow of information and the information available on-line merely duplicated the layout and format of what had previously been available in paper form.

ATI

Similarly with the RTOnet system there was also a mismatch between the technology and the people who use it, and again the mismatch occurs on two fronts, that is with people responsible for contributing material for RTOnet, and also with the end users in the member companies and other customers.

First, in terms of producing content for RTOnet, while there was a content management team whose role was to populate the system with information and knowledge, the people actually responsible for producing the content were expert engineers and researchers. They are the prime source of information for RTOnet. However, currently these experts do not produce content in a form that can be imported directly into RTOnet. Thus, the content management team acts as an intermediary between the experts and RTOnet. Also in terms of keeping the content up to date the team needs to consult with the engineers and researchers and solicit updates as appropriate. The situation is compounded by the fact that currently there is no mechanism to fund the time expended by the engineers and researchers in performing activities related to either directly preparing material for RTOnet or for reviewing existing content and keeping it up to date.

The second mismatch occurs between the technology and the end users. The reason for this mismatch is that engineers in the member companies do not appear to have the capability to access and exploit fully the material available on RTOnet. In theory they have the capability, however, in practice the situation is rather different. In the case of the two member companies visited, access to the Internet and thence to RTOnet was less than ideal. In one case, Internet access was via a single terminal, which had a potential user audience of over 100 engineers. In the second case the company had a policy that any machine connected to the Internet was not permitted to be connected to any internal networks. Also, the engineering manager pointed out that most of the PCs used by engineers were actually 'clunky Pentium Ones', and thus would not be very suitable for accessing material in RTOnet. Also in both of these companies it was clear that senior management were not of the opinion that the use of the Internet was a useful and legitimate source of information for engineers.

In summing up the relationship or 'fit' between the technology and the people who use it, there is clear evidence of a mismatch in all three cases. In the case of the ATI and Neotany systems this mismatch was present right from the early stages. However, with the CoreTech intranet, there was no mismatch to begin with. However, as the importance of the system grew and its use became more widespread, the degree of mismatch began to grow. Also when senior managers recognised the growing importance of the intranet and decided that the time was ripe for imposing some control over the content, a mismatch between the early adopters and the 'new approach' to using the technology started to appear. However, it is true to say that initially this mismatch did not actually exist. Whether the initial zero mismatch was a result of the fact that the intranet grew bottom-up with users actually driving the technology, or the fact that in the early stages there were no controls on usage, or a combination of both is an interesting issue that would probably require further research to resolve.

Drifting

A second key theme in the Groupware literature is the notion of drifting (Ciborra 1996), where as organisations experiment with and learn from their use of the technology, the role of the technology will also evolve. The significance of drifting is that it can indicate that the users in the organisation are learning how to make use of the technology in context. This can entail 'discovery' and exploitation of features or new applications of the technology as well as learning that certain features and functionalities did not fit with existing work practices. In the three case studies presented here, evidence of drifting occurred with the CoreTech and Neotany systems. With respect to the CoreTech case, a prime example is the use of the intranet to facilitate widespread access to and integration of the existing IT systems and databases. This was not envisaged initially and perhaps was one of the key reasons for the rapid rise in importance of the intranet.

Perhaps the prime example of drifting in CoreTech is the use of the internal newsgroups to support communities of interests. One of the reasons for such a positive level of drifting (positive in this sense referring to 'finding' additional uses for the technology) and indeed the high level of integration of the technology into work practices in CoreTech is the fact that because the organisation is involved in the software and IT industry, there was already a high level of awareness and familiarity with the capabilities of Internet technologies and software in general. The fact that the intranet in CoreTech and in particular the newsgroups grew from the bottom-up is good evidence of this. This correlation between drifting and prior familiarity with the capabilities of software and collaborative network tools is corroborated by Orlikowski (1996) in a case study of Groupware within a software company and by Failla (1996) in a case study of Groupware in IBM. However, in the CoreTech case there were also examples of 'negative' drifting, negative being used in this sense to denote the case where features or functionalities of the system were not being used. The best instance of this is the reluctance of new users, who through a combination of lack of training and a fear of falling foul of the policy on intranet use, fail to exploit fully the capabilities of the intranet and instead restrict themselves to use the 'safe' applications such as the Desktop Directory.

With the Neotany case, the most obvious example of drifting concerned the 'confidential' reports prepared by the Neotany field engineers. These contain information that is really only intended for use within Neotany but they are being incorporated into a system whose initial objective was to improve the efficiency of sending information to the dealerships. A second example is the use by dealers of the e-mail component of the extranet to 'advertise' to other dealerships, their surplus spare parts and accessories. However, the Neotany case also provides a good example of 'negative' drifting. There is strong evidence that people in the dealerships are not using the extranet and indeed this is a prime concern with people at Neotany HQ. This 'non-use' includes those dealerships who see downloading bulletins as very time consuming, as well as those dealerships where HITEQ technicians are not actually permitted to use the system. 'Negative' drifting where features and functionalities of collaborative technology are bypassed or not used, is not uncommon and has been reported by Ciborra and Patriotta (1996) and Ciborra and Suetens (1996).

With respect to the ATI case and the use of RTOnet, there is no evidence of drifting having occurred. This is most likely due to the fact that the use of the RTOnet system is still in its infancy.

Thus in two out of the three case studies (CoreTech and Neotany), drifting was seen to have occurred, and examples of 'positive' and 'negative' drifting were evident. The significance of this is that it highlights those areas where the respective 'organisations' have modified the features and functionalities of the systems so that they fit more readily into the appropriate context of use.

8.1.5   The role and effect of intranet/extranets

Fulk and DeSanctis (1995) note that the capabilities of new communications technologies (including Internet technologies) contribute to a large variety of changes in organisations and in organisational forms. As presented in Chapter 2, these changes in organisational form can be referred to as changes in 'vertical control', 'horizontal coordination', 'organisation and unit size', 'new types of coupling' and 'communication cultures'. A discussion of the types of changes and the accompanying changes in organisational form in each of the three case studies is presented below.

CoreTech

With respect to the CoreTech case, perhaps the most striking aspect of the use of an intranet is the range of resultant changes in working practices, many of which were actually unforeseen. As discussed in the case study the use of the intranet facilitates information sharing in the company on a scale that previously was impossible and this has led to effects such as information bypassing the hierarchies (an example of a change in 'vertical control'), informal networks supporting communities of interests (an example of a change in communications culture) and the expectation by employees that they have access to information by right (an example of a change in 'vertical control').

Many people's roles have also changed. For example, some middle managers whose power no longer resides in the information they once controlled (change in 'vertical control'), the adoption of the technology by senior managers to increase the level of direct feedback from employees (change in communication cultures), the numerous people for whom the use of the intranet has become a key part of their role, and the people whose jobs will no longer exist. One of the factors in the success of the CoreTech intranet is its ease of use and this appears to have contributed to the high degree of acceptance of a relatively new technology. Similarly the ease with which the intranet allows integration with existing IT systems appears to be a major factor in its success and in its emergent role as a strategic IT system. Evidence from the case study is that the integration into existing systems and the resultant ubiquitous browser front end is a major advantage of the intranet.

Other types of changes that have occurred include the use of the intranet to support cross-divisional working. The Desktop Directory and individuals' 'home pages' are seen as useful in locating information about work being performed by colleagues in other divisions in the organisation. In terms of Fulk and DeSanctis' (1995) dimensions of change in organisational form this is an example of a new type of coupling within the organisation.

Neotany

It is interesting to compare the above with the changes that occurred in the Neotany case. While similar changes occurred in that the roles of the service manager and the DOM were undermined (changes in vertical control), and also that the extranet facilitated the sharing of much more information than was the case previously other changes such as supporting communities of interest and knowledge sharing did not occur. It is not just the case that these changes did not happen but rather they were prevented from happening. The decision not to support newsgroups or similar discussion forums precluded the formation of communities of interest. Also the fact that the Neotany extranet essentially facilitated a one-way flow of information inhibited not only knowledge and information sharing amongst the dealerships but also the sharing with Neotany of knowledge and information located in the dealerships. The net effect of this was to constrain the changes to those roles which involved simply relaying information.

While there were changes to the roles of people who produce the bulletins these changes were minimal, the difference being that rather than preparing a paper bulletin, it was now produced and distributed electronically, the on-line bulletins having an identical layout to the paper version. Perhaps as the people who produce information for the extranet become more familiar with and accustomed to electronic publishing they may develop more innovative uses of the extranet. The main role affected by the Neotany extranet was that of the field engineer. The extranet enables them to have a much more flexible role. They can now work remotely from Neotany HQ using dial-in access to the extranet rather than having to maintain a small library of bulletins and technical information or having to repeatedly call Neotany HQ to request that information be faxed to them (this is what Fulk and DeSanctis (1995) refer to as a change in form of 'horizontal coordination').

Finally, the other change that is evident is the use by dealers of the e-mail component of the extranet to advertise surplus parts and accessories. While this is an example of a change in 'communication cultures', it can actually have a negative effect in that the more it is used then the more e-mail traffic is generated and this can cause disillusionment with the extranet. Indeed one of the parts managers interviewed commented that he simply does not have the time to process all the e-mail he receives and this can mean he may miss important e-mails from Neotany or TNT as discussed in the case study.

ATI

With respect to the ATI system, for those people directly involved in developing the system and for preparing the content of the system, there has been a major change in role. They have moved from the 'predictable' world of contributing to publications to the role of processing and customising electronic content. The roles of other people not directly involved in RTOnet are also beginning to change. Engineers and other experts are being encouraged strongly to contribute their knowledge for dissemination via RTOnet. Not surprisingly there has been some resistance from those who subscribe to the notion that the best way for them to maintain their status as an expert is to keep rather than divulge freely their knowledge. This situation is not helped by the fact that there is no funding available for experts who wish to spend time 'transferring' their knowledge to RTOnet.

In terms of changes in organisational form, there is no evidence in the ATI case of changes to vertical control, horizontal coordination, or organisation and unit size. Although there is an implicit objective of the RTOnet product manager that the 'deep wells of knowledge' in ATI can be linked via the use of technologies such as RTOnet, this has not actually occurred yet. Perhaps, as mentioned before, it is too soon to identify changes in the ATI example. However, there is evidence of new types of coupling being facilitated between ATI and third party information providers who supply information for inclusion on RTOnet. The significance of this from ATI's perspective is that it will help to consolidate the role of RTOnet as a key source of information on all aspects related to materials technologies.

Relationships

Another interesting aspect of change associated with RTOnet is that it will reduce the level of face-to-face contact that experts will have with existing members and prospective clients. In a sense their exchanges of information will become 'electronic', information will be shared electronically and they may never meet the customer face-to-face (this is an example of what Nohria and Berkley (1994) refer to as an interorganisational coupling facilitated by technology). This is a major change especially as managers in ATI acknowledge that a key part of their business is actually relationship management. The idea of information exchange becoming more electronic also arose in the CoreTech case. However, senior managers in CoreTech stressed that while information exchange is an important component of maintaining relationships with colleagues, such 'relationships' should not be 'allowed' to become electronic and that the use of the intranet should allow people more time to manage relationships with colleagues and customers. With respect to the Neotany extranet, the effect on the relationships between Neotany HQ and people in the dealerships, of information exchange becoming 'electronic' is also an issue. However, the extent to which they are being affected depends on the perspective. For example, people in Neotany HQ believe that the use of the extranet to exchange information is strengthening their relationships with dealers, the easier and more immediate flow of information being cited as a key element of this. On the other hand the view from the dealerships is that because the information exchange component of the relationship is becoming more electronic, they feel more distant from Neotany and thus the overall relationship is actually weakening. The fact that dealers feel they receive fewer visits from DOMs (who send information via the extranet) and that bulletins are 'unsigned' whereas previously they had an individual contact name, serves to reinforce this conclusion.

Thus of the three cases, two of them (ATI and Neotany) are seeing 'relationships' becoming less personal and more electronic. However, in the third case (CoreTech), while it is recognised that 'relationships' can become more electronic, senior managers are anxious that this should not actually happen. Perhaps it is because they see the intranet as facilitating knowledge management and that a key element of this (as cited by a number of people) is that the system supports personal interaction rather than just putting people into contact with information. The more advanced nature and wider experience with intranets in CoreTech may justify this.

However, it could also be argued that a key aspect of intranets and Internet technology is that they facilitate an electronic exchange of information with people who have no need, or even no desire, to meet in order to exchange or share information and knowledge, and this information exchange can form the basis for a rudimentary 'relationship' between the parties involved. The case of the newsgroups in CoreTech is a good example of this. However, the Neotany case contradicts this and suggests that relationships are weakened by information exchange becoming electronic (both in terms of information in the form of bulletins and information received from DOMs). The conclusion therefore is that there is a balance between the personal (face-to-face) means and the 'electronic' means of exchanging information in sustaining a relationship. Going too far towards the 'electronic means' may weaken the relationships, whereas going too far towards the 'personal means' may improve the relationship but at the expense of time and effort.

Table 8.3 summarises the above discussion of the findings in terms of changes in the dimensions of organisational form.

Examination of the contents of Table 8.3 shows that there is no clear pattern of change across the three case studies. In fact the only common characteristic across the three is that no changes in organisation and unit size were evident. However, bearing in mind that the three systems have not been in use for very long (CoreTech approximately – three years, Neotany approximately – two years, ATI less than a year) it is perhaps the case that such organisational-level changes have yet to manifest themselves, despite the fact that in each of the case studies the effect of the use of the intranet on individuals is evident. This finding mirrors that noted by Jurison (1996) who points out that the impact of IT on the individual precedes that on the organisation and that it may take many years before the impact of an IT system is felt at the organisational level.

Table 8.3 Summary of discussion of forms of organisational change

	CoreTech	ATI	Neotany
Changes in vertical control	Information bypassing hierarchies Employees expecting access to information Some middle managers being isolated	No changes evident	Information bypassing the 'traditional' route of service managers and DOMs Roles of service managers and DOMs being undermined
Changes in horizontal coordination	No changes evident	No changes evident	Field engineers having remote access to intranet
Changes in organisation and unit size	No changes evident	No changes evident	No changes evident
New types of coupling	No changes evident	Inclusion of third party information on RTOnet	No changes evident
Changes in communications cultures	Informal networks, especially newsgroups Use of the intranet by senior managers to solicit feedback	No changes evident	Dealers advertising surplus parts and accessories via e-mail

The above discussion about the changes in organisational form that resulted from the implementation and use of intranet/extranet essentially presented the 'technological determinism' perspective, which takes the view that IT is a cause of organisational change. Although the implementation and use of intranet/extranet did result in changes in each case, the nature of those changes was determined by the complex interaction between the technology and its organisational users. To gain a better understanding of the 'forces' that shaped these changes it is useful to examine the 'social determinism' perspective. This involves looking at the issues of 'power and politics' and is discussed below.

8.1.6   Power and politics

As the initial motives for deploying an intranet/extranet in the three cases were concerned with improving the efficiency of existing ways of sharing information and the facilitation of new ways of sharing information, it is useful to examine the political aspects from the perspective of the use of information and the control of access to information.

Walsh and Ungson (1991) note that organisational memory and the use of knowledge contained therein can play a political role. In the case studies there were instances of political actions with respect to the use of knowledge and information. This relates to how individuals can wield 'power' over others in the organisation through either filtering information from organisational memory or by controlling access to information. Filtering in this sense can also mean 'owners' of information not transferring their knowledge to organisational memory. Examples of these are evident in the three case studies and are discussed below.

CoreTech

With respect to the CoreTech intranet the move towards a licensed or official intranet, although supposedly done for purposes of information management, could be interpreted as a political move in that it entailed the establishment of 'ownership' of the intranet and the component of organisational memory contained therein. Those whose information or knowledge content did not conform to the rules (as defined for the 'Framework for Information Management') were denied the opportunity to contribute to the 'official' component of organisational memory as represented by the licensed intranet. The fact that the official search engine no longer indexed the unlicensed intranet pages meant that even the existence of the content of 'unlicensed' information was denied to users and this represents a further indication of a political motivation. Also of relevance to this discussion is some data that was collected during a visit to the company subsequent to the main phase of data collection. There now appears on the official intranet, the 'story' behind the development of the CoreTech intranet. This purports to be the real story of how the CoreTech intranet was developed, implemented and managed. The 'story' conveys the notion that the 'success' of the intranet in CoreTech was as a result of the foresight of people in the CRU, who right from the very early stages planned and managed the deployment of the intranet (sic). No mention is made of the role of the unofficial intranet or the early adopters at CoreTech Labs who were instrumental in publishing information and knowledge in the early stages, and developing intranet applications that helped to create the surge in widespread interest in and use of the intranet. The author of the above 'story' is a senior manager in the CRU which by sheer 'coincidence' was the unit that introduced the 'Framework for Information

Management' and effectively assumed control of the intranet and its content as a result. This rewriting of history by the 'victors' is perhaps the strongest indication of how the use of knowledge and organisational memory as represented by the intranet can actually play a political role.

Neotany

With respect to the Neotany extranet there is also evidence of a political role with reference to the content of the extranet. For example, unlike the CoreTech case where the use of newsgroups facilitated an informal means of sharing information and represented an alternative voice to the use of the extranet, with respect to the Neotany case the capability of the extranet to facilitate newsgroups was purposely not implemented. The reason being that, from the perspective of managers in Neotany, it was not possible to identify a non-controversial use of the newsgroups. There was also a fear that the dealerships would use facilities such as newsgroups to 'gang up' on Neotany. Preventing the implementation of the newsgroups can thus be viewed as an attempt to control the degree to which people in the dealerships could share and use knowledge and also as an attempt to limit their potential contribution to 'organisational' memory.

Another interesting example from the Neotany case is the issue of access to the reports that field engineers submit in response to a visit to a dealership when all other avenues of resolving the issue have been exhausted. As noted in Chapter 7, the contents of these reports can often identify a dealer's incompetence as being the source of the problem. Also as pointed out, these reports are now being entered into a database accessible via the extranet. Thus should the full repertoire of such information be available to all users of the extranet there is a large potential for conflict. Restricting access to such information while strictly speaking is an example of the use of organisational memory to fulfil a political role, actually serves to hide information from those who would react strongly, and thus there is actually less conflict than there is potential for.

A final example from the Neotany case relates to the expectation that the individual departments in Neotany should generate their own web pages for the extranet and use whatever structures they saw fit to disseminate information to the dealerships. As noted in the case study, this was a deliberate decision by the head of IT, taken in order to make it clear that the IT department was not attempting to control the flow of information on the extranet. This decision is itself a political act, and it means that the head of IT chose not to use the extranet as an opportunity to control the flow of information from Neotany to the dealerships. He pointed out that as his department had never controlled the flow of information, he did not see why they should start doing so now. This is in marked contrast to the CoreTech case where similarly, prior to the intranet, the CRU did not control the flow of information within CoreTech, but seized upon the opportunity to do so with the implementation of the intranet.

ATI

In the ATI case a clear example of the use of knowledge and organisational memory to fulfil a political role in terms of restricting access to information and knowledge, is the reluctance of some experts to divulge their knowledge. Having recognised that information/knowledge is 'power' which they wish to retain and only dole out information and knowledge as they see fit, they are in effect pursuing a political agenda.

Finally, in addition to the above examples of using intranets to facilitate a political role for knowledge and organisational memory, there are also examples of how the use of intranets can reduce or eliminate such power held previously. For example, the use of the intranet in CoreTech as an important mechanism for the distribution of information and knowledge undermines the role of middle managers who previously saw the control of information flow as an important element of their role. With respect to the Neotany extranet, the role of sales managers in controlling the flow and timing of information to the HITEQs and other technicians is also undermined. In addition, in the ATI case the ability of experts to divulge information and knowledge as they see fit is undermined by the fact that a significant proportion of their information and knowledge is being made available via RTOnet. At present their only protection against this and the further undermining of their role is to refuse to or to delay divulging their knowledge. However, as pointed out in Chapter 6, as the momentum increases towards the use of RTOnet as (potentially) the key mechanism for transferring knowledge to members (and others), these reluctant experts will be isolated, marginalised, and eventually will be required to divulge their information and knowledge. Thus, while the use of intranets/extranets cannot force an unwilling employee to share knowledge, it can play a role in terms of allowing others to identify those people who are unwilling to share knowledge or in terms of isolating those who seek to control access to information.

Thus in all the three cases there are clear examples of political acts concerning the use and access to information and knowledge. This corroborates the earlier work of Walsh and Ungson (1991) who discuss how knowledge and organisational memory can play a political role in an organisation.

8.1.7 Summary of findings in relation to the IT literature

In summarising the discussion of the findings in the context of the IT literature, illustrated in Table 8.4, while there are similarities across the three cases, there is no clear pattern of outcomes. This finding strongly supports the earlier work of Ciborra (1996: 9) who talks of the 'plasticity of the artefact' and the crucial role of context in determining outcomes. Thus, the implementation of an intranet/extranet will not lead to any predictable outcomes. Even the notion, most often touted by consultants, that the implementation of intranets/extranets can be justified on the basis of cost savings accrued from the 'removal of paper' from an organisation, is now seen as questionable to say the least. The Neotany case showed that cost savings in one area can be offset by increased costs elsewhere (i.e. in the dealerships). Similarly, the ATI case showed that there is value in retaining paper as a means of transferring information to members as this helps to maintain the relationship between ATI and its members.

However, in comparing the outcome with respect to the benefits in each case, there are some interesting results. For example, in comparing the CoreTech and ATI cases, both systems show potentially strong benefits overall. However, in the ATI case there was a strong element of formal planning whereas in the CoreTech case there was very little. This suggests that it may be useful to examine whether existing planning and implementation procedures need to be revisited in the light of intranets. However, when the Neotany case is taken into consideration, where there was also a lack of formal planning, there were few overall benefits. Perhaps this was because with respect to the Neotany extranet, the application was very focused and well defined and integration of the system into corporate strategy did not occur.

Table 8.5 summarises the discussion of the changes in dimensions of organisational forms (as proposed by Fulk and DeSanctis (1995)). Again it is evident that there is no clear pattern of outcomes common across the three cases.

The significance of the findings presented in the above set of tables and the implications of this for further research into intranets will be addressed in Chapter 9, which presents the conclusions of the research.

Table 8.4   Summary of discussion of IT issues

	CoreTech	ATI	Neotany
Integration into corporate strategy	High	High	Low
Integration with existing systems	High	Low	Low
Planning/ Implementation			
Facilitators to implementation	'Informal' approach Use of open standards	Senior management approval	'Informal' approach Use of open standards
Inhibitors to implementation	None initially	Lack of funding Internal resistance	None initially
The involvement of external expertise in planning and implementation	None	Prototype developed in conjunction with BT	None
Evaluation			
Main benefits	Cost savings, easier and more open access to information	Potential cost savings, additional revenue	Little overall benefit, but potentially easier access to information
Main downside	Less 'face-to-face' interactions	Members may not have capability to access the system	Not being used sufficiently
Groupware Issues			
Integration and Appropriation	High for some users (e.g. software engineers) Low for new users	Low at member companies Low at ATI	Low at dealerships Low at Neotany HQ
Examples of drifting Positive	Integration with existing systems	No evidence at this stage	Access to field engineers' reports
	Use of newsgroups		Dealers advertising via e-mail
Negative	New users and 'safe' applications		Dealers not downloading information HITEQs not granted access

Table 8.5 Summary of discussion of changes in organisational forms

	CoreTech	ATI	Neotany
Changes in vertical control	Information bypassing hierarchies Some middle managers being 'isolated'	No changes evident	Roles of service managers and DOMs being undermined
Changes in horizontal coordination	No changes evident	No changes evident	Field engineers having remote access to extranet
Changes in organisation and unit size	No changes evident	No changes evident	No changes evident
New types of coupling	No changes evident	Inclusion of third party information on RTOnet	No changes evident
Changes in communications cultures	Informal networks, especially newsgroups Use of the intranet by senior managers to solicit feedback	No changes evident	Dealers advertising surplus parts and accessories via e-mail

Having reviewed and discussed the findings in the context of the IT literature, the following section evaluates the findings with respect to the knowledge management literature.

8.2 Evaluating the findings in the context of the knowledge management literature

As mentioned in Chapter 4, during the early stages of looking at the IT literature it became apparent that various issues relating to the flow of information and knowledge were important to the study of intranets/extranets. Thus, in order to understand better the issues that surround the use of intranets/extranets, this section situates the findings in the context of the knowledge management literature. As noted in Chapter 3, the approach taken here is to treat knowledge as a 'physical substance', as this approach lends itself to recognising and making use of the information systems aspect of knowledge management and the role that technology can play in facilitating the process.

However, before discussing these issues it is useful to reflect on whether knowledge 'delivered' or transferred via an intranet/extranet is the 'same' as knowledge transferred face-to-face. According to Nonaka (1994) there are two types of knowledge, tacit and explicit. As discussed in Chapter 3, tacit knowledge (or the 'knowing how') is difficult to communicate to others whereas explicit knowledge (or the 'knowing what') can be easily communicated and shared. Thus, the knowledge that is transferred or delivered via an intranet/extranet must be more explicit in nature. This does not actually cause a problem in terms of the role of intranets/extranets in knowledge management for although tacit knowledge is not transferred, the use of an intranet/extranet facilitates a greater degree of knowledge transfer than would have otherwise been the case. The use of an intranet can also assist in identifying and locating those in the organisation who actually possess tacit knowledge and face-to-face meetings can then be set up to assist with the transfer of this knowledge, thus increasing the potential for the transfer of tacit knowledge between individuals in the organisation.

The issues to be addressed in this discussion, as noted in Chapter 3, include various aspects of knowledge creation, storage, transfer, and use. These themes were also used to guide the data collection, as noted in Chapter 4. The role of the intranet/extranet in facilitating or supporting these various aspects is discussed below.

8.2.1 Knowledge creation

As noted in Chapter 3, in simple terms knowledge creation is the process of adding value to information (Ponelis and Fairer-Wessels 1998). However, a more useful approach to considering knowledge is that provided by Nonaka and Takeuchi (1995) who suggest four basic patterns for creating knowledge, based on the dynamic interaction between tacit knowledge and explicit knowledge, and explanations of these were presented earlier in Chapter 3. Each of the four patterns is discussed below in the context of the three case studies and also in the context of how the use of an intranet/extranet affects each pattern.

From tacit to tacit

This pattern of knowledge creation refers to the situation where individuals acquire knowledge directly from others. Of the three cases, ATI provides the best example of this, with ATI experts working, typically face-to-face, with engineers in the member companies. However, as RTOnet will essentially replace a lot of the face-to-face contact between ATI and the member companies, this pattern of knowledge creation is likely to be undermined severely. It could be argued that if this pattern of knowledge creation is undermined by RTOnet, then a way of compensating for this would be to increase the involvement of ATI engineers and researchers in the various training programmes that ATI operate. However, this is beyond the scope of this discussion, and besides it is envisaged that in the future a lot of ATI training programmes will be delivered through RTOnet.

Similarly in the Neotany case, the degree of knowledge creation based on a tacit-to-tacit pattern is again decreasing. There are two prime examples of this. Firstly, in the case of field engineers, prior to the extranet, if there was an issue that could not be resolved via a telephone conversation, then a field engineer would visit the dealership in order to resolve the problem. With the advent of the extranet, there is the potential to resolve such problems without the engineer having to physically visit the dealership. While this may appear to be a more efficient use of the engineer's time, it practically eliminates any possibility of knowledge creation via tacit knowledge being appropriated by people in the dealership. Secondly, prior to the extranet there was a great deal of interaction between the DOMs and the sales managers and/or dealer principals in the dealerships and visits to the dealerships afforded opportunities for knowledge creation via the tacit-to-tacit pattern. Now that the extranet is in place, such opportunities are reduced markedly as there is less need for a DOM to visit a dealership simply to 'deliver' information.

However, with respect to the CoreTech intranet, the situation is somewhat different. Here the intranet facilitates a greater degree of contact between people and while not all such contact will actually be face-to-face, the opportunities for knowledge creation are improved greatly. A prime example is the use of the Desktop Directory, which allows people to search on items such as job title and work area, and then to follow this up by looking at the web pages of the appropriate sections, teams, and individuals. The appropriate person can then be contacted and the opportunity for tacit-to-tacit knowledge transfer and creation has been made. Given that senior managers in CoreTech see knowledge management as a key objective, perhaps this is why they stress that the intranet should be used to put people into contact with people rather than making the information exchange component of relationships electronic. Indeed the Organisational Development Manager jokingly suggested that once people have used the intranet to locate someone who appears to have the knowledge they require or which could be of use, there should be a spring-lever in their chair to make them go and talk to that person. A second example of where the CoreTech intranet facilitates greater opportunities for knowledge creation is the use of newsgroups. Many enquiries on the newsgroups are from people trying to find others in the company who have worked on problems similar to the one they are trying to solve. Again, this facilitates an increased level of contact with people right across the company and thus this increases greatly the opportunities for knowledge creation. Whether people having been contacted in this way are then willing to share their knowledge is a different matter and is addressed below in the discussion of knowledge transfer.

From explicit to explicit

This pattern of knowledge creation refers to the combination of discrete pieces of explicit knowledge into a new 'whole'. In all three case studies this process is supported by the intranet/extranet, but to a different extent. For example, in the CoreTech case, the fact that there is now a great deal of material on the intranet, including both information and knowledge on a wide variety of topics, procedures, and work areas, and also the fact that people have easy access to this content, significantly increases their ability to locate and combine discrete pieces of knowledge. It is interesting to note that in the early stages of the CoreTech intranet, people were free to publish, within reason, whatever content they saw fit. With the introduction of the framework for information management, where content now needs to be approved by a franchise holder, this has made people more reluctant to publish content on the official intranet. This is partly due to the fact that the framework essentially imposes a structure on the information and many people were not too happy with this (hence the 'Campaign for intranet Freedom') or may feel that the structure is not appropriate to the kind of content that they wish to publish. Another key aspect of the framework is that the unofficial or unlicensed servers are no longer indexed by the 'official' intranet search engine. The net effect of this is that the content of such pages are denied to other users and thus it reduces the amount of knowledge 'available' for combination. Thus, overall the CoreTech intranet supports the explicit-to-explicit pattern of knowledge creation, but the effect of the framework for information management means that there is a smaller quantity of knowledge available to facilitate this pattern of knowledge creation. On the other hand, it could be argued that a positive effect of the framework is that it ensures that the content on the official intranet meets certain criteria in terms of ownership, validity, and that it is up to date. Thus, the content on the official intranet is actually a higher 'quality' and this should lead to a more effective and efficient knowledge creation process.

In the case of the ATI system, it again supports the explicit-to-explicit knowledge creation process. Here, there is more information and knowledge easily available than was the case prior to RTOnet. Examples include data sheets and best practice guides. Also search engines in the system allow users to locate and combine knowledge and thus contribute to the knowledge creation process. However, the fact that users cannot contribute material to the site means that in a sense the knowledge creation process is rather restricted.

Similarly in the case of the Neotany extranet, there is more information and knowledge easily available than was the case previously, but again the fact that people in the dealerships cannot publish information restricts the quantity of knowledge available, and thus reduces the opportunities for combining knowledge.

From tacit to explicit

This pattern of knowledge creation involves the externalisation of tacit knowledge, that is it involves the articulation of tacit knowledge through dialogue into explicit knowledge. However, as noted by Nonaka (1991) the nature of tacit knowledge renders it highly personal and hard to formalise and communicate. In terms of discussing how the intranet/extranet in each of the three cases supports this pattern of knowledge creation it is necessary to examine how it supports the dialogue part of the process. This is because the presence and use of intranets/extranets will not affect how tacit knowledge is articulated but rather can facilitate and support the dialogue process by making it easier for people to communicate.

For example, with respect to the CoreTech intranet, the use of newsgroups is a prime example of where a much greater degree of dialogue can be facilitated. Typical enquiries on these groups, especially ones such as *ct.pc* (PC related discussions) and *ct.www* (general Internet and www discussions) involve users looking for help with a particular technical problem. The use of the newsgroups supports a dialogue between the enquirer and those who articulate their tacit knowledge in order to help solve the problem. The interesting aspect of this dialogue is that it can be seen by all users of the group, potentially anyone in the company who has intranet access. Users can contribute to the dialogue, either by asking for clarification, raising related issues, or even contributing their knowledge. Even those users who choose not to participate in the dialogue (the so called 'lurkers') can still see what is being discussed. Thus, when one looks at the dialogue on a particular issue on a newsgroups it may appear that only one or two

people are benefiting from the discussion, but in fact there are potentially thousands of other users taking advantage of the knowledge that
has been articulated.

In the case of the ATI system, as mentioned in Chapter 6 RTOnet will
also contain a number of interactive software packages which are essentially interactive expert systems. These systems already contain the
articulated tacit knowledge of ATI experts and thus while RTOnet does
not play a role in the articulation process it facilitates the dialogue that
will support the tacit-to-explicit pattern of knowledge creation.

Finally, in the case of the Neotany extranet, the system actually
contributes little more to the process of facilitating dialogue than was
the case when material was sent in paper format to dealerships. While
the information and knowledge contained in the bulletins is easier to
access now because it is on the extranet, many bulletins are now
'anonymous', whereas when they were in paper format they always had
a contact name. Thus, if a technician in a dealership had a query about
a bulletin or wanted to understand more about the content of the bulletin, the fact that there is no contact name may actually deter him
from establishing a dialogue with the originator. The net effect of this is
that the opportunities for dialogue to support a tacit-to-explicit pattern
of knowledge creation are very much reduced. The fact that there are no
discussion forums available on the Neotany extranet reduces the opportunities still further.

From explicit to tacit

This pattern of knowledge creation refers to the use of new explicit
knowledge to broaden, extend and reframe one's tacit knowledge. Again
while intranets/extranets cannot help with the process of internalisation,
they can certainly facilitate and support the process by allowing access
to explicit knowledge on a scale that previously was just not possible. In
this context the role of intranet/extranet is essentially the same as that
played in the explicit-to-explicit pattern of knowledge creation as
discussed above.

Table 8.6 summarises the above discussion of the role of intranet/
extranet in each pattern of knowledge creation.

Organizational learning

As knowledge creation is related to the process of organisational learning
(Huber 1991), it is useful at this stage to look briefly at the role of intranet/
extranet in supporting organisational learning in the three companies
studied.

As noted in Chapter 3, Argyris and Schon (1978) refer to two types of organisational learning; single-loop learning and double-loop learning. Single-loop learning is concerned primarily with effectiveness, that is modifying an organisation's theory-in-use so as to best keep organisational performance within the range specified by the existing norms. This essentially means performing existing processes more effectively. With this in mind, it is clear that all three companies studied have undergone this type of learning. Indeed it was the desire to seek ways to become more efficient that led to the use of intranet/extranet in the three companies. In the CoreTech case, much efficiency was derived from the changes in information distribution from paper to intranet. People in the organisation have learned the value, in terms of efficiency, of publishing information electronically. In the ATI and Neotany case, similar changes have taken place.

Double-loop learning refers to the case where the organisational norms themselves are modified. However, it was not possible to obtain data that were robust enough to support a discussion of double-loop learning. This is a result of the difficulties in establishing what the existing norms are and in trying to ascertain whether they have changed. Participant observation combined with a longitudinal approach to the research may have helped to overcome some of these difficulties.

Table 8.6 Role of intranet/extranet in knowledge creation

	CoreTech	ATI	Neotany
Tacit-to-Tacit	Increasing the opportunities for face-to-face interaction	Decreasing the amount of face-to-face interaction	Decreasing the amount of face-to-face interaction
Explicit-to-Explicit	Increases availability and access to explicit knowledge	Increases availability and access to explicit knowledge	Increases availability and access to explicit knowledge
Tacit-to-Explicit	Supports the dialogue process by making it easier to communicate	Supports the dialogue process by making it easier to communicate	Reduces opportunities for dialogue
Explicit-to-Tacit	Increases availability and access to explicit knowledge	Increases availability and access to explicit knowledge	Increases availability and access to explicit knowledge

8.2.2   Knowledge storage

While the previous section looked at various aspects of knowledge creation, this section focuses on the role of intranets in storing not only the existing knowledge but also that which is newly 'created'.

In each of the three case studies the intranet/extranet acts as a repository of large amounts of knowledge, and as such the intranet/extranet can be viewed as a component of organisational memory. With respect to the CoreTech intranet, the various newsgroups and discussion forums also represent instances of collective memory where, as noted by Stein and Zwass (1995), collective memory refers to the social process of articulating, exchanging, and sharing information leading to shared interpretations. The 'community spirit' and 'sense of togetherness' on the ct.misc newsgroup is a good example of this. The archives of the newsgroups in particular are thus an important element of organisational memory. The newsgroups and discussion forums also provide a valuable role in that they help to make people more aware of the existence or whereabouts of information and knowledge stored by other members of the organisation. The storing of information and knowledge in an electronic format also means that searching for it becomes much easier, although it must be remembered that in the CoreTech case, some people had reservations about the effectiveness of the current search engine in use on the intranet.

Similarly, in the ATI case, RTOnet also represents an important element of organisational memory. Key components include the ATI 'archives' of information and knowledge, previously only available in paper form, best practice guides, and interactive expert-system software packages. With respect to the Neotany extranet, it too represents an element of organisational memory as it now contains all the contents of previous technical and service bulletins, new bulletins as they are published, and field engineers' reports that at the time of conducting the data collection were being entered into a database accessible via the extranet. However, while the field engineers' reports will thus be available via the extranet, access to them will be restricted to people in Neotany HQ. This is because, as noted in the case study, these often contain 'sensitive' information about particular people in the dealerships which may cause conflict if the information was freely available.

Content management

An interesting aspect of the use of intranet/extranet in facilitating easy storage and greater exploitation of organisational knowledge is that it also makes it easier to actually 'manage' the information and knowledge contained therein. In each of the three case studies there are examples of different approaches to managing the content on the intranet/extranet.

First, in the CoreTech case, content management is achieved via the guidelines and operation of the framework for information management. Franchise holders in each division thus actually control and have responsibility for the content of the material published on the intranet. When an employee wishes to publish information he needs to seek approval from his franchise holder who will ensure that the information to be published meets the guidelines as set out in the framework for information management. There is no pressure on employees to publish information on the intranet and similarly the franchise holders do not solicit for information or knowledge to be published. Thus, in a sense the franchise holder performs the role of 'censor' in that information that does not meet the guidelines does not get published. While the guidelines may have a legitimate purpose in that they ensure that content published on the 'official' intranet meets the requirements of the framework for information management, they may actually act as a barrier and deterrent to people who would like to publish information on the intranet. The fact that the intranet search engine only indexes and searches pages that are on the official intranet is another example of 'censorship' of intranet content. The net effect of this is that less content is actually published that would otherwise have been the case.

In contrast, with respect to the ATI case, the process of content management is rather different. First, there is a content management team responsible for soliciting and actually managing the content of RTOnet so as to ensure that the content is up to date. In a sense there is pressure on the relevant experts to contribute material for publication on RTOnet and also to periodically revisit their material so as to ensure that it remains up to date. In this context the content management team may be viewed as a facilitator rather than as a censor of extranet content.

Finally, in the case of the Neotany extranet, because the system permits only a one-way flow of information from Neotany HQ to the dealerships, there is by default a restriction on the content and who can publish. Contributions to the content of material on the intranet can only be made by people in Neotany HQ, who are also responsible for acquiring and compiling the material that is to be published.

Of the three approaches to content management, it is difficult, without further research, to ascertain which approach is optimal. The CoreTech approach has merits in that once the content has been published, users can be sure that it meets certain guidelines and requirements, but on the other hand the need to seek approval to publish may deter from publishing, people who have very valuable information and knowledge. Also the search engine only permits users to search content on licensed pages and this has the effect of reducing the amount of organisational memory that they can exploit. Similarly the ATI approach has merits in that the valuable time of researchers and experts is not consumed in preparing content for publication on RTOnet, but on the other hand the content is very much dependent on what the researchers and experts actually choose to make available. Finally in the Neotany case, the approach differs from that taken in the CoreTech and ATI cases because here the people responsible for compiling the content are the same people who are responsible for managing the content of the extranet. However, while this means that, in general, there is no censorship of content, it also means that the layout and format of information published differs little from what would have been published the 'old' way on paper.

In summary, the above discussion shows that intranet/extranet can act as a component of organisational memory but that there is a need for managers to recognise this aspect of the use of intranets/extranets and to develop appropriate strategies for managing the content. This is corroborated by Stein and Zwass (1995) who point out that the need to recognise and develop the information-systems aspect of organisational memory is growing ever stronger with the increasing weight of knowledge work and because of the capabilities offered by advanced information technologies, which are increasingly being used by organisations.

8.2.3   Knowledge transfer

As discussed in Chapter 3, knowledge transfer encompasses two aspects. The first aspect involves the transfer of information and knowledge as part of the processes of creating and storing knowledge. The role of the intranet in facilitating these processes was discussed above. The second aspect of knowledge transfer is as a constituent of the retrieval of information and knowledge from organisational memory so that it may be used by people in the organisation (Miles *et al.* 1998). In all three case studies the use of the intranet/extranet plays a key role in this process and allows users near instantaneous access to the information and knowledge stored therein.

With respect to the CoreTech case, there are two key ways in which the use of the intranet can facilitate knowledge transfer. The first way takes advantage of the information published on web pages on the intranet. Anyone with access to the intranet can easily retrieve the contents of these pages and use the information and knowledge as appropriate. Intranet access also supports access to the wider Internet, and thus users can exploit this to transfer 'external' knowledge for use within the company. However, as noted earlier the net effect of the CoreTech policy for Internet access may mean that users do not actually use the Internet and thus lose the benefits of knowledge that may be transferred in from the Internet. The second way takes advantage of the newsgroups and other discussion forums as a mechanism for transferring knowledge either 'live' via an on-line dialogue or by searching the archives of these discussions.

In the ATI case, the actual objective of the RTOnet system is to facilitate and support the transfer of knowledge, for a price of course. Users connect to the system via the Internet and retrieve whatever knowledge is desired/appropriate to their requirements. Similarly in the Neotany case the initial objective of the extranet was to facilitate a more efficient transfer of information and knowledge to people in the dealerships. However, unlike the CoreTech case where users could actually publish their own information on the intranet, the Neotany system only supports a one-way transfer of information from Neotany to the dealerships. Admittedly, the system does allow dealers to send information via e-mail to Neotany and to each other, but unless such messages are copied to all dealers, this is essentially a means of private communication and does not represent a form of electronic publishing and thus such information is not available to all users. Also the fact that the facility to support discussion groups was deliberately not implemented, because managers in Neotany could not see a non-controversial use for them (i.e. there was a fear that dealers would use the discussion groups to 'gang-up' on Neotany) meant that yet another form of open communications and knowledge transfer was denied to users. In contrast, the CoreTech case showed that newsgroups were very much valued by users and were influential in facilitating an open environment for information sharing and knowledge transfer.

The fact that the use of the intranet/extranet in each case facilitates easier transfer of knowledge and information means that users may be more motivated to retrieve information from the system than they might have otherwise been. They may also be more motivated to retrieve information that they did not have access to previously. However, the situation in each case differs slightly. As noted by Stein (1995) an individual is motivated to retrieve information if:

* *The enquirer has knowledge that the required information exists* – in all three cases, users are well informed of what information is available on the respective systems.

- *The enquirer values that information and believes that it has a bearing on the current situation* – again this applies in all three cases.
- *The enquirer has the ability to search, locate and decode the desired information* – all three systems provide this capability. Although in the CoreTech case there were some concerns expressed about the effectiveness of the intranet search engine, this is balanced by the fact that employees can make use of the newsgroups to solicit assistance in locating information on the intranet.
- *The cost of locating the information is less than that of recomputing the solution from scratch* – again this applies in all three cases. Indeed in many instances the intranet/extranet will be the only source of such information.

Thus, according to the above criteria users of the three systems under discussion should be highly motivated to retrieve information from their respective intranet/extranet. However, there are also a number of demotivators which may temper their enthusiasm. For example, in the CoreTech case, new users in particular who are not familiar with the way the intranet works may be 'scared' of using the system for fear of falling foul of the policy for intranet and Internet use. In the ATI case, engineers in the member companies may be 'scared' off or discouraged from using RTOnet because access to and use of the system incurs usage charges. Also, engineers may not actually have ready access to the Internet to be able to access RTOnet. The example in one member company of where the terminal facilitating Internet access is actually shared by potentially hundreds of engineers is a case in point. With respect to the Neotany case, HITEQs and other technicians may not actually be allowed to access the extranet and this obviously impedes their ability to retrieve information and knowledge from the system.

Thus, although in theory the motivation of people to use the intranet/extranet to retrieve information and knowledge is potentially very high, in practice there are barriers which act as demotivators. Thus, users may not actually be in a position to retrieve and subsequently exploit knowledge which is readily available on the three systems under discussion.

However, while intranets/extranets can facilitate greater access to organisational information and make it easier for individuals to share knowledge, employees may or may not be willing to share information as widely as technology makes possible or as much as managers might desire. Although the intranet/extranet may reduce the personal cost (in terms of time and opportunity) to sharing information and knowledge, the view adopted by Skyrme (1997a), Davenport and Prusak (1998),

Davenport *et al.* (1998) appears to be that the barriers to knowledge sharing are personal and cultural and are centred around an unwillingness of individuals to share knowledge. While the use of intranets/extranets cannot force an unwilling employee to share knowledge, it can play a role in terms of allowing others to identify those people who are unwilling to share knowledge or in terms of isolating those who seek to control access to information. These issues are related to aspects of knowledge use (discussed below) and the politics of knowledge as discussed earlier.

8.2.4   Knowledge use

As noted in Chapter 3, facilitating the transfer of knowledge or even transferring knowledge does not guarantee that such knowledge will actually be used. As noted by Davenport and Prusak (1998) access to knowledge is a necessary condition for knowledge use but it is not sufficient to ensure that the knowledge will be used. Also there may be barriers present which prevent users from having access to the full repertoire of organisational knowledge, for example, because some people have decided not to 'transfer' their knowledge to the component of organisational memory represented by the intranet.

Walsh and Ungson (1991) note that organisational memory, the knowledge contained therein and its use plays three important roles within organisations:

1. it plays an informational role
2. organisational memory fulfils a control function
3. organisational memory can play a political role.

The first two of these roles are discussed below in the context of the three case studies. The third role was addressed earlier in the wider context of a discussion of the politics associated with the implementation process as evidenced in the case studies.

Informational role

According to Walsh and Ungson (1991) the information content that is housed in organisational memory can contribute to decision making. This was evident in the three case studies although perhaps more so in the ATI and Neotany cases than in the CoreTech case. For example, in the ATI case the information contained on RTOnet can be used by an engineer in a member company, to decide how best to utilise a new materials technology. Similarly, in the Neotany case, information

contained on the extranet could be used by a HITEQ or other technician to decide how to identify and how best to resolve a problem on a
vehicle. In the CoreTech case, although there was ample evidence of
people using the intranet to retrieve and use information, there does
not appear to be specific examples of how information was used to
contribute to decision-making. Perhaps this is a limitation of the data
collection process, but on the other hand as noted by many of those
interviewed, use of the intranet is fast being taken for granted (and thus
is fully appropriated according to Ciborra (1996)) and therefore its role in
contributing to decision making, while potentially important, may not
actually be immediately apparent to users.

Organisational memory fulfilling a control function

The use of knowledge from organisational memory can reduce transaction
costs that are often associated with the implementation of new decisions (Walsh and Ungson 1991). Retrieval from organisational memory,
via the intranet, of information on the 'what to do' and 'how to do' of
implementing decisions in the organisation can serve to efficiently
shape desired behaviours without incurring expensive monitoring costs.
It can also serve to increase the efficiency of existing processes or work
procedures in that the easy availability of the information on the intranet/
extranet can mean that people actually follow procedures as intended.

CoreTech

For example, in the CoreTech case, a communications manager (Networks) commented that with reference to his work area, prior to the
intranet many details of work procedures were not performed simply
because people were either not aware of them or because the information was just too difficult or too time consuming to locate. Now
through the widespread use of the intranet, people are much more
aware of work procedures and processes because they are easy to access
and easy to look at on the intranet, and are actually attending to the
processes and procedures as required.

Neotany

With respect to the Neotany case, the need for technicians to refer to
technical and service bulletins in order to repair and maintain vehicles
provides a good example of how the extranet can support the role of
organisational memory in fulfilling a control function. Prior to the
extranet, it was not uncommon for technicians in some dealerships to
be unaware of recently issued bulletins, partly because the bulletins

may have still been with the service managers or because the bulletins may not have been processed correctly at the dealership and perhaps were filed away incorrectly. If the technician in trying to resolve a problem with a vehicle could not locate relevant information in the files he would have contacted the product support people in Neotany HQ who having discussed the problem with the technician would have retrieved from their files the appropriate bulletin and faxed it to the technician. Given that technical bulletins were supposed to be relayed to technicians as soon as possible and that faxing bulletins through was intended as a last resort, not only did this mean that procedures were not being followed but also the attempt to 'repair' the procedure resulted in a lot of wasted time at the dealership and also at Neotany HQ. Now, with the deployment of the extranet, technicians have been made aware that *all* bulletins are to be found on the system. If they telephone the product support people at Neotany HQ seeking assistance in resolving a problem with a vehicle, something which is now discouraged strongly, and if the information they need is actually in a bulletin that has been published, then they are 'told off' and are referred to the appropriate bulletin on the extranet. This now helps to ensure that the procedure relating to the use of bulletins, whether stored on paper or on the extranet, is adhered to, and thus facilitates the removal of previous inefficiencies that resulted from the procedures not actually being followed.

ATI

Finally, in the ATI case a good example of the use of the extranet to facilitate the role of organisational memory as a control function is the case of dealing with non-member enquiries. Prior to RTOnet, handling and dealing with enquiries from non-members could tie up resources, particularly experts, at ATI, despite the fact that ATI strive to abide by the membership principle in that information and knowledge should not be transferred to non-members until such time as they actually pay the appropriate fee to become members. Thus, prior to the deployment of RTOnet, the procedures associated with the membership principle were not being followed, but also as mentioned in Chapter 6, in some circumstances such as dealing with health and safety issues, it was actually difficult to enforce the membership principle. However, now that RTOnet has been deployed, it is possible to utilise a standard response to non-member enquiries, which is to refer them directly to RTOnet. Thus, in accessing RTOnet to retrieve information and knowledge non-members will have to register and pay to retrieve content from the

Table 8.7   Overall summary of key knowledge management issues from the case studies

	CoreTech	ATI	Neotany
Knowledge creation	Positive role overall	Positive role overall	Little or no role
Knowledge storage	Valuable repository of organisational memory	Valuable repository of organisational memory	Valuable repository of organisational memory
Knowledge transfer	Very positive role	Very positive role	Positive but limited role
Knowledge use informational role control function	yes yes	yes yes	yes yes

system, thus enforcing the membership principle. Also, the rote response to refer non-member enquiries to RTOnet means that the previous difficulty associated with dealing with health and safety enquiries has now been eliminated.

Thus, in all three case studies there are examples of organisational memory fulfilling a control function, corroborating the findings of Walsh and Ungson (1991). In each case this is facilitated by the respective intranet/extranet.

8.2.5   Summary of findings in relation to the knowledge management literature

In summarising the discussion of the findings in the context of the knowledge management literature, illustrated in Table 8.7, there is little overall difference between the three cases.

The main difference is the extent to which the intranet/extranet facilitates and supports the process of knowledge creation. In both the CoreTech and ATI cases, it provides a positive role, whereas in the Neotany case the overall role is fairly neutral. While the Neotany extranet actually has a positive role with respect to the explicit-to-explicit and the explicit-to-tacit patterns of knowledge creation it has a negative role with respect to the tacit-to-tacit and tacit-to-explicit patterns. This is a direct result of the fact that the extranet has essentially automated the process of sending information to the dealerships at the expense of personal contact.

In terms of the overall role of intranets/extranets in the knowledge management process, it can be seen from Table 8.7 that the role is positive.

It is also interesting to note that in addition to representing a component of organisational memory, intranets/extranets can also play valuable roles in knowledge creation, transfer and use.

Furthermore, the evaluation of intranet/extranet in the context of knowledge management has served to provide a different perspective and to enhance the understanding of the issues that arise with the implementation and use of intranet/extranet.

8.3 Summary

This chapter presented detailed discussions of the findings of the case studies in relation to the context of the IT literature and the knowledge management literature. However, while the IT and knowledge management perspectives were useful in helping to understand the role and context of intranets, these perspectives did not actually address all the issues that arose in the case studies. This is discussed in Chapter 9 which presents a commentary on this and provides some suggestions for areas of the literature which may illuminate further the understanding of the role and effect of intranets. This commentary is included as a part of the overall conclusions of the research.

9
Conclusions

This chapter presents the conclusions of the research. It begins by looking at the methodological issues and assesses the appropriateness of the research methodology employed. Following the discussion of the methodological issues, the chapter then moves on to look at the significance and relevance of the findings in terms of 'situating' intranets/extranets in the overall context of IT in general, and knowledge management in particular. Finally, as this is a relatively new area being subjected to in-depth analysis, some suggestions for further work are presented.

9.1 Methodological issues

Two issues are addressed here: the use of Table 4.2 (showing initial motives for the use of intranets) as a way of 'structuring' the research, and the use of an interpretive case study approach.

9.1.1 Initial motives for using intranet/extranet

The use of Table 4.2 as a way of 'structuring' the research may seem to be rather simplistic and to a certain extent could be viewed as trivialising the use of intranets. Indeed the table does not even begin to capture the full repertoire of issues that arise from the use of intranets, and the case studies presented in Chapters 5, 6 and 7 bear testament to this. Also, as the three systems that form the basis of the case studies were implemented for similar but not identical reasons, and different stakeholders in each case pursued different outcomes, such a 'single reason' classification of the case is inherently partial.

However, the value of the table lies in its simplicity. It provided a neat way of 'structuring' the research based on the initial motives for using intranets/extranets (as derived from the preliminary research) as well as a basis for selecting companies within which to conduct the research. It also provides the basis for a multiple case research design where complementary *and* contradictory results are to be expected. The selection for the case studies of companies in different industries contributes significantly to this.

Furthermore, as noted in Chapter 4, this research was intended to be exploratory in design and interpretive in nature and the use of Table 4.2 is compatible with these objectives whereas a more deterministic table or approach would have detracted from these objectives.

It is also worthwhile reflecting on the execution of the case studies themselves and the order in which they were conducted. The case studies were actually conducted in the order in which they are presented in the book, that is CoreTech was performed first, followed by ATI, and then Neotany. In terms of conducting the case studies, the CoreTech case proved more challenging in research terms, due to a combination of the fact that it was such a large organisation, the fact that the initial introduction of the intranet was not really a planned affair, and also because it was the first case that was conducted. By the time the Neotany case was conducted there was a greater sense of exactly what data were required and how best to obtain such data. Also, the fact that ATI and Neotany are much smaller organisations meant that it was easier to envisage the role of the extranet in the overall context of the activities of the respective organisation. Thus, in writing the ATI and Neotany case studies it was easier to convey a greater degree of sharpness and precision of data that was more difficult to convey in the CoreTech case.

If the opportunity existed to conduct this research again, it would perhaps be more beneficial to conduct one of the smaller more focused case studies first before moving onto the rather larger CoreTech case. Investigating and understanding the issues arising from, for example, the Neotany case before tackling the CoreTech case may have led to a more focused approach to data collection for the CoreTech case and may thus have resulted in a greater precision of data and a 'crisper' case study. Therefore, perhaps the lesson here is to conduct a small case study first, which would allow one to grasp quickly some of the key issues involved, before moving onto the larger cases. As noted above, this may have led to more precise data in the CoreTech case but it would not necessarily have led to any additional issues arising. Indeed, upon reflection it is felt that conducting the CoreTech case after the Neotany and ATI cases, may have actually led to some issues being omitted. A prime example of this is the use of newsgroups, which because this was a very 'emotive' issue in CoreTech led me to specifically seek data on the use (or otherwise) of newsgroups in Neotany and ATI. As seen in the Neotany case the decision not to implement newsgroups was an important example of the power that Neotany could 'exert' in its relationship with dealerships. If the Neotany case had been conducted first it is likely that the issue of the use (or non-use) of newsgroups would have been omitted from the Neotany case since it would have been rather difficult to be in a position to collect data about an issue that at the time I was not aware was actually 'absent'. Thus, while there may have been benefits in first conducting a smaller case study, this may have had disadvantages in that some issues may have been omitted or at the very least have appeared with less emphasis than what is actually included in this book.

However, the above discussion is done with the benefit of hindsight and is coloured by actually knowing what issues have occurred in each of the three cases. Therefore, perhaps the lesson here is that where little is actually known about the area being investigated (as was the case with intranets at the beginning of this research) a small pilot study can help to identify and illuminate some of the issues that may appear in the later larger cases. However, in order not to 'miss' issues it is very important to be open to new phenomena in each case and to use the findings from a pilot study to act as an initial guide rather than as constraints to later stages of data collection.

9.1.2   Use of an interpretive case study approach

As pointed out in Chapter 1, the use of intranets/extranets is a relatively recent phenomenon and apart from the 'journalistic' anecdotes little was known of the issues that may arise from the deployment of such technologies. In order to build up a rich description and an understanding of such issues, an interpretive philosophy combined with a case study approach was adopted. The use of alternative methods such as questionnaires and surveys would not have served to capture all the issues that actually arose in the case studies presented earlier. Also, judging by the comments below from the RTOnet product manager, a more deterministic research approach may have made it more difficult to solicit companies to participate in the research. He commented that:

> I think the methodology you're using is very interesting...the system you're using because it's essentially a free space approach to pulling the information out, it allows you to pull up some of the human issues that are there. I think if you'd done it a different way with questionnaires and all that sort of stuff well frankly you'd have

got a very different response from me. I'd have been bored to death filling the bloody thing in. I wouldn't have learned anything, but equally I've learned something from the discussions we've had which is what's in it for me.

Thus, given the objective of building rich descriptions of the use of a relatively new technology, the adoption of an interpretive case study approach proved to be an appropriate approach.

9.2   Key contributions of this research

This research provides a valuable in-depth insight into the implementation and use of intranets and extranets, an area which continues to grow in importance to managers in organisations and which provides a solid basis on which firms can begin to develop and exploit collaborative applications. The work presented here will also prove valuable to other researchers who may wish to explore the use of these technologies as it provides the basis on which specific hypotheses may be identified concerning intranets/extrancts, their positioning among IT systems in general, and their role in organisational knowledge management. The key findings of this research are discussed below under a number of headings.

9.2.1   Intranets/extranets and IT in general

The evidence from the case studies and the discussion and analysis presented in Chapter 8 is that from one perspective intranets/extranets, in general, are not substantially different to other forms of IT. In practice many forms of new IT systems have been adopted by organisations without systematic strategy formulation and evaluation. Faxes, mobile phones, 'palmtop organisers' and concepts like business process reengineering have all mushroomed in a short period of time with little formal planning but with major organisational effects. At first sight intranets/extranets appear to fit into this category. However, there are a number of key areas where they are significantly different.

Relatively low implementation costs (due to the emphasis being on open rather than proprietary technology standards) is one of these areas, as is the growing interest (as noted earlier) in using intranets to 'lubricate' the flow of information and knowledge within an organisation. Essentially, intranets are beginning to fulfil the promise made by the use of Groupware but at a significantly reduced cost. Furthermore, the role of intranets as an integrative system in terms of facilitating easier access to information stored on other IT systems in use in an organisation offers potentially significant benefits to organisations. Many authors discuss the advantages for companies in having an integrated IT solution, that is where the internal IT systems and the external IT systems are integrated or at a very minimum can actually share data. Unfortunately, in practice the goal of having an integrated IT solution has not proved to be easy to achieve, due to a combination of technical limitations and the sheer cost of integration, particularly for small companies. Based on the findings presented here, intranets can offer a solution to these problems. In terms of identifying the wider potential significance of intranets, Nunamaker and Briggs (1997) point out:

> with the advent of standard cross-platform web browsers, we may be advancing from the horse-and-buggy days to the Model-T days of the information age.

Perhaps the importance of intranets can be best measured by the large number of organisations that now claim to have an intranet/extranet in place and who are using them as the base on which to develop their strategy for electronic commerce and ultimately 'e-business'.

9.2.2   Three case studies – three different situations

In each of the case studies, although the common denominator was the use of intranet/extranet technology, and Table 4.2 was used as a convenient way of structuring the research, the cases themselves do not represent equivalent quadrants of a 2×2 matrix, but actually represent three very different situations.

For instance, the CoreTech case could best be described as an example of the very rapid diffusion of technology within an organisation. As noted in the case, in the first year of use of the intranet, usage grew at 100 per cent per month for much of the year, and approximately one year later the number of users had grown to an estimated 55 000. Such a level of growth in such a short period of time represents characteristics that are perhaps distinctive to intranets. Also distinctive to intranets is that this growth was driven by a combination of very low implementation costs, almost immediate cost savings compared to distributing information on paper, and interest in the use initially being driven from the bottom-up rather than 'dictated' from the top-down. The CoreTech case also highlights the issues that arise when the use of an intranet evolves beyond that originally intended. In this situation the taking of political action was quite evident in terms of establishing 'ownership' not only of the intranet but also of the content and the procedures for who could publish information on the intranet.

On the other hand, the Neotany case represents a rather different situation. With Neotany the situation is probably best represented as an example of application development, the application in this case being the extranet used to replace the paper-based mechanisms for distributing information from Neotany to the dealerships. Unfortunately, like many examples of application development where the users of the application were not involved or even consulted in the design and development stage, the usage of the application was not as 'popular' as the designers might have intended. An interesting comparison between the CoreTech case and the Neotany case is that in the CoreTech case those middle managers that were 'bypassed' by the flow of information on the intranet were unable to exert any control on such information flows, whereas in the Neotany case sales managers were actually able to exercise such control. Indeed the exercise of power is very strong in the Neotany case and this case actually mirrors 'classic EDI' implementations where one party (in this case Neotany) dictates the design and development of the system and the other parties (in this case the dealerships) have little or no choice but to accept what is 'offered'. However, if this case is treated as a 'classic EDI' case, it does have a distinguishing characteristic in that the development and implementation of the application did not actually incur any additional costs at the dealerships (usage costs are a different matter) whereas in 'traditional' EDI cases the cost of implementation is typically significant. Again this finding represents characteristics that are perhaps distinctive to intranets.

Finally, the ATI case represents a situation that perhaps lies somewhere in between the CoreTech and the Neotany case. The ATI case also represents an example of application development in the sense that RTOnet is an application that is intended to initially complement and eventually replace ATI's existing methods of transferring information and knowledge to members, but this case differs from Neotany in the sense that ATI is not in a position to 'dictate' to users in the member organisations. Indeed in this instance the ATI case represents a similar situation to the CoreTech case in that ATI is attempting to drive the diffusion and use of Internet technologies among their member companies. Unfortunately, from ATI's perspective, the potential reluctance of members and non-members to pay for information delivered via RTOnet is a cost of information problem that CoreTech did not have.

Thus, while there may be similarities in the three case studies, they do actually represent three very different situations. However, what is perhaps distinctive about the findings presented in this book is that each of the three 'organisations' individually can actually benefit and perhaps learn from the findings of the other two cases.

9.2.3   What is different about intranets/extranets?

One of the main contributions of this book is that it offers an in-depth insight into the issues that surround the implementation and operation of intranets. Of particular interest is the identification of how the findings presented here differ from other IT systems that have been reported in the past.

One of the findings that represents characteristics that are particularly distinctive to intranets is the decreasing relevance of and the increasingly problematic nature of formal 'traditional' planning procedures in a world where intranets and extranets are becoming so ubiquitous. The 'old style' of preparing formal three- or five-year strategic plans for an organisation's information systems is being swept away and it is clear that planning procedures need to be completely revised in the light of the results reported here and in light of the Internet in general.

If the planning procedures need to be revised then so too do implementation procedures. In all three cases reported here the hardware infrastructure necessary to support the intranet/extranet was already in place and the intranet/extranet application was therefore relatively easy and inexpensive to deploy. This finding is again perhaps distinctive when compared to the other IT systems that typically required a roll out of hardware on which the new system would operate. Furthermore, it is clear from the findings presented here that once the intranet/extranet has been deployed it can act as a platform for further application development, and again future applications can benefit from the fact that the basic infrastructure is already in place. Examples of this from the case studies include the move towards intranet 'facilitated' knowledge management in CoreTech, and the shift away from developing applications for the Neotany mainframe and instead using the extranet as the platform for future application development. It is clear from the findings presented here that the use of intranets permits the IT implementation process to be potentially very low cost and to be very rapid. Again, this finding represents characteristics that are distinctive to the use of intranets/extranets.

Perhaps the area where intranets/extranets excel is in terms of the cost benefits that can result from replacing paper-based mechanisms of distributing information. In the CoreTech case the cost savings were substantial and were achieved in a remarkably short period of time.

Similarly in the Neotany case, large cost savings were being accrued by Neotany almost from day one. ATI also stands to potentially benefit from large cost savings. What is particularly distinctive here is the combination of the fact that not only can tangible benefits be measured easily and directly but also the period of time over which these benefits can be realised is almost instantaneous when compared to more 'traditional' IT systems. Indeed one of the problems that plagued more 'traditional' IT systems was the fact that it was often very difficult to directly measure the benefits that an IT system gave to an organisation, and the fact that it often took years before any change was measurable did not help matters. The fact that the use of intranets/extranets can deliver large benefits (in terms of measurable cost savings) in a very short space of time is perhaps one of the reasons why they have attracted so much interest.

Finally, it is clear from the findings presented here that the use of intranet/extranets will influence significantly the use of IT in the corporate environment. It is readily replacing existing technology at a much lower operating cost and with a significant number of additional advantages. It offers companies new opportunities for sharing and distributing information both internally amongst employees and also externally with customers and suppliers.

9.2.4   The politics of intranets/extranets

The findings reported here present an interesting perspective on the politics of intranets. It was seen in the case studies and the subsequent discussion that the implementation and operation of intranets and extranets permits a degree of 'openness' concerning the use of information in organisations and thus helps to expose to a wider audience the exercise of power and the taking of political action. For example, in the CoreTech case the introduction of the framework for information management as a mechanism for controlling what information is published on the intranet was a political act that was visible to those 80 000 employees who actually had access to the intranet at the time. What is perhaps unique about this particular example is that the intranet was then actually used as a vehicle by which those opposed to such a move could actually air their views (as evidenced in the 'Campaign for Intranet Freedom').

When compared to the Neotany case the decision not to support newsgroups in order to prevent dealers 'ganging-up' on Neotany is an example of how rapidly the politics of intranets have matured. Managers in CoreTech (being early movers in implementing intranets) soon realised the importance of establishing ownership of the intranet and controlling what information could be published on the intranet, whereas by the time Neotany came to implement their extranet (just over a year later) managers in Neotany had recognised the need for control.

Comparing the findings from the three case studies, it is clear that the use of intranets has the potential to both undermine and/or reinforce existing power relations. For example, in the CoreTech case the role and power held by some middle managers is being undermined by the fact that they no longer control the flow of information to their subordinates. In the Neotany case, some sales managers and indeed the DOMs are being similarly affected. However, although these are examples of where existing power relations are being undermined, there are also instances of where existing power relations have been reinforced. The Neotany case provides the best example of this and it is clear that the use of the extranet has strengthened Neotany's power over the dealerships.

In addition to having the potential to reinforce as well as undermine existing power relations, the findings also illustrate that the use of intranets can facilitate the 'seizing' of power (as in the CRU establishing their ownership of the CoreTech intranet) where it did not exist before. In retrospect the 'Campaign for Intranet Freedom' was a short-lived affair and when employees in CoreTech now talk of 'the intranet', by default this refers to the official licensed intranet. So it would appear that the 'seizing' of power by the CRU was a successful venture. Although as the Neotany case illustrates the 'seizing' of power just because it is now possible does not mean that it will actually happen, and the decision of the Neotany Head of IT not to take the opportunity to control the flow of information to the dealerships provides the best example.

Thus, the findings presented in this book illustrate that the use of intranets has numerous political implications and as was seen in the case studies, an awareness of the political issues associated with the implementation and use of an intranet/extranet is crucial in understanding the nature of the factors that shape the role of the intranet/extranet. Thus, in terms of considering intranets/extranets from a political perspective, there is no clear pattern of outcomes and hence the implementation of an intranet/extranet will not have a consistent effect on the balance of power in an organisation.

9.2.5   Intranets/extranets and knowledge management

This research also contributes significantly to an understanding of the role that intranets and extranets can play in facilitating knowledge management in an organisational context. Again, this is an area that continues to grow in importance and the research reported here provides important insights both to managers and other researchers. Indeed an important contribution of this research is that the link between knowledge management and the use of intranets, that was made at the inception of this research, has since been validated by practice. This serves to further enhance the importance of the findings reported in this book as they provide a valuable early insight into the role of intranets in knowledge management.

However, as noted earlier, while knowledge management (and indeed the use of Internet technologies) may still be viewed by some as simply the latest business phenomena, trend analysis and recent research suggest that neither the Internet nor knowledge management are 'fads' but rather that they are of more enduring significance. Looking ahead it is evident that they will be fundamental factors in future business strategies for most organisations. The apparent ease with which new forms of communication within organisations can be facilitated by intranets, has led to a surge in interest in their potential role in knowledge management. The growth of interest in knowledge management has essentially been contemporary with that of intranets/extranets. Fundamentally intranets/extranets have altered the discussion of knowledge management by putting the theory into practice. Scott (1998) points out that possibly the most far-reaching impact of the intranet is on organisational knowledge.

As seen in the case studies intranets/extranets can indeed play a role in facilitating knowledge management and as shown they can represent a significant component of organisational memory, and can also play valuable roles in the processes of knowledge creation, transfer and use.

However, as evidenced by the findings reported here it is clear that the nature of the challenge of knowledge management is much more about the interrelationship of content, context, and people, and thus it is inevitable that the technology will not be enough. These findings show that effective knowledge management cannot take place without extensive behavioural, cultural, and organisational change.

9.3 Some suggestions for further work

There are a number of areas where it is felt that further research would be both informative and useful. Although there were benefits (in terms of cross-case comparison and a wider understanding) to the research presented here in selecting companies operating in different industries, further research would benefit by selecting companies operating in the same industry. This would eliminate the contextual differences that may be introduced by virtue of the fact that the companies participating would be operating in different industries and thus would be likely to provide a deeper understanding of the role of intranets and extranets.

In the time since the inception of this research and the preparation of this book there has been significant technological maturity (as expected) in the field of intranets/extranets and thus a second specific area that would provide scope for future research is an investigation of the nature of the diffusion of intranet technology. The CoreTech case represents an example of the rapid diffusion of intranet technology. However, managers in organisations that have recently implemented an intranet/ extranet have had the opportunity to learn from the early movers in intranets, indeed a significant portion of CoreTech's product and service portfolio now concerns intranets. Also, given the recent rapid advancements in intranet technology, it is now the case that intranets that have been implemented recently are much more 'feature-rich' than those reported in this book. Such features include the capability to monitor very closely how employees are making use of the intranet and indeed can easily monitor their access to and use of the Internet from their work PCs. Thus, in addition to investigating the diffusion of intranet technology in other organisations, another fruitful area for future research would be an investigation of the political issues surrounding the use of such feature-rich intranets. This research should include an examination of how employees feel about their use of the intranet and/ or Internet being under surveillance and also how this may affect their use of the technology.

As was seen in the findings reported here an understanding of the politics surrounding the implementation and operation of intranets is crucial to understanding their organisational role. Thus, an additional potential topic for future research would be a more in-depth investigation of the nature of the politics of intranets. Specifically this should encompass an investigation of the impact of existing power relationships on the intended role of an intranet and the subsequent influence of the use of the intranet on the power relationships between the affected parties to the implementation. This would provide a useful complement to the findings reported here.

Finally, future research in this area could also involve a more focused economic analysis. The findings reported here probably only touched the surface in terms of trying to understand the economic issues associated with the implementation and use of intranets, that is it was difficult to substantiate any claim that the use of intranets can be justified on the basis of potential cost savings. For example, in the Neotany case although there were substantial cost savings accrued to Neotany HQ these were partly offset by increased costs of printing material in the dealerships. But in terms of assessing the cost benefit where should the boundary be drawn? How do the 'economics' of intranets change as the boundary or area of attention is altered? Particularly in the case of extranets an investigation based on transaction cost analysis would be a useful approach.

Given the recent rapid increase in the implementation of intranets/ extranets, future research will certainly benefit from there being a greater number of organisations that could form the basis for such research. Having provided an in-depth insight into the key issues that accompany the implementation and use of intranets, the findings reported in this book should certainly be of assistance to other researchers interested in this fast growing area.

9.4 Closing words

In the past few years the nature of intranets has changed markedly. What began as a simple extension of the use of the Internet has blossomed beyond all expectation. Yet, as noted earlier, this has been a quiet but very significant revolution. The functionality and capability of intranets has grown rapidly, the adoption by organisations has flourished and the use by employees has almost become second nature. When one considers the fact that the intranet is to all intents and purposes a sibling of the Internet, it is not surprising that just as the Internet has had a major effect on how people access information (and also to what information they have access) then similarly intranets are having a major effect on how employees access information within organisations and also to what information they now have access. Unfortunately, in some organisations the response to the intranet as a vehicle that can be used to efficiently and effectively disperse information far and wide within the organisation, has been to populate the intranet with as much information as possible. The growth in the use of external information content feeds has not helped. Rather than being a positive approach this has detracted somewhat from how employees view the intranet. Employees are beginning to feel overloaded with information and will find it increasingly difficult to find what information they require from the intranet. There are two key directions that managers in organisations may take in resolving this issue. First, they may decide to segment the information to which employees have access in order to make it easier for them to find the information they require. While this may seem to be an acceptable solution it raises a significant issue in that there is a very high likelihood that it will lead to a return to the 'traditional' departmental stovepipes of information within an organisation rather than the ubiquitous access to corporate information as triumphed by the early introduction of intranets. Secondly, they may possess sufficient managerial foresight to recognise the importance and significance of the tenets of knowledge management and start to realise that the sharing and reuse of knowledge within the organisation is too important to leave to chance. Hopefully, the latter direction will prevail. It will then be the case that what has happened so far with intranets and knowledge management is merely the raiding party – the real revolution is just getting underway.

References

Alvesson, M. (1993) 'Organizations as Rhetoric: Knowledge-Intensive Firms and the Struggle with Ambiguity', *Journal of Management Studies*, 30(6): 997–1015.

Amidon, D.M. (1998) 'The Evolving Community of Knowledge Practice: The Ken Awakening', *International Journal of Technology Management*, 16(1–3): 45–63.

Argyris, C. and Schon, D.A. (1978) *Organizational Learning: A Theory of Action Perspective*, Addison-Wesley, Reading, MA.

Attewell, P. and Rule, J. (1984) 'Computing and Organizations: What We Know and What We Don't Know', *Communications of the ACM*, 27: 1184–92.

Avison, D.E. and Fitzgerald, G. (1995) *Information Systems Development: methodologies, technologies, tools,* 2nd edn, McGraw Hill, London.

Bakos, J.Y. (1991a) 'Information Links and Electronic Marketplaces: The Role of Interorganizational Systems in Vertical Markets', *Journal of Management Information Systems*, 8(2): 31–52.

Bakos, J.Y. (1991b) 'Strategic Implications of Interorganizational Systems', in E. Sutherland, and Y. Morieux, (eds), *Business Strategy and Information Technology, Routledge*, London, pp. 163–74.

Bakos, J.Y. and Brynjolfsson, E. (1993) 'Why information technology hasn't increased the optimal number of suppliers', in T.N. Mudge, V. Milutinovic and L. Hunter (eds), *Proceedings of 26th Hawaii International Conference on Science Systems*, IEEE, Los Alamitos, CA, USA, 4: 799–808.

Bakos, J.Y. and Treacy, M.E. (1986) 'Information Technology and Corporate Strategy: A Research Perspective', *MIS Quarterly*, 10(2): 107–191.

Bariff, M.L. and Galbraith, J.R. (1978) 'Intraorganizational Power Considerations for Designing Information Systems', *Accounting, Organizations and Society*, 3(1): 15–27.

Barley, S.R. (1986) 'Technology as an Occasion for Structuring: Evidence from Observation of CT scanners and the social Order of Radiology Departments', *Administrative Science Quarterly*, 31: 78–108.

Basker, J. (1998) 'Intranets: Who's Doing What', *Business Information Review*, 15(2): 94–103.

Bayyigit, A.C., Inman, O.L. and Kuran, E.D. (1997) 'New Product Introduction: Reducing Time to Market Using Internet and Intranet Technology', IEEE, pp. 454–9, 27–31 July 1997, *Innovation in Technology Management – The Key to Global Leadership. PICMET '97.*

Bellinger, G. (2001) 'Knowledge Management', http://www.outsights.com/systems/kmgmt /kmgmt.htm.

Benbasat, I., Goldstein, D.K. and Mead, M. (1987) 'The Case Study Research Strategy in Studies of Information Systems', *MIS Quarterly*, 11(3): 369–88.

Benjamin, R.I. and Scott-Morton, M.S. (1988) 'IT, Integration, and Organizational Change', *Interfaces*, 18(3): 86–98.

Blackler, F. (1993) 'Knowledge and the Theory of Organizations: Organizations as Activity Systems and the Reframing of Management', *Journal of Management Studies*, 30(6): 863–84.

Blackler, F. (1995) 'Knowledge, Knowledge Work and Organizations: An Overview and Interpretation', *Organization Studies*, 16(6): 1021–46.

Bloomfield, B.P. and Coombs, R. (1992) 'Information Technology, Control and Power: The Centralisation and Decentralisation Debate Revisited', *Journal of Management Studies*, 29(4): 459–84.

Bock, G.E. and Marca, D.A. (1995) *Designing Groupware – A Guidebook for Designers, Implementors, and Users*, McGraw-Hill, New York.

Bohm, D. (1994) *Thought as a System*, Routledge, New York.

Boland, R.J. (1997) 'The In-Formation of Information Systems', in R.J. Boland and R.A. Hirschheim (eds), *Critical Issues in Information Systems Research*, John Wiley, Chichester, pp. 363–79.

Boland, R.J. and Tenkasi, R.W. (1995) 'Perspective Making and Perspective Taking in Communities of Knowing', *Organization Science*, 6(4): 350–72.

Bonoma, T.V. (1985) 'Case Research in Marketing: Opportunities, Problems, and a Process', *Journal of Marketing Research*, XXII: 199–208.

Brancheau, J.C. and Wetherbe, J.C. (1987) 'Key Issues in Information Systems Management', *MIS Quarterly*, 11: 23–45.

Brown, J.S. (1998) 'Organizing Knowledge', *California Management Review*, 40(3): 90–111.

Bruno, L. (1996) 'Groupware Vs. Webware: Forget the Hype. Can Web servers and browsers really make the Groupware grade?', *Data Communications*, 25(3): 123–30.

Brynjolfsson, E. (1993) 'The Productivity Paradox of Information Technology', *Communications of the ACM*, 36(12): 67–77.

Burrel, G. and Morgan, G. (1979) *Sociological Paradigms and Organizational Analysis*, Heinemann, London.

Callaghan, J.G. and Flavin, P.G. (1996) 'Intranets – Corporate Nirvana: The End of the Traditional Organization?', *Journal of the Institution of British Telecommunications Engineers*, 15(3): 224–29.

Cameron, B., DePalma, D.A., Herron, R.O. and Smith, N. (1995) 'Where Does Groupware Fit?', *Forrester Software Strategies Report*, 6(3).

Campalans, A., DeVito, E. and Honig, C. (1997) 'Exploiting Intranets for Knowledge Management and Information Sharing', *Journal of Business & Finance Librarianship*, 3(1): 27–39.

Cash, J.I. and Konsynski, B. (1985) 'IS Redraws Competitive Boundaries', *Harvard Business Review*, 63(2): 134–142.

Cash, J.I., Eccles, R.G., Nohria, N. and Nolan, R.L. (1994) *Building The Information-Age Organization: Structure, Control, and Information Technologies*, Irwin, Boston.

Chatfield, A.T. and Bjørn-Andersen, N. (1997) 'The Impact of IOS-Enabled Business Process Change on Business Outcomes: Transformation of the Value Chain of Japan Airlines', *Journal of Management Information Systems*, 14(1): 13–40.

Checkland, P. and Holwell, S. (1998) *Information, Systems and Information Systems – Making Sense of the Field*, John Wiley & Sons, Chichester.

Ciborra, C. (1994) 'The Grassroots of IT and Strategy', in C. Ciborra, and T. Jelassi, (eds), *Strategic Information Systems – A European Perspective*, John Wiley and Sons, Chichester, pp. 3–24.

Ciborra, C.U. (ed.) (1996) *Groupware and Teamwork – Invisible Aid or Technical Hindrance?* John Wiley & Sons, Chichester.

Ciborra, C.U. and Patriotta, G. (1996) 'Groupware and Teamwork in New Product Development: The Case of a Consumer Goods Multinational', in C. Ciborra (ed.), *Groupware and Teamwork – Invisible Aid or Technical Hindrance?* John Wiley & Sons, Chichester.

Ciborra, C.U. and Suetens, N.T. (1996) 'Groupware for an Emerging Virtual Organization', in C. Ciborra (ed.), *Groupware and Teamwork – Invisible Aid or Technical Hindrance?* John Wiley & Sons, Chichester.

Clark, T.H. and Stoddard, D.B. (1996) 'Interorganizational Business Process Redesign: Merging technological and Process Innovation', in J.F. Nunamaker, and R.H. Sprague, (eds), *Proceedings of the 29th Hawaii International Conference on System Sciences*, IEEE Computing Society Press, Los Alamitos, CA., USA, 4: 349–58.

Clemons, E. (1986) 'Information systems for sustainable competitive advantage', *Information and Management*, 11: 131–6.

Clemons, E. and Row, M. (1992) 'Information Technology and Industrial Co-operation: The Changing Economics of Co-ordination and Ownership', *Journal of Management Information Systems*, 9(2): 9–28.

Cohen, D. (1998a) 'Toward a Knowledge Context: Report on the First Annual U.C. Berkeley Forum on Knowledge and the Firm', *California Management Review*, 40(3): 22–39.

Cohen, S. (1998b) 'Knowledge Management's Killer App', *Training and Development*, 52(1): 50–7.

Cole, B. (1996) 'One year, $3.5 billion later . . . ', *Network World*, 13(24): 1, 68–9.

Cole, R.E. (1998) 'Introduction to Special Issue', *California Management Review*, 40(3): 15–21.

Coleman, D. (1997a) 'Collaborating on the Internet and Intranets', *Proceedings of the 30th Hawaii International Conference On Systems Sciences*, IEEE Computer Society, 2: 350–8, 7–10 January 1997.

Coleman, D. (1997b) 'Knowledge Retrieval', Collaborative Strategies', http://www.collaborate.com/mem/hot_tip /tip0697.php3.

Constant, D., Kiesler, S. and Sproull, L. (1994) 'What's Mine Is Ours, or Is It? A Study of Attitudes about Information Sharing', *Information Systems Research*, 5(4): 400–21.

Cropley, J. (1998) 'Knowledge Management: A Dilemma', *Business Information Review*, 15(1): 27–34.

Daft, R.L. and Weick, K.E. (1984) 'Toward a Model of Organizations as Interpretation Systems', *Academy of Management Review*, 9: 284–95.

Datamonitor (1998a) *Intranets in Pharmaceuticals*, Datamonitor, London, February.

Datamonitor (1998b) *Intranets in US Financial Services*, Datamonitor, London, March.

Datamonitor (1999) *European Intranet and Extranet Survey*, Datamonitor Plc, London, March.

Davenport, T.H. and Short, J.E. (1990) 'The New Industrial Engineering: Information Technology and Business Process Redesign', *Sloan Management Review*, 32: 11–27.

Davenport, T.H., DeLong, D.W. and Beers, M.C. (1998) 'Successful Knowledge Management Projects', *Sloan Management Review*, 39(2): 43–57.

Davenport, T.H., Jarvenpaa, S.L. and Beers, M.C. (1996) 'Improving Knowledge Work Process', *Sloan Management Review*, 38: 53–65.

Davenport, T.H. and Prusak, L. (1998) *Working Knowledge – How Organizations Manage What They Know*, Harvard Business School Press, Boston, MA.

Dennis, A.R., Pootheri, S.K. and Natarajan, V. (1998) 'Lessons from the Early Adopters of Web Groupware', *Journal of Management Information Systems*, 14(4): 65–86.

Doyle, D.B. and du Toit, A.S.A. (1998) 'Knowledge-based Enterprises: An Overview', *South African Journal of Library and Information Science*, 66(3): 90–8.

Dreifus, S.B. and Daniels, N.C. (1993) *Strategic Planning for IT – Improving Productivity, Profitability and Customer Satisfaction*, Economist Intelligence Unit, New York, NY., ISBN 0–850–58749–2.

Earl, M.J. (1993) 'Experiences in Strategic Information Planning', *MIS Quarterly*, 17: 1–24.

EFQM (1997) *Knowledge Management in Europe –'Current Practice' Survey Results*, European Foundation for Quality Management, September.

Eisenhardt, K.M. (1989) 'Building Theories from Case Study Research', *Academy of Management Review*, 14: 532–50.

Failla, A. (1996) 'Technologies for Co-ordination in a Software Factory', in C. Ciborra (ed.), *Groupware & Teamwork – Invisible Aid or Technical Hindrance?* John Wiley & Sons, Chichester, pp. 61–88.

Forrester Research (1996), *Computing Strategies*, 13(9), July.

Foucault, M. (1983) 'The Subject and Power', Critical Inquiry, 8(4): 777–95.

Foucault, M. (1980) In C. Gordon (ed.), *Power/Knowledge: Selected Interviews and Other Writings*, Pantheon Books, New York, 147–65.

Fulk, J. and DeSanctis, G. (1995) 'Electronic Communication and Changing Organizational Forms', *Organization Science*, 6(4): 337–49.

Galbraith, J.R. (1974) 'Organization Design: An Information Processing View', *Interfaces*, 4(3): 28–36.

Gallie, D. (1978) *In Search of the New Working Class*, Cambridge University Press, Cambridge, UK.

Galliers, R.D. (1995) 'A Manifesto for Information Management Research', *British Journal of Management*, 6: 45–52.

Galliers, R.D. (1994) 'Strategic information system planning: myths, reality and guidelines for successful implementation', in R.D. Galliers, and B.S.H. Baker, (eds), *Strategic Information Management*, Butterworth-Heineman, Oxford, pp. 129–47.

Gick, M.L. and Holyoak, K.J. (1987) 'The Cognitive Basis of Knowledge Transfer', in S.M. Cormier and J.D. Hagman (eds), *Transfer of Learning: Contemporary Research and Applications*, Academic Press, San Diego, CA.

Gilbert, M., Seaton, R. and Jensen, K. (1999) 'Why managing individual knowledge is crucial for organizational efficiency and effectiveness', *Cranfield University*, unpublished working paper.

Gill, T.G. (1995) 'High-Technology Hidebound: Case Studies of Information technologies That Inhibited Organizational Learning', *Accounting, Management and Information Technologies*, 5(1): 41–60.

Ginzberg, M.J. (1981) 'Key Recurrent Issues in the MIS Implementation Process', *MIS Quarterly*, 5(2): 47–59.

Glyn-Jones, F. (1995) 'The Groupware Grapevine', *Management Today*, pp. 83–6, April.

Gogan, J.L. and Cash, J.I. (1992) 'IT-based innovation: managing a disorderly process', in Milutinovic, V. *et al.* (eds), *Proceedings of 25th Hawaii International*

Conference on System Sciences, IEEE Computing Society Press, Los Alamitos, CA., USA, 4: 257–67, ISBN: 0–818–62420–5.

Goodhue, D. (1992) 'User Evaluations of MIS Success: What are we really measuring?', 25th Hawaii International Conference on System Sciences, in Milutinovic, V. *et al.* (eds), *Proceedings of 25th Hawaii International Conference on System Sciences*, IEEE Computing Society Press, Los Alamitos, CA., USA, 4: 303–14, ISBN: 0–818–62420–5.

Gottschalk, P. (1997) *A Review of Literature on the Implementation of Strategic Information Systems Plans*, The Henley Research Centre Working Paper Series, HWP 9708, Henley Management College, Oxfordshire.

Grant, R.M. (1996) 'Towards a Knowledge-Based Theory of the Firm', *Strategic Management Journal*, 17: 109–122.

Grint, K. and Woolgar, S. (1997) *The Machine at Work: Technology Work and Organization*, Polity Press, Cambridge, UK.

Gundry, J. and Metes, G. (1998) *Team Knowledge Management: A Computer-Mediated Approach*, Knowledge Ability Ltd, February.

Haapaniemi, P. (1996a) 'Cyber-strategy', *Journal of Business Strategy*, 17(1): 22–7.

Haapaniemi, P. (1996b) 'Going global: Exploring the Intranet', *Journal of Business Strategy*, 17(1): 26.

Hamilton, S. and Chervany, N.L. (1981) 'Evaluating Information System Effectiveness Part I: Comparing Evaluation Approaches', *MIS Quarterly*, 5(3): 55–69.

Harris, D.B. (1996) 'Creating a Knowledge Centric Information Technology Environment', Technology in Education Institute, http://www.dbharris.com/ckc.htm, 15 September.

Hayes, N. and Walsham, G. (2000) 'Safe enclaves, political enclaves and knowledge working', in C. Prichard, R. Hull, M. Chumer and H. Willmott (eds), *Managing Knowledge: Critical Investigations of Work and Learning*, Macmillan, Basingstoke, pp. 69–87.

Hedberg, B., Edstrom, A., Muller, W. and Wilpert, B. (1975) 'The Impact of Computer Technology on Organizational Power Structures', in E. Grochla and N. Szyperski (eds), *Information Systems and Organizational Structure*, published by Walter de Gruyter, Berlin, pp. 131–48.

Henderson, J.C. and Venkatraman, N. (1993) 'Strategic Alignment: Leveraging Information Technology for Transforming Organizations', *IBM Systems Journal*, 31(1): 4–16.

Hildebrand, C. (1996) 'A Little of That Human Touch', *CIO*, 9(10): 64–70.

Holland, C., Lockett, G. and Blackman, I. (1992) 'Planning for Electronic Data Interchange', *Strategic Management Journal*, 13(7): 539–50.

Holland, C.P. and Lockett, G. (1994) 'Strategic Choice and Interorganizational Information Systems', in J.F. Nunamaker, and R.H. Sprague, (eds), *Proceedings of the 27th Hawaii International Conference on System Sciences*, IEEE Computing Society Press, Los Alamitos, CA., USA, 4: 405–15, ISBN: 0–818–65080–X.

Hollis, D.R. (1996) 'The Shape of Things to Come: The Role of IT', *Management Review* (AMA), 21: 62.

Hook, M. and Baker, H.M. (1997) 'Groupware: A Tool for Collaborative Computing and Knowledge Management', *Proceedings of National Annual Meeting to the Decision Sciences*, Decision Sci. Inst. (USA), 2: 822–4.

Horvath, A.T. and Fulk, J. (1994) 'Information Technology and the Prospects for Organizational Transformation', in B. Kovacic (ed.), *New Approaches to*

Organizational Communication, State University of New York Press, Albany, pp. 117–41.

Huber, G.P. (1990) 'A Theory of the Effects of Advanced Information Technologies on Organizational Design, Intelligence, and Decision Making', *Academy of Management Review*, 15(1): 47–71.

Huber, G.P. (1991) 'Organizational Learning: The Contributing Processes and the Literature', *Organization Science*, 2(1): 88–115.

Hughes, J.A., O' Brien, J., Sharrock, W., Rouncefield, M., Rodden T. and Calvey, D. (1994) *Field Studies and CSCW*, COMIC Deliverable 2.2, The COMIC Project, Esprit Basic Research Action 6225, University of Lancaster, October.

International Data Corporation (IDC) (1997) *The Intranet: Slashing the Cost of Business*, available at http://big.ids.net/intranetdev/idc/ report.html.

Ives, B. and Olson, M.H. (1984) 'User involvement and MIS success: A review of research', *Management Science*, 30: 586–603.

Jennex, M., Olfman, L., Panthawi, P. and Park, Y. (1998) 'An Organizational Memory Information Systems Success Model: An Extension of DeLone and McLean's IS Success Model', *Proceedings of 31st Annual Hawaii International Conference on System Sciences*, IEEE, pp. 157–65.

Johansen, R. (1988) *Groupware*, Free Press, New York.

Johansson, H.J., McHugh, P., Pendlebury, A.J. and Wheeler, W.A. (1993) *Business Process Reengineering – Breakpoint Strategies for Market Dominance*, John Wiley & Sons, Chichester.

Johnson-Lentz, P. and Johnson-Lentz, T. (1982) 'Groupware: The Process and Impacts of Design Choices', in E.B. Kerr and S.R. Hiltz (eds), *Computer-Mediated Communication Systems: Status and Evaluation*, Academic Press, New York, NY.

Johnston, H.R. and Vitale, M.R. (1988) 'Creating Competitive Advantage with Interorganizational Information Systems', *MIS Quarterly*, 12(2): 153–65.

Jones, M. (1999) 'Information Systems and the Double Mangle: Steering a Course Between the Scylla of Embedded Structure and the Charybdis of Strong Symmetry', in T.J. Larsen, L. Levine and J.I. DeGross (eds), *Information Systems: Current Issues and Future Changes*, IFIP (International Federation for Information Processing), Laxenburg, Austria, pp. 287–302.

Jones, M. (1995) 'Organizational Learning: Collective Mind or Cognitivist Metaphor', *Accounting, Management and Information Technologies*, 5(1): 61–77.

Jurison, J. (1996) 'The Temporal Nature of IS Benefits: A Longitudinal Study', *Information & Management*, 30(2): 75–9.

Keen, P.G.W. (1981) 'Information Systems and Organizational Change', *Communications of the ACM*, 24(1): 24–33.

Kiely, T. (1993) 'Learning to Share, *CIO*, 6(15): 38–44.

King, W.R. (1996) 'Strategic Issues in Groupware', *Information Systems management*, 13(2): 73–75.

King, W.R. and Grover, V. (1991) 'The Strategic Use of Information Resources: an exploratory study', *IEEE Transactions on Engineering Management*, 38(4): 293–305.

King, W.R. and Thompson, S.H.T. (1996) 'Key Dimensions of Facilitators and Inhibitors for the Strategic Use of Information Technology', *Journal of Management Information Systems*, 12(4): 35–53.

King, W.R., Grover, V. and Hufnagel, E.H. (1989) 'Using Information and Information Technology for Competitive Advantage: Some Empirical Evidence', *Information and Management*, 17(2): 87–93.

Klinte, T.J.B. and Gardiner, H. (1997) 'The Successful Adoption of Groupware: Perceptions of the Users', *Human Systems Management*, 16(4): 301–6.

Knights, D. and Murray, F. (1992) 'Politics and Pain in Managing Information Technology: A case study from Insurance', *Organization Studies*, 13(2): 211–29.

Knights, D. and Roberts, J. (1982) 'The Power of Organization or the Organization of Power?' *Organization Studies*, 3(1): 47–63.

Konsynski, B.R. and McFarlan, F.W. (1990) 'Information Partnerships – Shared Data Shared Scale', *Harvard Business Review*, pp. 114–20.

Konsynski, B.R. (1993a) 'Strategic Control in the Extended Enterprise', *IBM Systems Journal*, 32(1): 111–42.

Konsynski, B.R. (1993b) 'A Perspective on the 'Case Study Approach' to IT Investment Evaluation', in R.D. Banker, R.J. Kauffman, and M.A. Mahmood, (eds), *Strategic Information Technology Management: Perspectives on Organizational Growth and Competitive Advantage*, Idea Group Publishing, Harrisburg PA, pp. 15–24.

KPMG Management Consulting (1998a) *Intranet Research Report 1998*.

KPMG (1998b) *Knowledge Management Research Report 1988*, KPMG Management Consulting.

KPMG (1998c) *The Power of Knowledge*, KPMG Management Consulting, 1998.

Kwon, T.H. and Zmud, R.W. (1987) 'Unifying the fragmented models of information systems implementation', in R.J. Boland, and R.A. Hirschheim, (eds), *Critical Issues in Information Systems Research*, John Wiley & Sons, Chichester.

Lederer, A.L. and Salmela, H. (1996) 'Toward a Theory of Strategic Information Systems Planning', *Journal of Strategic Information Systems*.

Lederer, A.L. and Sethi, V. (1988) 'The Implementation of Strategic Information Systems Planning Methodologies', *MIS Quarterly*, 7: 445–61.

Leonard, D. and Sensiper, S. (1998) 'The Role of Tacit Knowledge in Group Innovation', *California Management Review*, 40(3): 112–32.

Leonard, D.C. (1998) 'Electronic Evolution: From Technical Communication to Knowledge Management', *Proceedings of 1998 IEEE International Communication Conference: IPCC 1998 – Contemporary Renaissance: Changing the Way we Communicate*, 2: 9–20.

Leonard-Barton, D. (1995) *Wellsprings of knowledge: Building and Sustaining the sources of innovation*, Harvard Business School Press, Boston, MA.

Levine, L. and Monarch, I. (1998) 'Collaborative Technology in the Learning Organization: Integrating Process with Information Flow, Access, and Interpretation', *Proceedings of 31st Annual Hawaii International Conference on System Sciences*, IEEE, pp. 444–59.

Levitt, B. and March, J.G. (1988) 'Organizational Learning', *Annual Review of Sociology*, 14: 319–40.

Lines, D. and Finlay, P. (1995) 'Investment Appraisal and Lotus Notes: the use and usefulness of traditional financial appraisal techniques', Loughborough University Business School Research Series, Working Paper No. 1995: 17, Loughborough University, July.

Lucas, H.C. (1981) *Implementation: The Key to Successful Information Systems*, McGraw-Hill, New York.

MacDonald, H. (1991) 'Business strategy development, alignment, and redesign', in M. Scott-Morton (ed.), *The Corporation of the 1990s*, Oxford University Press, New York, pp. 159–86.

Mackiewicz, A. and Daniels, N.C. (1994) *The Successful Corporation of the year 2000*, Economist Intelligence Unit, New York, NY., ISBN 0–850–58760–3.

Malhotra, Y. (1998) 'Deciphering the Knowledge Management Hype', *Journal for Quality and Participation*, Special Issue on Learning and Information Management, 21(4): 58–60.

Malhotra, Y. (1997) 'Knowledge Management in Inquiring Organizations', *Proceedings of 3rd Americas Conference on Information Systems*, pp. 293–295, August.

Malhotra, Y. (1996) 'Organizational Learning and Learning Organizations: An Overview', Brint Research Institute, http://www.brint.com/papers/orglrng.htm.

Malone, T.W., Yates, J. and Benjamin, R.I. (1987) 'Electronic Markets and Electronic Hierarchies', Communications of the ACM, 30(6): 484–97.

Markus, M.L. and Bjørn-Andersen, N. (1987) 'Power over Users: its exercise by System Professionals', *Communications of the ACM*, 30(6): 498–504.

Markus, M.L. and Pfeffer, J. (1983) 'Power and the Design of Accounting and Control Systems', *Accounting, Organizations and Society*, 8(2/3): 205–18.

Markus, M.L. and Robey, D. (1988) 'Information Technology and Organizational Change: Causal Structure in Theory and Research', *Management Science*, 34(5): 583–98.

Markus, M.L. and Robey, D. (1983) 'The Organizational Validity of Management Information Systems', *Human Relations*, 36(3): 203–25.

Markus, M.L. (1983) 'Power, Politics and MIS Implementation', *Communications of the ACM*, 26(6): 430–44.

Marlow, E. and O'Connor-Wilson, P. (1997) *The Breakdown of Hierarchy – Communicating in the Evolving Workplace*, Butterworth-Heinemann, Boston, MA.

Marshall, L. (1997) 'Facilitating Knowledge Management and Knowledge Sharing. New Opportunities for Information Professionals', *Online*, 21(5): 92–8.

Martin, C. and Powell, P. (1992) *Information Systems – A Management Perspective*, McGraw-Hill, Maidenhead.

Martiny, M. (1998) 'Knowledge Management at HP Consulting', *Organizational Dynamics*, 27(2): 71–7.

McKenney, J.J., Copeland, D.C. and Mason, R.O. (1995) *Waves of Change – Business Evolution through Information Technology*, Harvard Business School Press, Boston, Massachusetts.

Miles, G., Miles R.E., Perrone, V. and Edvinsson, L. (1998) 'Some Conceptual and Research Barriers to the Utilization of Knowledge', *California Management Review*, 40(3): 281–8.

Miles, M.B. and Huberman, A.M. (1984) *Qualitative Data Analysis – A Sourcebook of New Methods*, Sage Publications, Newbury Park, California.

Monteiro, E. and Hanseth, O. (1996) 'Social Shaping of Information Infrastructure: On Being Specific about the Technology', in W.J. Orlikowski, G. Walsham, M.R. Jones and J.I. DeGross (eds), *Information Technology and Changes in Organizational Work*, Chapman & Hall, London, 1996, pp. 325–43.

Monteiro, E. and Hepsø, V. (1999) 'Diffusion of Infrastructure: Mobilization and Improvisation', in T.J. Larsen, L. Levine and J.I. DeGross (eds), *Information Systems: Current Issues and Future Changes*, IFIP (International Federation for Information Processing), Laxenburg, Austria, pp. 255–74.

Mooney, J., Gurbaxani, V. and Kraemer, K. (1995) 'A Process Oriented Framework for Assessing the Business Value of Information Technology', in J. DeGross *et al.* (eds), *Proceedings of the Sixteenth International Conference on Information Systems*, ACM, New York, pp. 17–27.

Morgan, G. (1986) *Images of Organization*, Sage, Beverly Hills.

Nandhakumar, J. (1996) 'Design for Success?: critical success factors in executive information systems development', *European Journal of Information Systems*, 5(1): 62–72.

Network News (1997) 'BT Pulls if off – development of an Intranet', Case Study, VNU Business Publications Limited, 13 August 1997.

Nohria, N. and Berkley, J.D. (1994) 'The Virtual Organization: Bureaucracy, Technology, and the Implosion of Control', in C. Heckscher and A. Donnelon (eds), *The Post-Bureaucratic Organization: New Perspectives on Organizational Change*, Sage, Thousand Oaks, CA, pp. 108–28.

Nonaka, I. and Takeuchi, H. (1995) *The Knowledge-Creating Company – How Japanese Companies Create the Dynamics of Innovation*, Oxford University Press, New York.

Nonaka, I. (1994) 'A Dynamic Theory of Organizational Knowledge Creation', *Organization Science*, 5(1): 14–37.

Nonaka, I. (1991) 'The Knowledge-Creating Company', *Harvard Business Review*, 69: 96–104.

Nunamaker, J.F. and Briggs, R.O. (1996–1997) 'Information Technology and Its Organizational Impact', *Journal of Management Information Systems* (Special Issue), 13(3): 3–6.

Opper, S. and Fersko-Weiss, H. (1992) *Technology for Teams: Enhancing Productivity in Networked Organizations*, Van Nostrand Reinhold, New York.

Orlikowski, W.J. (1992) 'The Duality of technology: Rethinking The Concept of Technology In Organizations', *Organization Science*, 3(3): 398–427 (1193).

Orlikowski, W.J. (1996) 'Evolving with Notes: Organizational Change around Groupware Technology' in C. Ciborra (ed.), *Groupware and Teamwork – Invisible Aid or Technical Hindrance?* John Wiley & Sons, Chichester, pp. 23–59.

Orlikowski, W.J., Yates, J., Okamura, K. and Fujimoto, M. (1995) 'Shaping Electronic Communication – The Metastructuring of Technology in the Context of Use', *Organization Science*, 6(4): 423–44.

Pancucci, D. (1995) 'Groupware Users Missing Boat', *FT Business Computing Brief*, Issue 275, 6–7, 6 July 1995.

Parker, A. and Attwood, R. (1997) *Intranets – The Evolution of a New management Tool*, *Financial Times* – Media & Telecoms Publishing, London, March, ISBN 1–853–34790–6.

Petreley, N. (1996) 'The Domino Effect: Lotus stages impressive comeback with Notes 4.5', *Infoworld*, 18(33): 102.

Pincince, T.J., Goodtree, D. and Barth, C. (1996) 'The Full Service Intranet', *Forrester Research Report*, 10(4): xxx.

Polanyi, M. (1997) 'The Tacit Dimension', in L. Prusak, (ed.), *Knowledge in Organizations*, Butterworth-Heinemann, Boston, MA.

Polanyi, M. (1966) *The Tacit Dimension*, Doubleday, New York.

Ponelis, S. and Fairer-Wessels, F.A. (1988) 'Knowledge Management: A Literature Overview', *South African Journal of Library and Information Science*, 66(1): 1–9.

Poon, S. and Swatman, P.M.C. (1996) 'Small Business Alliances: A Framework for Internet-Enabled Strategic Advantage', in J.F. Nunamaker and R.H. Sprague (eds), *Proceedings of the 29th Hawaii International Conference on System Sciences*, IEEE Computing Society Press, Los Alamitos, CA., USA, 4: 359–67.

Porter, M.E. and Millar, V.E. (1985) 'How Information Gives You Competitive Advantage', *Harvard Business Review*, pp. 149–60, July–August.

Pralahad, C.K. and Hamel, G. (1992) 'The Core Competence of the Corporation', *Harvard Business Review*, 68: 79–91.

Prusak, L. (1998) 'The Eleven Deadliest Sins of Knowledge Management', *California Management Review*, 40(3): 265–76.

Pumo, J.M. (1996) 'Delivering IT Value in Three Easy Steps', *Planning Review*, 24(1): 42–3.

Pycock, J. (1995) 'Process or Practice: Elements of An Ethnographic Orientation to Process Models', *IEE Colloquium on CSCW and the Software Process*, Digest No. 1995/036, IEE, London, pp. 3/1–3, 20 February.

Radosevich, L. (1996) 'Internet Plumbing Comes to Groupware', *Datamation*, 42: 58–62.

Raisinghani, M.S., Ramarapu, N. and Simkin, M. (1997) 'The Analysis and Study of the Impact of Technology on Groups: A Conceptual Framework', *Proceedings of National Annual Meeting of the Decision Sciences*, 2: 518–20, Decision Sciences Institute, USA.

Raymond, L. (1990) 'Organizational Context and Information Systems Success: A Contingency Approach', *Journal of Management Information Systems*, 6(4): 5–20.

Reich, B.H. and Benbasat, I. (1996) 'Measuring the Linkage between Business and Information Technology Objectives', *MIS Quarterly*, 20(1): 55–81.

Remenyi, D. (1995) 'So You Want To Be An Academic Researcher in Business And Management Studies', *Henley Working Paper* HWP 9531, The Henley Research Centre.

Riggins, F.J. and Rhee, H. (1998) 'Towards a Unified View of Electronic Commerce', *Communications of the ACM*, 41(10): 88–95.

Robey, D. (1995) 'Theories that Explain Contradiction; Accounting for the Contradictory Organizational Consequences of Information Technology', in J. DeGross *et al.* (eds), *Proceedings of the Sixteenth International Conference on Information Systems*, ACM, New York, pp. 55–63.

Rockart, J.F., Earl, M.J. and Ross, J.W. (1996) 'Eight Imperatives for the New IT Organization', *Sloan Management Review*, 38(1): 43–5.

Rockart, J.F. and Scott-Morton, M.S. (1984) 'Implications of Changes in Information Technology for Corporate Strategy', *Interfaces*, 14(1): 84–95.

Rose, C. (1996) 'Netscape adopts the Lotus position', *Communications Week International*, p. 25, 4 November.

Ross, J.W., Beath, C.M. and Goodhue, D.L. (1996) 'Develop Long-Term Competitiveness through IT Assets', *Sloan Management Review*, 38(1): 31–42.

Ruggles, R. (1998) 'The State of the Notion: Knowledge Management in Practice', *California Management Review*, 40(3): 80–9.

Russell, J. (1996) 'An Approach to Organizational Ethnographic Research: Strategy, Methods and Processes', *Discussion Papers in Accounting and Management Science*, Number 96–122, ISSN 1356–3548, University of Southampton, March.

Sabherwal, R. and King, W.R. (1991) 'Towards a Theory of Strategic Use of Information Resources', *Information and Management*, 20(3): 191–212.

Sayer, K. (1998) 'Denying the technology: middle management resistance in business process re-engineering', *Journal of Information Technology*, 13(4): 247–57.

Schein, E.H. (1984) 'Coming to a New Awareness of Organizational Culture', *Sloan Management Review*, 25: 3–16.

Schrage, M. (1996) 'The Future of Groupware', *American Programmer*, 9(8): 2–6.

Schultze, U. (1999) 'Investigating the Contradictions in Knowledge Management', in T.J. Larsen, L. Levine and J.I. DeGross (eds), *Information Systems and Future Changes*, IFIP, Laxenburg, Austria, pp. 155–74.

Scott, J.E. (1998) 'Organizational Knowledge and the Intranet', *Decision Support Systems*, 23(1): 3–17.

Scott-Morton, M.S. (1991) *The Corporation of the 1990s – Information Technology and Organizational Transformation*, Oxford University Press, New York, ISBN 0-195-06358-9.

Shapiro, D. (1994) 'The Limits of Ethnography: Combining Social Sciences for CSCW', in *Transcending Boundaries, CSCW '94, Proceedings of the Conference on Computer Supported Cooperative Working*, ACM, New York, NY USA, pp. 417–28, October.

Short, J.E. and Venkatraman, N. (1992) 'Beyond Business Process Redesign: Redefining Baxter's Business Network', *Sloan Management Review*, 34: 7–21.

Skyrme, D. and Amidon, D. (1997) *Creating the Knowledge-based business*, Business Intelligence, London.

Skyrme, D.J. (1995) 'Getting to Grips with Groupware', Management Insight No.7, David Skyrme Associates, http://www.skyrme.com/insights/7gw.htm.

Skyrme, D.J. (1997a) 'From Information to Knowledge Management – Are You Prepared?' *Proceedings of 21st International Online Information Meeting*, pp. 109–17, 9–11 December 1997.

Skyrme, D.J. (1997b) 'Knowledge Management: Making Sense of an Oxymoron', http://www.skyrme.com/insights/22km.htm, June 1997.

Sproull, L. and Kiesler, S. (1991) *Connections – New Ways of Working in the Networked Organization*, MIT Press, Cambridge, MA.

Srinivasan, A. (1985) 'Alternative Measures of Systems Effectiveness: Associations and Implications', *MIS Quarterly*, 9(3): 243–53.

St. John Bate, J. and Travell, N. (1994) *Groupware – Business Success with Computer Supported Cooperative Working*, Alfred Waller Ltd., Henley on Thames.

Stein, E.W. (1995) 'Organizational Memory: Review of Concepts and Recommendations for Management', *International Journal of Information Management*, 15(2): 17–32.

Stein, E.W. and Zwass, V. (1995) 'Actualizing Organizational Memory with Information Systems', *Information Systems Research*, 6(2): 85–117.

Stewart, T.A. (1998) *Intellectual Capital – The New Wealth of Organizations*, Doubleday/Currency, New York.

Sutherland, F., Brown, A. and Remenyi, D. (1995) 'Towards a Model for Benchmarking Information Technology Effectiveness', *2nd European Conference on Information Technology Investment Evaluation*, Operations Research Society, Birmingham, pp. 118–32, 11–12 July.

Sveiby, K.E. (1998) 'Tacit Knowledge', http://www.sveiby.com.au/polanyi.html.

Taninecz, G. (1996) 'The Web Within', *Industry Week*, 245(5): 45–51.

Taylor, B. (1994) *Successful Change Strategies – Chief Executives in Action*, Director Books (Fitzwilliam Publishing Limited), Hemel Hempstead.

Technology Strategies (1996) 'What is Best for the Group', *Technology Strategies*, No.125, pp. 15–17, July–August.

Teece, D.J. (1998) 'Capturing Value from Knowledge Assets: The New Economy, Markets for Know-How, and Intangible Assets', *California Management Review*, 40(3): 55–79.

Thibaut, J.W. and Kelly, H.H. (1959) *The Social Psychology of Groups*, Wiley, New York.

Thong, J.Y.L., Yap, C. and Raman, K.S. (1996) 'Top Management Support, External Expertise and Information Systems Implementation in Small Businesses', *Information Systems Research*, 7(2): 248–267.

Tomasula, D. (1996) 'Wall Street's Invisible Intranets', *Wall Street & Technology*, 14(1): 54 and 56.

Tsoukas, H. (1996) 'The Firm as a Distributed Knowledge System: A Constructionist Approach', *Strategic Management Journal*, 17: 11–25.

Vadapalli, A. and Ramamurthy, K. (1997–1998) 'Business Use of the Internet: An Analytical Framework and Exploratory Case Study', *Journal of Electronic Commerce*, 2(2): 71–94.

Van Maanen, J. (1979) 'The Fact of Fiction in Organizational Ethnography', *Administrative Science Quarterly*, 24: 539–50.

Vandenbosch, B. and Ginzberg, M.J. (1996–7) 'Lotus Notes and Collaboration: Plus ca change . . .', *Journal of Management Information Systems* (Special Issue), 13(3): 65–82.

Venkatraman, N. (1991) 'IT-Induced Business Reconfiguration' in Scott-Morton, M. (ed.), *The Corporation of the 1990s – Information Technology and Organizational Transformation*, Oxford University Press, New York, pp. 122–58.

Venkatraman, N. (1994) 'IT-Enabled Business Transformation – From Automation to Business Scope Redefinition', *Sloan Management Review*, 36: 73–87.

Walsh, J.P. and Ungson, G.R. (1991) 'Organizational Memory', *Academy of Management Review*, 16(1): 57–91.

Walsham, G. (1993) *Interpreting Information Systems in Organizations*, John-Wiley, Chichester.

Walsham, G. (1995) 'Interpretive Case Studies in IS Research: nature and method', *European Journal of Information Systems*, 4(2): 74–81.

Walsham, G. (1997) 'Actor-Network Theory and IS Research: Current Status and Future Prospect', in A.S. Lee, J. Liebenau and J.I. DeGross (eds), *Information Systems and Qualitative Research*, Chapman and Hall, London, pp. 466–80.

Warren, L. (1998) 'Know What You Know', *Information Week*, 22(4): 18–23.

Weick, K.E. (1991) 'The Nontraditional Quality of Organizational Learning', *Organization Science*, 2(1): 116–24.

Wen, H.J., Yen, D.C. and Lin, B. (1998) 'Methods for Measuring Information Technology Investment Payoff', *Human Systems Management*, 17(2): 145–53.

Wiig, K.M. (1997) 'Knowledge Management: Where did it come from and where will it go?' *Expert Systems with Applications*, 13(1): 1–14.

Wiig, K.M., DeHoog, R. and Van Der Spek, R. (1997) 'Supporting Knowledge Management: A Selection of Methods and Techniques', *Expert Systems with Applications*, 13(1): 15–27.

Williams, A. (1996) 'Groupware: The Next Wave of Office Automation?' *Industrial Management & Data Systems*, 96(6): 11–13.

Yates, J. and Orlikowski, W.J. (1992) 'Genres of Organizational Communication: A Structurational Approach to Studying Communication and Media', *Academy of Management Review*, 17: 299–326.

Yin, R.K. (1994) *Case Study Research – Design and Methods*, 2nd edn, Sage Publications, Thousand Oaks, California.

Zona Research, Internet and Intranet (1997) Markets, Opportunities, and Trends, Zona Research Inc, Redwood City, CA., http://www.zonaresearch.com.

Index